OPERA SCENES
FOR CLASS AND STAGE

Mary Elaine Wallace
Robert Wallace

Southern Illinois University Press
Carbondale and Edwardsville

Feffer & Simons, Inc.
London and Amsterdam

Library of Congress Cataloging in Publication Data

Wallace, Mary Elaine.
    Opera scenes for class and stage.

    Bibliography: p.
    1. Opera—Production and direction. I. Wallace,
Robert, 1945-   joint-author. II. Title.
MT955.W24   782.1.071   78-11095
ISBN O-8093-0903-3

Contents

Preface

SCENES extracted from the wealth of available operatic literature have served for many years as an educational and performance resource for professional and collegiate opera workshops, private voice studios, and summer opera institutes. Scenes may range from the solo aria enacted by a vocalist in a recital situation to an extended excerpt requiring a company of singing actors and actresses performing on stage with all the accouterments of a complete production—orchestra, costumes, makeup, props, scenery, and lighting. In every circumstance, the selection is dependent upon a director, conductor, or teacher who knows the vast operatic repertory and can select appropriate material with ease. Such selection requires more than a general knowledge of operas and their casts.

Some years ago, faced with the problem of having to make such selections of scenes literally overnight, we began notating appropriate excerpts on cards and filing them for quick reference. These cards were our computer; they were indexed to remind us of scenes which used various combinations of voices, and they also contained additional pertinent information. How long was the excerpt? What were the vocal ranges, not of the entire opera role, but of the portion included in the scene? On what pages of readily accessible piano-vocal scores would we find this scene? The demand for this kind of information has not diminished, and at the urging of opera directors, conductors, voice teachers, students, and friends, this book has become a reality.

For most persons involved in selecting opera excerpts, the time-consuming task begins with a list of the voices available. More than one opera director has walked into a workshop situation to find a number of women with fine voices and only a few mature male singers. What scenes would be appropriate? Teachers have even called us long distance asking such questions as: What can I choose that will use two excellent sopranos but will also include a young tenor who should not attempt a major aria until his vocal production is more secure, but who does need maximum exposure to opera and to acting? In the Table of Voice Categories one may even find the suitable scene in which the leading tenor of the opera has a small amount of music in a comfortable tessitura while the burden of the singing falls on the two sopranos.

Frequently persons participating in short-term opera workshops have a repertory of arias or duets already memorized; a choice of scenes using these may be the answer when rehearsal time is at a premium. Certainly it will be advantageous for the singer to perform the aria in its proper setting within the opera. An in-depth study of the character the singer is portraying and a development of the emotions and physical tensions inherent in the action and interaction of the scene can result in a more convincing performance of an aria. For this reason, we have included an index showing the excerpts in which familiar arias, duets, and ensembles appear.

The short synopsis of the action of each excerpt should whet the imagination of the person using this book. For some this may be unnecessary information; the mere title of the opera may be enough to visualize the time, place, characters, and action of the excerpt. For those who wish to pursue it further, we have included page numbers for the published piano-vocal scores most frequently found on library shelves. If the reader has access to other piano-vocal scores of the same opera, it is not difficult to find the excerpt. The page numbers are approximately the same in all scores—they may even have come from the same original plates—and certainly the plot outlined by us can be found by looking through the text of any published score of the opera.

In timing the scenes only an approximation of the length is given but in planning a workshop program, or excerpts for a voice recital, it is easy to have too much material. Some cuts have been suggested and other cuts may be made to reduce the scene to an appropriate length. We have shown the scene in its entirety as a numbered excerpt and then have used the letters *a*, *b*, *c*, etc., to indicate smaller segments of the same scene. Improvised final measures may be necessary to make an excerpt sound complete, especially those from through-composed operas.

Staging suggestions are not included because it is our premise that only those movements created by the director and brought to life by the cast will prove convincing. It is suggested, however, that persons preparing the scene spend time with the necessary research. This includes a study of the opera libretto, a study of the music, a study of historical style, and the development of a viable stage plan which will make the action believable. Doorways, even if marked only by two chairs, should be imagined to lead to another room or to the outside; that geography should remain consistent. At times it seems advantageous to have set props and hand props, while at other times pantomime is most effective. Leotards and tights may be used in lieu of costumes; in some cases, rehearsal skirts or hoops would be valuable in training the singers to walk properly.

It should be pointed out that when contemporary scores or copyrighted translations are used in public performance, permission must be obtained from the publisher holding the copyright. The royalties for such performances will vary depending upon the publisher and the length of the excerpt. Using operas which are public domain and singing these excerpts in the original language or in your own translation are certainly permissible; in fact, there is real merit in being able to work with a scene in the original language as preparation for the vocalist who will eventually need to learn entire operatic roles in foreign languages. For this reason we have included an indication of the languages found in each published score mentioned.

Opera scenes with a theme (see *The Opera Journal* 5, no. 3 [Summer 1972]) have proven to be a popular vehicle for opera workshops. Mozart Minatures, Shakespeare in Opera, Opera Americana, Puccini Portraits, Verdi Vignettes, and dozens of less confining titles—Opera Matinee, Opera Buffet, Spotlight on Opera, and Accent on Opera—have been umbrella titles for opera scenes presented on the same program. Although we have not indexed this book in that way, it would not be difficult to decide upon a theme, publicize it early, and then choose the scenes to fit the title and the singers available.

Almost any opera in the vast repertory could probably be excerpted in some way, although through-composed operas and those needing special effects and difficult stage settings are less likely to lend themselves to this treatment. In setting limitations for this volume we have used very few of Wagner's operas and have carefully indicated other operas requiring mature dramatic voices, as these voices are less likely to be found in the opera workshop as we know it today. We have included few excerpts from chamber operas; most short operas would be usable in their entirety by the same individuals and organizations using programs of scenes. We do hope we have compiled enough material to make it easier for students, teachers, and opera directors to choose opera excerpts for class and stage.

Mary Elaine Wallace
Robert Wallace

Carbondale, Illinois
September 1978

A Note on the Text

THE Index of Operas and the Index of Arias and Ensembles have been alphabetized by the commonly recognized titles without consideration for articles, e.g., *The Abduction from the Seraglio*, *Un Ballo in Maschera*, "La luce langue." The Index to Editions of Piano-Vocal Scores provides the publication date or issue number by which each score cited in the text may be found.

PUBLISHERS' ABBREVIATIONS

Al	Alkor-Edition Kassel	Int	International Music Co.
Bel	Belwin Mills	Jou	Joubert
B&H	Boosey & Hawkes, Inc.	Kal	Edwin F. Kalmus
Br	Broude Brothers, Ltd.	Nov	Novello & Co.
Chap	Chappell & Co., Inc.	Ox	Oxford University Press
Chou	Choudens	Pet	C. F. Peters Corp.
Col	Colombo	Ric	G. Ricordi
Dur	Durand	Sch	Schott und Söhne
Fab	Faber Music, Ltd.	SZ	Casa Musicale Sonzogno
Gal	Galaxy Music Corp.	UE	Universal Edition
GS	G. Schirmer, Inc.		

LANGUAGE ABBREVIATIONS

e = English, f = French, g = German, i = Italian, r = Russian

PAGE REFERENCES

opt. = optional cut   trad. = traditional cut

pp. 21-36   The excerpt begins at the top of page 21
                           and concludes with the last bar of page 36.

pp. 114/2/1-31/1/3   The excerpt begins on page 114, second
                           score, first bar, and concludes on page 131,
                           first score, third bar.

pp. 98; 101/4/2-16;   The excerpt includes all of page 98; then
120-31/1/3   cuts to page 101, fourth score, second bar,
                           and continues through the last bar of page
                           116; then cuts again to the top of page 120
                           and continues through page 131, first score,
                           third bar.

pp. 35-71 (trad.   The excerpt begins on page 35, first score,
(trad. cut 45/1/3-   first bar, and continues through page 45,
48/1/1)   first score, third bar; then traditionally cuts
                           to page 48, first score, first bar, and con-
                           tinues to the end of page 71.

VOCAL RANGES

S = Soprano,   M-S = mezzo-soprano,   C = contralto,   T =
tenor,   BAR = baritone,   BS = bass

The system used to notate vocal ranges is the one used by
Quaintance Eaton in her reference works, *Opera Production* and
Opera Production II, as diagramed below:

Soprano: Bb2-C5   Bass: F1-E3

Table of Voice Categories

VOICE CATEGORIES are grouped by range beginning with Soprano (first), Mezzo-Soprano (second), Tenor (third), Baritone (fourth), Bass (fifth), and then in combinations thereof.

In the Chorus column, F = Female, M = Male, X = Mixed, C = Children, and O = Offstage.

For the speaking roles, SpF = Female, SpM = Male, SpC = Child. For the silent roles, SF = Female, SM = Male, SC = Child, SX = Extras. "Ad lib" following a letter abbreviation indicates any number of persons in that category.

Opera	Excerpt	Lesser Roles	Chorus
	SOPRANO		
Cavalleria Rusticana	1	M-S	
Don Giovanni	6	BAR or BS	
	8a	BAR or BS	
Die Fledermaus	6	M-S, BAR	
La Forza del Destino	1a	M-S	
L'Infedeltà Delusa	5a	S, T	
Lakmé	3	M-S	
Lucia di Lammermoor	1	M-S	
Macbeth	3	BAR	
	4	S or M-S, BS	
Madama Butterfly	1a		F
Manon	3	BAR	X

Opera	Excerpt	Lesser Roles	Chorus
Medea	1	2S or S, M-S	F
	5	M-S, 2SC	
Otello	5a	M-S	
I Puritani	3a	BAR, BS	
The Seagull	3	BAR	
Il Trovatore	1a	S or M-S	
Wuthering Heights	3c	M-S	

MEZZO-SOPRANO

Opera	Excerpt	Lesser Roles	Chorus
The Ballad of Baby Doe	4	2S, 2M-S	
Carmen	2	SM or SpM	X
The Consul	3	2S or S, M-S	
L'Italiana in Algeri	4a	S, M-S	
The Rake's Progress	4a	T	

TENOR

Opera	Excerpt	Lesser Roles	Chorus
Lucia di Lammermoor	6	BS	M

BARITONE

Opera	Excerpt	Lesser Roles	Chorus
The Ballad of Baby Doe	6	2T, BAR, BS	
Otello	2	T	

BASS

Opera	Excerpt	Lesser Roles	Chorus
Il Barbiere di Siviglia (Paisiello)	3	BS	
Il Barbiere di Siviglia (Rossini)	2b	BS	
L'Elisir d'Amore	2a		X

2 SOPRANOS

Opera	Excerpt	Lesser Roles	Chorus
Ariadne auf Naxos	1		
Les Dialogues des Carmé-lites	3		
	9		F, X
Der Freischütz	2a		
	3	1-4S	F
Lohengrin	2		

Opera	Excerpt	Lesser Roles	Chorus
Norma	3a		
	4	M-S, 2SC opt.	
	4a	2SC opt.	
Le Nozze di Figaro	9		
Summer and Smoke	2	BS, SpF	

SOPRANO, MEZZO-SOPRANO

Opera	Excerpt	Lesser Roles	Chorus
Aïda	2		F, XO opt.
	2a		XO opt.
Ariadne auf Naxos	1		
The Ballad of Baby Doe	3b		
The Consul	4a	SM; S, M-S, BS opt.	
Così Fan Tutte	2a		
Les Dialogues des Carmé- *lites*	2		
	6		F
	8		
Eugene Onegin	2		
	2a		
Der Fliegende Holländer	2a		F
La Gioconda	4		
Hänsel und Gretel	1a		
L'Incoronazione di Poppea	2		
	9a		
Lakmé	1	T, BS	
	1a		
Lizzie Borden	2	SO	
	5		
Lohengrin	2		
Die Lustigen Weiber von *Windsor*	1		
Madama Butterfly	3		
	5		
	6b	SC, T	
Martha	1a		F
The Medium	1	SM	
	2	SM	

Opera	Excerpt	Lesser Roles	Chorus
The Mother of Us All	5a		
Norma	3a		
	4	M-S, 2SC opt.	
	4a	2SC opt.	
Le Nozze di Figaro	3		
The Old Maid and the Thief	1a		
	3a		
	3b	BAR	
Orfeo ed Euridice	1		
	2a		
Pique Dame	2	S, M-S or 2M-S	F
The Rape of Lucretia	4a		
Der Rosenkavalier	1	2T, BAR, BS, SC	
Suor Angelica	1	SF opt.	
The Tender Land	1a		
	5	SpC	
Werther	4a		
Wuthering Heights	3c		

SOPRANO, TENOR

Opera	Excerpt	Lesser Roles	Chorus
Aïda	3b		
Andrea Chénier	1		
	3	2BAR, 2BSO	
	3a	SpM	
Un Ballo in Maschera	2a		
The Bartered Bride	1		
	3		
	5	T, BS, SX ad lib	
	7		
La Bohème	1		
Carmen	3		
Le Comte Ory	3a		
Les Contes D'Hoffmann	3b		
Così Fan Tutte	7	S, M-S	
	7a	S	
Les Dialogues des Carmé- lites	7a		

Opera	Excerpt	Lesser Roles	Chorus
Don Carlos	2b		
	5	3BS, 4BS opt.	
Don Pasquale	7		
L'Elisir d'Amore	1		
	2c		
	4a		F
	5		
Die Entführung aus dem Serail	6		
La Fanciulla del West	2	T	
	3a	M-S	
Faust	2c		
Fidelio	1a		
La Fille du Régiment	2		
Die Fledermaus	5		
Der Fliegende Holländer	2b		
La Forza del Destino	1b		
	1c	M-S	
L'Incoronazione di Poppea	1a		
	4		
	6		
L'Infedeltà Delusa	5	S, T, BS	
	6		
Lakmé	4		
	6		
	7a		XO
	7b		
	7c	BAR or BS	MO
	7d		MO
Lohengrin	3	5SM, 2SF	
Louise	3		XO
Lucia di Lammermoor	2		
Die Lustigen Weiber von Windsor	5a		
Madama Butterfly	2	M-S	
Manon	1	2S, M-S, SpM, SM	

Opera	Excerpt	Lesser Roles	Chorus
Manon	2a		
	4c	SpM	XO
	4d		
	5a		
Manon Lescaut	3a		
	5		
	5a		
	5b		
Martha	2a		
	3a		
Il Matrimonio Segreto	1		
Medea	2		
	4a		
Mignon	1c		
	2c		
Norma	2		
Otello	1		
	4		
Les Pêcheurs de Perles	2a		
Pelléas et Mélisande	3		
	5	BAR	
	5a		
	9	SM	
La Périchole	1	SpF, 3SpM	X
	4a	SpM	
Pique Dame	3	S, M-S or 2M-S	
	4		
I Puritani	4		
Roméo et Juliette	1a	M-S, BAR	
	2a		
	4		
	6		
La Rondine	3a		
	3c		
The Saint of Bleecker Street	1b		
La Sonnambula	1		

Opera	Excerpt	Lesser Roles	Chorus
Susannah	1a		
	3		
The Taming of the Shrew	5		
The Tender Land	2		
	3		
Tosca	1a		
	4		
La Traviata	1	T	X
	1a		
	3b	S or M-S	
Il Trovatore	3	T	MO
Vanessa	3		
Wuthering Heights	3	M-S	
	3a	M-S	
	3b		

SOPRANO, BARITONE

Opera	Excerpt	Lesser Roles	Chorus
Aïda	3a		
Andrea Chénier	2a		
The Ballad of Baby Doe	1	M-SO	
Un Ballo in Maschera	3a		
Il Barbiere di Siviglia (Rossini)	2a		
La Bohème	2a		
Carmen	1		M
Cavalleria Rusticana	3		
The Crucible	3		
Don Giovanni	3a		
	8	BAR or BS, SM ad lib	
Don Pasquale	3		
Eugene Onegin	3		F
	3a		
	5		
La Fanciulla del West	1		
Die Fledermaus	5		
Der Fliegende Holländer	3a		

Opera	Excerpt	Lesser Roles	Chorus
La Gioconda	6b		
Giulio Cesare	4	BS	
	4a	BS	
L'Incoronazione di Poppea	5a		
	8a		
Lohengrin	1		
Lucia di Lammermoor	3		
Die Lustigen Weiber von Windsor	6a	2 or more SM	
Macbeth	2	BS	
	2a	SM	
Madama Butterfly	4	SF, SC	
Manon Lescaut	2	SX ad lib	
Il Matrimonio Segreto	8		
Le Nozze di Figaro	1		
	7	BAR or BS O	
The Old Maid and the Thief	2a	M-S O	
I Pagliacci	1a		
	1b		
Les Pêcheurs de Perles	3	BS	
	3a		
Pelléas et Mélisande	1		
	3		
	4		
	5	BAR	
	5a		
	7		
	9	SM	
La Périchole	1	SpF, 3SpM	X
	4a	SpM	
Peter Grimes	3a		
Rigoletto	2a		
	3a	M-S, 2T, BAR or T, 2BAR, 2BS	M
	3b	T or BAR, BS	
	3c		

Opera	Excerpt	Lesser Roles	Chorus
The Seagull	4		
Summer and Smoke	1	T, BS, SpF, SF, SX opt.	
	3	BS	
The Taming of the Shrew	6		
Tosca	2	T, BS, SX ad lib	X, C
	3b	T	
	3c		
La Traviata	2a		
Il Trovatore	4		
Werther	1		
Wuthering Heights	1a		
	2	S, T, SX opt.	
	2a		
Die Zauberflöte	2a		

SOPRANO, BASS

Opera	Excerpt	Lesser Roles	Chorus
Don Giovanni	2a		
	3a		
	8	BAR or BS, SM ad lib	
Don Pasquale	5		
Die Entführung aus dem Serail	3		
La Fille du Régiment	1		
Der Fliegende Holländer	3a		
La Forza del Destino	2	BAR or BS	MO
	2a		
Giulio Cesare	4	BS	
	4a	BS	
L'Infedeltà Delusa	2		
	3		
Lakmé	5		X opt.
Lucia di Lammermoor	5	T, BAR	X
Il Matrimonio Segreto	8		

Opera	Excerpt	Lesser Roles	Chorus
Die Meistersinger von Nürnberg	2	M-S O opt.	
Mignon	1d		
	3		
Norma	1		X
Le Nozze di Figaro	1		
I Puritani	1		
Roméo et Juliette	5a		
Susannah	4		
Vanessa	4a	SF	

2 MEZZO-SOPRANOS

Opera	Excerpt	Lesser Roles	Chorus
The Ballad of Baby Doe	7		
Don Carlos	2a		F
Giulio Cesare	1	BS	
	3a		

MEZZO-SOPRANO, TENOR

Opera	Excerpt	Lesser Roles	Chorus
Aïda	4a		
Boris Godounov	6		
Carmen	4a		
	7		
	9		XO opt.
La Cenerentola	2	S, M-S O opt.	
Le Comte Ory	1a		
La Favorita	2a	S opt.	
	5a		XO
La Gioconda	3	BAR O opt.	
Giulio Cesare	1	BS	
	3a		
Mignon	1c		
	2c		
Norma	2		
La Périchole	1	SpF, 3SpM	X
	4a	SpM	

Opera	Excerpt	Lesser Roles	Chorus
The Saint of Bleecker Street	2a		XO
Samson et Dalila	3	SM ad lib	
	3a		
Il Trovatore	2	T, BS	X
	2a	T	
	5a		
Vanessa	1a		
Werther	2	SpM O	
	4b		
	5	SO	FO or CO
	5a		

MEZZO-SOPRANO, BARITONE

Opera	Excerpt	Lesser Roles	Chorus
The Ballad of Baby Doe	2	M-S	
Il Barbiere di Siviglia (Rossini)	2a		
Boris Godounov	4		F
	4a		
Carmen	5	2S or S, M-S, BAR, BS	X
Così Fan Tutte	6		
The Crucible	2a		
Falstaff	2a		
La Favorita	3	S, T	
L'Italiana in Algeri	2		
Lizzie Borden	1		
Lohengrin	1		
Martha	3b		
Il Matrimonio Segreto	8		
La Périchole	1	SpF, 3SpM	X
	4a	SpM	
Samson et Dalila	2		
The Seagull	2		
	5	B	

Opera	Excerpt	Lesser Roles	Chorus
	MEZZO-SOPRANO, BASS		
La Gioconda	5a		
L'Italiana in Algeri	2		
Lizzie Borden	1		
Martha	3b		
Il Matrimonio Segreto	8		
Mignon	1d		
	3		
Le Nozze di Figaro	2		
The Rape of Lucretia	4d		
Der Rosenkavalier	3		M
	2 TENORS		
L'Incoronazione di Poppea	7		
	TENOR, BARITONE		
Il Barbiere di Siviglia	1a		
(Paisiello)	1b		
Il Barbiere di Siviglia	1	S or M-S, BS	
(Rossini)	1a		
La Bohème	3a		
Boris Godounov	5		
Don Carlos	1		
L'Elisir d'Amore	3		
Eugene Onegin	4	BS, SM	
Die Fledermaus	2		
La Forza del Destino	3		
	4	BAR or BS, 2SM	
	5		
La Gioconda	2	S, T, SF	
	2a		
	2b		
Il Matrimonio Segreto	4		
Otello	3a		
Les Pêcheurs de Perles	1		

Opera	Excerpt	Lesser Roles	Chorus
Pelléas et Mélisande	6		
Peter Grimes	1		
Pique Dame	1a		
The Rake's Progress	2		
	5	SO	
The Tender Land	4		

TENOR, BASS

Opera	Excerpt	Lesser Roles	Chorus
The Bartered Bride	4		
Boris Godounov	1		XO
	3b	2SM opt.	
Don Pasquale	2		
L'Elisir d'Amore	2b		
Die Entführung aus dem	1	SpM	
Serail	1a		
	4		
	4a		
Faust	1		FO, MO
La Favorita	1		
Der Freischütz	1	SM	
L'Italiana in Algeri	1		
Die Lustigen Weiber von	2		
Windsor			
Manon	4a		F
	4b		
Il Matrimonio Segreto	4		
Mefistofele	1		
Die Meistersinger von	3a		
Nürnberg	3b		

2 BARITONES

Opera	Excerpt	Lesser Roles	Chorus
Falstaff	2b		
Die Fledermaus	2		
Pelléas et Mélisande	6		

Opera	Excerpt	Lesser Roles	Chorus
BARITONE, BASS			
La Cenerentola	5		
Don Carlos	2c		
Don Pasquale	1		
	6		
Fidelio	2		M
Der Fliegende Holländer	1		MO opt.
Die Lustigen Weiber von	4	T opt.	M
Windsor	4a		
Macbeth	1		F, M
Il Matrimonio Segreto	6		
Die Meistersinger von	4		
Nürnberg			
I Puritani	3b		
Rigoletto	1		
2 BASSES			
Don Carlos	4a		
Fidelio	2		M
Der Fliegende Holländer	1		MO opt.
Il Matrimonio Segreto	6		
3 SOPRANOS			
Dido and Aeneas	1a		X
Le Nozze di Figaro	5b		
2 SOPRANOS, MEZZO-SOPRANO			
Ariadne auf Naxos	2a		
Carmen	8		
Così Fan Tutte	3a		
	5		
Les Dialogues des Carmé-	5		
lites			
Dido and Aeneas	1a		X
Hänsel und Gretel	1b		
	2	SF, SC ad lib opt.	FO

Opera	Excerpt	Lesser Roles	Chorus
Louise	2a	5S, 3M-S	F
Il Matrimonio Segreto	2		
Le Nozze di Figaro	5b		
The Old Maid and the Thief	1b		
	3	BAR	
	4		
Orfeo ed Euridice	2		
	2b		
Der Rosenkavalier	2a	T, BAR, BS	
	4	BAR, SC	
The Saint of Bleecker Street	4	BS, SM, SC, SF	F
The Seagull	1	T	

SOPRANO, 2 MEZZO-SOPRANOS

Carmen	8		
Les Dialogues des Carmélites	4	BAR	
Dido and Aeneas	1a		X
	2		X
Giulio Cesare	2	BS	
Hänsel und Gretel	1b		
Il Matrimonio Segreto	2		
The Rape of Lucretia	4b		

SOPRANO, MEZZO-SOPRANO, TENOR

Aïda	1		
	5		XO
Un Ballo in Maschera	1	T, BAR	F
	1a		
Cavalleria Rusticana	2		
Le Comte Ory	3	T, BAR, BS O	F
	5	S, M-S or 2 M-S	
Dido and Aeneas	3		X
La Favorita	2		F
Der Fliegende Holländer	2		F

Opera	Excerpt	Lesser Roles	Chorus
La Gioconda	6a	T, BS	XO
Giulio Cesare	2	BS	
Il Matrimonio Segreto	7		
Medea	4		
Mignon	2b		
	4b		
Norma	3	M-S, 2SC	
Otello	5	T, BAR, 2BS	
Pelléas et Mélisande	2		XO
The Rake's Progress	3	SM ad lib	X opt.
Rigoletto	2c		
Vanessa	1	SF	

SOPRANO, MEZZO-SOPRANO, BARITONE

Opera	Excerpt	Lesser Roles	Chorus
The Ballad of Baby Doe	3	T, BAR, SF, SM	
	3a		
	5	M-S, SM, SX ad lib	
The Consul	1a		
Così Fan Tutte	2c		
Dido and Aeneas	3		X
La Gioconda	1		
L'Incoronazione di Poppea	8		
Lizzie Borden	3a		
	4		
Louise	4		XO
The Old Maid and the Thief	2		
	5		
	6a		
Pelléas et Mélisande	2		XO
Rigoletto	2b		

SOPRANO, MEZZO-SOPRANO, BASS

Opera	Excerpt	Lesser Roles	Chorus
Les Contes D'Hoffmann	3d		
Così Fan Tutte	2c		
La Fille du Régiment	3	SpF, SpM opt.	M

Opera	Excerpt	Lesser Roles	Chorus
La Gioconda	5		XO
Lizzie Borden	3a		
Louise	4		XO
Martha	1	T, BAR, BS	F
Il Matrimonio Segreto	9		
Medea	3		M
Rigoletto	4b		MO opt.
La Traviata	3a		
2 SOPRANOS, TENOR			
Dido and Aeneas	3		X
Die Fledermaus	3		
Der Freischütz	2		
Norma	3	M-S, 2SC	
La Rondine	3b	BS	
The Saint of Bleecker Street	3	BS	
SOPRANO, 2 TENORS			
Die Fledermaus	1		
	7		
Manon Lescaut	1	BAR O	
Mignon	1a		
Susannah	1		
	2		
	5	2T, BAR, BS	X
SOPRANO, TENOR, BARITONE			
Aïda	3	M-S, BS	
Un Ballo in Maschera	2		
Il Barbiere di Siviglia (Rossini)	5		
Les Dialogues des Carmélites	1	BAR	
L'Elisir d'Amore	2d		
La Fanciulla del West	4		

Opera	Excerpt	Lesser Roles	Chorus
Die Fledermaus	1		
	4		
	7		
Help! Help! The Globolinks!	1		
L'Incoronazione di Poppea	1	2T	
Lakmé	7	BAR or BS	XO
Manon	5		M
Rigoletto	3	M-S, 2T, BAR or T, 2BAR, 2BS	M
	4c	BS	
Roméo et Juliette	1	M-S, BAR	M
Il Tabarro	2	S, T opt.	
Tosca	3	T, BAR	XO
	3a	T, BAR	
La Traviata	2	S or M-S, T, BS	
Il Trovatore	1	S or M-S	
	1b		
Die Zauberflöte	2		

SOPRANO, TENOR, BASS

Opera	Excerpt	Lesser Roles	Chorus
Il Barbiere di Siviglia (Paisiello)	4		
	4a		
	5a		
Il Barbiere di Siviglia (Rossini)	4a		
Faust	3		XO
Fidelio	4a		
La Fille du Régiment	4		
La Forza del Destino	1	M-S	
	6	BAR O	
Manon	4	SpM	F, XO
Manon Lescaut	3b		
Mefistofele	3		XO
Mignon	1b	BS	
	4c		
Les Pêcheurs de Perles	2		

Opera	Excerpt	Lesser Roles	Chorus
La Périchole	4	2SM, 2SpM or T, SpM	
Die Zauberflöte	5	SpF	
	7a		

2 SOPRANOS, BARITONE

Dido and Aeneas	3		X
Don Giovanni	4		
Die Fledermaus	3		
L'Incoronazione di Poppea	5		
Orfeo ed Euridice	2		
(seldom performed in this version)	2b		
Summer and Smoke	4	S, M-S	

SOPRANO, BARITONE, BASS

Il Barbiere di Siviglia (Rossini)	2c		
Don Giovanni	2		
	7		
Der Fliegende Holländer	3		
Pelléas et Mélisande	8a		
La Périchole	4	2SM, 2SpM or T, SpM	
I Puritani	3		
The Taming of the Shrew	2a	T, BAR opt.	

2 SOPRANOS, BASS

Don Giovanni	4		
Fidelio	1b		
The Taming of the Shrew	4		

SOPRANO, 2 BASSES

Don Giovanni	2		
	7		
Der Fliegende Holländer	3		

Opera	Excerpt	Lesser Roles	Chorus
2 MEZZO-SOPRANOS, TENOR			
Cavalleria Rusticana	2		
Mignon	2b		
MEZZO-SOPRANO, TENOR, BARITONE			
Albert Herring	2		
Il Barbiere di Siviglia (Rossini)	5		
Don Carlos	3		
La Favorita	4	T	
Giulio Cesare	3	2SM	
Madama Butterfly	6a	SF	
The Rake's Progress	4		
MEZZO-SOPRANO, TENOR, BASS			
Aïda	4		M
Il Barbiere di Siviglia (Rossini)	4a		
Carmen	4		F
Le Comte Ory	1	S	F
Faust	2a		
La Favorita	5		XO
Mignon	1b	BS	
	4c		
La Périchole	4	2SpM or T, SpM	
Samson et Dalila	1		F
2 MEZZO-SOPRANOS, BARITONE			
Giulio Cesare	3	2SM	
MEZZO-SOPRANO, 2 BARITONES			
Falstaff	2	T, BS	
Lizzie Borden	3b	SO	

Opera	Excerpt	Lesser Roles	Chorus
MEZZO-SOPRANO, BARITONE, BASS			
The Devil and Daniel Webster	1		
Lizzie Borden	3b	SO	
La Périchole	4	2SpM or T, SM	
2 MEZZO-SOPRANOS, BASS			
Il Matrimonio Segreto	9		
2 TENORS, BARITONE			
La Périchole	2		
	3	SpM	
2 TENORS, BASS			
Die Entführung aus dem Serail	2		
Die Meistersinger von Nürnberg	3		
TENOR, BARITONE, BASS			
Il Barbiere di Siviglia (Paisiello)	2		
Così Fan Tutte	1		
L'Italiana in Algeri	5		
The Taming of the Shrew	1		
TENOR, 2 BARITONES			
Così Fan Tutte	1		
La Périchole	2		
	3	SpM	
TENOR, 2 BASSES			
Il Barbiere di Siviglia (Paisiello)	2		
L'Italiana in Algeri	5		

Opera	Excerpt	Lesser Roles	Chorus
3 SOPRANOS, MEZZO-SOPRANO			
Ariadne auf Naxos	2		
Hänsel und Gretel	3		
The Saint of Bleecker Street	1a		
2 SOPRANOS, 2 MEZZO-SOPRANOS			
Falstaff	1a		
Hänsel und Gretel	3		
The Rape of Lucretia	2a		
Die Zauberflöte	6	2SM	
	8		
2 SOPRANOS, MEZZO-SOPRANO, TENOR			
Dido and Aeneas	1		X
Hänsel und Gretel	3		
Louise	2	5S, 3M-S, SM ad lib	F
2 SOPRANOS, MEZZO-SOPRANO, BARITONE			
Dido and Aeneas	1		X
Hänsel und Gretel	1		
L'Incoronazione di Poppea	9		
Il Matrimonio Segreto	3		
The Mother of Us All	1		
Le Nozze di Figaro	5a		
The Old Maid and the Thief	1		
	6		
2 SOPRANOS, MEZZO-SOPRANO, BASS			
Il Matrimonio Segreto	3		
SOPRANO, 2 MEZZO-SOPRANOS, TENOR			
Dido and Aeneas	1		X

Opera	Excerpt	Lesser Roles	Chorus
SOPRANO, 2 MEZZO-SOPRANOS, BARITONE			
La Cenerentola	1a		M
Dido and Aeneas	1		X
Hänsel und Gretel	1		
Il Matrimonio Segreto	3		
The Mother of Us All	1		
SOPRANO, 2 MEZZO-SOPRANOS, BASS			
Boris Godounov	3a		
La Cenerentola	1a		
Il Matrimonio Segreto	3		
SOPRANO, MEZZO-SOPRANO, 2 TENORS			
Die Meistersinger von Nürnberg	1		
Mignon	2a		
SOPRANO, MEZZO-SOPRANO, TENOR, BARITONE			
La Cenerentola	4		
Les Contes D'Hoffmann	2	T, BAR or BS	
La Gioconda	6	T, BS	XO
Louise	1		
Madama Butterfly	6	M-S, SC	
Martha	2		
	3		
A Midsummer Night's Dream	2		
Le Nozze di Figaro	4a		
Otello	3		
The Rape of Lucretia	3		
Rigoletto	2		
	4a		
Roméo et Juliette	2		M
Il Trovatore	5		
Werther	3		
	4	SM	

Opera	Excerpt	Lesser Roles	Chorus
SOPRANO, MEZZO-SOPRANO, TENOR, BASS			
Les Contes D'Hoffmann	1		
	2	T, BAR or BS	
L'Elisir d'Amore	4		F
La Fanciulla del West	3		
Faust	2b		
Louise	1		
Martha	2		
	3		
Mefistofele	2		
Mignon	4	BS	XO
	4a		
Roméo et Juliette	3		
The Saint of Bleecker Street	2	S, BAR, BS	X
SOPRANO, MEZZO-SOPRANO, BARITONE, BASS			
The Bartered Bride	2		
The Consul	1	S or M-S, 2SM	
Don Carlos	4b		
SOPRANO, MEZZO-SOPRANO, 2 BASSES			
Roméo et Juliette	5		
3 SOPRANOS, TENOR			
Dido and Aeneas	1		X
2 SOPRANOS, 2 TENORS			
Die Entführung aus dem Serail	5		
Mignon	2a		
La Rondine	2	SM	X opt.
	3	BS	

Opera	Excerpt	Lesser Roles	Chorus
2 SOPRANOS, TENOR, BARITONE			
La Bohème	2 2b	2BS, SF	X
Don Giovanni	5		
Le Nozze di Figaro	4a		
La Rondine	1	2S, M-S, T, BAR, BS	
2 SOPRANOS, TENOR, BASS			
Don Giovanni	5		
L'Elisir d'Amore	4		F
Fidelio	1		
Mignon	4 4a	BS	XO
La Rondine	1	2S, M-S, T, BAR, BS	
SOPRANO, 2 TENORS, BARITONE			
Die Lustigen Weiber von Windsor	5		
Madama Butterfly	1	M-S, 2SM	F
Manon Lescaut	4		
SOPRANO, 2 TENORS, BASS			
Les Contes D'Hoffmann	3a		
Die Lustigen Weiber von Windsor	5		
SOPRANO, TENOR, 2 BARITONES			
Manon	2	SF	
SOPRANO, TENOR, BARITONE, BASS			
Amahl and the Night Visi- tors	1		
Il Barbiere di Siviglia (Paisiello)	1		

Opera	Excerpt	Lesser Roles	Chorus
Don Pasquale	4	T or BS, SM	
L'Elisir d'Amore	2		X
Fidelio	4		
Manon Lescaut	3	BS, SM ad lib	
Pelléas et Mélisande	8		
The Rake's Progress	1		
The Tender Land	1b		
Wuthering Heights	1	M-S, T	
Die Zauberflöte	7	SpF, SpM	M

SOPRANO, TENOR, 2 BASSES

Les Contes D'Hoffmann	3c	T opt.	
Fidelio	4		
Tosca	1		

3 SOPRANOS, BARITONE

Dido and Aeneas	1		X
Le Nozze di Figaro	5a		

2 SOPRANOS, BARITONE, BASS

The Bartered Bride	2		

SOPRANO, 2 BARITONES, BASS

Don Giovanni	3		X
Pelléas et Mélisande	8		

SOPRANO, BARITONE, 2 BASSES

Un Ballo in Maschera	3b		
Il Barbiere di Siviglia (Rossini)	2		
Don Giovanni	3		X
Pelléas et Mélisande	10	SF ad lib opt.	

SOPRANO, 3 BASSES

Don Giovanni	3		X

Opera	Excerpt	Lesser Roles	Chorus
2 MEZZO-SOPRANOS, TENOR, BARITONE			
Les Contes D'Hoffmann	2	T, BAR or BS	
2 MEZZO-SOPRANOS, TENOR, BASS			
Les Contes D'Hoffmann	2	T, BAR or BS	
2 MEZZO-SOPRANOS, BARITONE, BASS			
Giulio Cesare	5	BS	
MEZZO-SOPRANO, 2 TENORS, BASS			
Boris Godounov	2	BS, SM ad lib	
MEZZO-SOPRANO, TENOR, BARITONE, BASS			
Amahl and the Night Visi-tors	1		
Giulio Cesare	5	BS	
MEZZO-SOPRANO, BARITONE, 2 BASSES			
Il Barbiere di Siviglia (Rossini)	2		
2 TENORS, BARITONE, BASS			
Le Comte Ory	4		M opt.
3 SOPRANOS, MEZZO-SOPRANO, TENOR			
Les Dialogues des Carmé-lites	7		
The Saint of Bleecker Street	1	SpC, SC, S, T, SF and SC ad lib	
2 SOPRANOS, 2 MEZZO-SOPRANOS, BARITONE			
Die Zauberflöte	9		

Opera	Excerpt	Lesser Roles	Chorus
2 SOPRANOS, MEZZO-SOPRANO, 2 TENORS			
Mignon	2		
2 SOPRANOS, MEZZO-SOPRANO, TENOR, BARITONE			
Carmen	6		
Lakmé	2		
Le Nozze di Figaro	4a		
Wuthering Heights	4		
2 SOPRANOS, MEZZO-SOPRANO, 2 BARITONES			
Le Nozze di Figaro	5		
2 SOPRANOS, MEZZO-SOPRANO, BARITONE, BASS			
Macbeth	1	BS or 2BS	
Il Matrimonio Segreto	10		
Le Nozze di Figaro	5		
2 SOPRANOS, MEZZO-SOPRANO, 2 BASSES			
Il Matrimonio Segreto	10		
SOPRANO, 2 MEZZO-SOPRANOS, 2 TENORS			
Mignon	2		
SOPRANO, 2 MEZZO-SOPRANOS, TENOR, BARITONE			
Carmen	6		
Le Nozze di Figaro	4a		
Die Zauberflöte	1a		
	1b		
	3	SX or SC ad lib	MO
	4a	T, BAR	
	4b		
SOPRANO, 2 MEZZO-SOPRANOS, TENOR, BASS			
Boris Godounov	3	T	FO opt.

Opera	Excerpt	Lesser Roles	Chorus
Faust	2		
Vanessa	2	SM	XO opt.
	4	SX ad lib	
	5	SX ad lib	
Die Zauberflöte	3	SX or SC ad lib	MO

SOPRANO, 2 MEZZO-SOPRANOS, BARITONE, BASS

Opera	Excerpt	Lesser Roles	Chorus
La Cenerentola	1		M
Macbeth	1	BS or 2 BS	
Il Matrimonio Segreto	10		
The Rape of Lucretia	4c		

SOPRANO, 2 MEZZO-SOPRANOS, 2 BASSES

Opera	Excerpt	Lesser Roles	Chorus
La Cenerentola	1		M
Il Matrimonio Segreto	10		

SOPRANO, MEZZO-SOPRANO, 3 TENORS

Opera	Excerpt	Lesser Roles	Chorus
The Mother of Us All	4	2M-S	X

SOPRANO, MEZZO-SOPRANO, 2 TENORS, BASS

Opera	Excerpt	Lesser Roles	Chorus
Die Meistersinger von Nürnberg	5		
Mignon	1	M-S, BS	

SOPRANO, MEZZO-SOPRANO, TENOR, BARITONE, BASS

Opera	Excerpt	Lesser Roles	Chorus
Andrea Chénier	2	2SM	F, MO
Così Fan Tutte	2		X or XO opt.
	2b		
The Crucible	2		
Help! Help! The Globolinks!	2	BAR	
L'Italiana in Algeri	4	M-S, SX ad lib opt.	
	4b		
Le Nozze di Figaro	4		X
Pique Dame	1	T, BS	

Opera	Excerpt	Lesser Roles	Chorus
I Puritani	2	T, BS	X
Rigoletto	4		MO opt.
The Tender Land	1		
La Traviata	3		XO opt.

SOPRANO, MEZZO-SOPRANO, TENOR, 2 BARITONES

Così Fan Tutte	2		X or XO opt.
	2b		
Le Nozze di Figaro	4		X
Pique Dame	1	T, BS	

SOPRANO, MEZZO-SOPRANO, TENOR, 2 BASSES

L'Italiana in Algeri	4	M-S, SX ad lib opt.	
	4b		

SOPRANO, MEZZO-SOPRANO, BARITONE, 2 BASSES

Don Carlos	4	T	

2 SOPRANOS, 2 TENORS, BASS

L'Infedeltà Delusa	1		
	4		
	7		
Mignon	1	M-S, BS	

2 SOPRANOS, TENOR, 2 BARITONES

Le Nozze di Figaro	4		X

2 SOPRANOS, TENOR, BARITONE, BASS

Fidelio	3	T, BAR or BS	M
Le Nozze di Figaro	4		X
La Traviata	3		XO opt.

Opera	Excerpt	Lesser Roles	Chorus
2 SOPRANOS, TENOR, 2 BASSES			
Fidelio	3	T, BAR or BS	M
2 SOPRANOS, BARITONE, 2 BASSES			
Un Ballo in Maschera	3		
SOPRANO, 2 TENORS, 2 BARITONES			
I Pagliacci	1		
SOPRANO, 2 TENORS, BARITONE, BASS			
Ariadne auf Naxos	3		
	3a		
SOPRANO, TENOR, 2 BARITONES, BASS			
The Rape of Lucretia	1		
SOPRANO, TENOR, BARITONE, 2 BASSES			
Il Barbiere di Siviglia (Paisiello)	5		
Il Barbiere di Siviglia (Rossini)	4		
Don Giovanni	1		
SOPRANO, TENOR, 3 BASSES			
Don Giovanni	1		
3 SOPRANOS, 2 BARITONES			
Le Nozze di Figaro	5		
3 SOPRANOS, BARITONE, BASS			
Le Nozze di Figaro	5		
MEZZO-SOPRANO, TENOR, 2 BARITONES, BASS			
La Cenerentola	3a		

Opera	Excerpt	Lesser Roles	Chorus
MEZZO-SOPRANO, TENOR, BARITONE, 2 BASSES			
Il Barbiere di Siviglia (Rossini)	4		
La Cenerentola	3a		
2 SOPRANOS, 2 MEZZO-SOPRANOS, TENOR, BARITONE			
The Rape of Lucretia	2		
Die Zauberflöte	1		
2 SOPRANOS, MEZZO-SOPRANO, 2 TENORS, BASS			
L'Incoronazione di Poppea	3		
2 SOPRANOS, MEZZO-SOPRANO, TENOR, 2 BARITONES			
Così Fan Tutte	3		
	4		
	8		X
	8a		XO opt.
Lizzie Borden	3		
2 SOPRANOS, MEZZO-SOPRANO, TENOR, BARITONE, BASS			
Albert Herring	1		
Così Fan Tutte	3		
	4		
	8		X
	8a		XO opt.
Lizzie Borden	3		
Il Matrimonio Segreto	5		
	11		
Der Rosenkavalier	2	2T, BAR, BS, SX ad lib	
2 SOPRANOS, MEZZO-SOPRANO, TENOR, 2 BASSES			
Il Matrimonio Segreto	5		
	11		

Opera	Excerpt	Lesser Roles	Chorus
SOPRANO, 3 MEZZO-SOPRANOS, TENOR, BARITONE			
Eugene Onegin	1		
SOPRANO, 2 MEZZO-SOPRANOS, TENOR, BARITONE, BASS			
La Cenerentola	6		
	6a		
Don Carlos	2	SF	F, M
			opt.
Il Matrimonio Segreto	5		
	11		
Die Zauberflöte	4	T, BAR	M
SOPRANO, 2 MEZZO-SOPRANOS, TENOR, 2 BASSES			
Il Matrimonio Segreto	5		
	11		
SOPRANO, MEZZO-SOPRANO, 2 TENORS, BARITONE, BASS			
Lucia di Lammermoor	4		X
Il Tabarro	1		
SOPRANO, MEZZO-SOPRANO, 2 TENORS, 2 BASSES			
Les Contes D'Hoffmann	3	M-S	
SOPRANO, MEZZO-SOPRANO, TENOR, 2 BARITONES, BASS			
Die Lustigen Weiber von Windsor	6	SpM, 2 or more SM	
Le Nozze di Figaro	8		
SOPRANO, MEZZO-SOPRANO, TENOR, BARITONE, 2 BASSES			
Il Barbiere di Siviglia (Rossini)	3	BAR	M
Die Lustigen Weiber von Windsor	6	SpM, 2 or more SM	
Le Nozze di Figaro	8		

Opera	Excerpt	Lesser Roles	Chorus
3 SOPRANOS, TENOR, BARITONE, BASS			
Don Giovanni	9		
	9a		
3 SOPRANOS, TENOR, 2 BASSES			
Don Giovanni	9		
	9a		
2 SOPRANOS, 2 TENORS, 2 BARITONES			
The Taming of the Shrew	3		
2 SOPRANOS, TENOR, 2 BARITONES, BASS			
La Bohème	3		
SOPRANO, 3 TENORS, BARITONE, BASS			
The Mother of Us All	2	SF, 2SM	
2 MEZZO-SOPRANOS, TENOR, BARITONE, 2 BASSES			
Il Barbiere di Siviglia (Rossini)	3	BAR	M
2 TENORS, 2 BARITONES, 2 BASSES			
A Midsummer Night's Dream	1		
	3		
	4	M-S, BS, SX ad lib all opt.	
3 SOPRANOS, 2 MEZZO-SOPRANOS, TENOR, BASS			
The Consul	2		
	4	SM	
3 SOPRANOS, MEZZO-SOPRANO, 2 BARITONES, BASS			
Peter Grimes	3		

Opera	Excerpt	Lesser Roles	Chorus
2 SOPRANOS, 2 MEZZO-SOPRANOS, TENOR, BARITONE, BASS			
Le Comte Ory	2		X
The Crucible	1a	M-S, BS	
The Rape of Lucretia	4		
2 SOPRANOS, MEZZO-SOPRANO, TENOR, BARITONE, 2 BASSES			
The Bartered Bride	6		
SOPRANO, 2 MEZZO-SOPRANOS, TENOR, BARITONE, 2 BASSES			
The Bartered Bride	6		
La Cenerentola	3		M
L'Italiana in Algeri	3		
SOPRANO, 2 MEZZO-SOPRANOS, TENOR, 2 BARITONES, BASS			
La Cenerentola	3		M
L'Italiana in Algeri	3		
SOPRANO, MEZZO-SOPRANO, TENOR, 2 BARITONES, 2 BASSES			
Die Lustigen Weiber von Windsor	3	2 or more SM	X
SOPRANO, MEZZO-SOPRANO, TENOR, BARITONE, 3 BASSES			
Die Lustigen Weiber von Windsor	3	2 or more SM	X
SOPRANO, 2 TENORS, 2 BARITONES, 2 BASSES			
Il Barbiere di Siviglia (Paisiello)	6		
SOPRANO, 2 TENORS, 3 BARITONES, BASS			
The Taming of the Shrew	2	T, BS	

Opera	Excerpt	Lesser Roles	Chorus
2 SOPRANOS, 2 MEZZO-SOPRANOS, 2 TENORS, 2 BARITONES			
Peter Grimes	2	S, BS, SM	X
2 SOPRANOS, MEZZO-SOPRANO, TENOR, 3 BARITONES, BASS			
Le Nozze di Figaro	6		
2 SOPRANOS, MEZZO-SOPRANO, TENOR, 2 BARITONES, 2 BASSES			
Le Nozze di Figaro	6		
2 SOPRANOS, MEZZO-SOPRANO, TENOR, BARITONE, 3 BASSES			
Le Nozze di Figaro	6		
2 SOPRANOS, 4 MEZZO-SOPRANOS, 2 TENORS, BASS			
The Mother of Us All	5		X
2 SOPRANOS, 2 MEZZO-SOPRANOS, 3 TENORS, BARITONE, BASS			
Falstaff	1		
2 SOPRANOS, 2 MEZZO-SOPRANOS, 2 TENORS, 2 BARITONES, BASS			
The Crucible	1	M-S, BS	
2 SOPRANOS, 4 MEZZO-SOPRANOS, 2 TENORS, BARITONE, 2 BASSES			
The Mother of Us All	3		X
3 SOPRANOS, MEZZO-SOPRANO, 4 TENORS, 2 BARITONES, BASS			
The Crucible	4	3S, 3M-S, or 2S, 4M-S, BS	

OPERA SCENES
FOR CLASS AND STAGE

AÏDA

Guiseppe Verdi (1813-1901)

Ancient Egypt

EXCERPT 1   GS/Kal i, e pp. 5/5/1-28   11 min.
                Ric   i pp. 5/5/1-28

    The role of Radamès, dramatic tenor requires a powerful mature voice of heroic quality for the important aria "Celeste Aïda" in this scene. Amneris must be a dramatic mezzo-soprano with strength at extremes of range (Bb2-C4) and Aïda, lyric spinto soprano with strong B4.

    In the hall of the King of Egypt's palace, the young warrior Radamès indulges in the hope that he may be chosen as the leader of the Egyptian forces against the invading Ethiopians. Furthermore, he hopes after returning victorious that he may ask for Aïda's hand in marriage. Radamès little suspects that Princess Amneris is in love with him and fiercely jealous of her Ethiopian slave Aïda. In a trio, Amneris, pretending friendship for Aïda, discloses her jealousy in asides while Aïda and Radamès voice their own disquieting thoughts.

EXCERPT 2   GS/Kal i, e pp. 79-110   13½ min.
                Ric   i pp. 77-107

    This scene, a dramatic dialogue between Amneris (B2-Ab4) and Aïda (to C5), also uses a chorus of slave girls (S-A), a dance of Moorish slaves which can be cut, and an offstage chorus which is doubled by the orchestra.

    The Egyptian Princess Amneris, attended by her slaves, has devised a plot to discover if her slave Aïda is indeed in love with Radamès. Aïda enters; Amneris informs her that Radamès has been slain. Aïda's reaction to the news leaves no doubt as to her feelings. Amneris then informs her that Radamès lives and that she herself is a rival for his love. Amid the sounds of the victory chorus,

Amneris commands Aïda to be present at the triumphal entry and kneel at her feet while she, Amneris, crowns Radamès with the victor's wreath.

EXCERPT 2a   GS/Kal   i, e   pp. 89/3/2-110   10 min.
                  Ric   i   pp. 86/3/3-107

Amneris and Aïda the same as above without girls' chorus. Off-stage chorus optional.

EXCERPT 3   GS/Kal   i, e   pp. 209-57   23½ min.
                 Ric   i   pp. 211-64

This scene includes Aïda's emotional aria "O patria mia" with high *pianissimo* phrases and a sustained C5. Her father, Amonasro, must be a dramatic baritone capable of maintaining the high tessitura of the famous duet "Riverdrai le foreste imbalsamate." A duet between Aïda and Radamès requires that both singers have dramatic strength and vocal maturity as well as subtlety. Amneris and Ramfis, high priest, bass, appear only briefly.

On the banks of the Nile, Aïda awaits a meeting with Radamès. She is surprised by the arrival of her father, the captive Ethiopian King Amonasro, who declares that Radamès's love for her may provide an escape for the Ethiopian captives and a victory over the Egyptians. Tearfully Aïda agrees to lure Radamès into revealing his military strategy. Radamès enters and embraces Aïda. She begs him to take flight with her and when he finally consents, she asks what route the Egyptian soldiers will be taking so they can avoid them. Radamès answers, not realizing that King Amonasro is listening and waiting to expose Radamès as a traitor to his country. Amneris appears with the cry of "traitor." Radamès surrenders himself to the high priest.

EXCERPT 3a   GS/Kal   i, e   pp. 209-32   12½ min.
                  Ric   i   pp. 211-37

The portion of excerpt 3 which contains Aïda's aria and her duet with Amonasro.

EXCERPT 3b   GS/Kal i, e   pp. 233-49/2/1   8 min.
               Ric   i   pp. 238-55/2/1

Only the duet between Aïda and Radamès from excerpt 3.

EXCERPT 4   GS/Kal i, e   pp. 258-95   18½ min.
               Ric   i   pp. 265-305

This is a demanding scene for Amneris and Radamès. Also included is Ramfis, the high priest, a bass (G1-E3) able to sing unaccompanied. The men's chorus is unison and *a capella*. Two silent
guards complete the scene.

In the hall of judgment, Amneris is desperate: Radamès is to be
tried as a traitor. When he is brought in she offers to save him if he
will only return her love. He refuses, declaring it a blessing to die
for Aïda's sake. Amneris's love is transformed into hate. As
Radamès is condemned to be buried alive, Amneris dominates the
scene with her frenzied curse of the priests, born out of her mixed
feelings of love, hate, and despair.

EXCERPT 4a   GS/Kal i, e   pp. 258-76   9 min.
               Ric   i   pp. 265-87

The portion of excerpt 4 for Amneris and Radamès, omitting
Ramfis and the other priests.

EXCERPT 5   GS/Kal i, e   pp. 296-310   11 min.
               Ric   i   pp. 306-21

This is the famous double scene, the upper floor of the stage
representing the Temple of Vulcan, and the lower, the tomb in
which Radamès has been condemned to be buried alive. The duet
for Aïda and Radamès is lyric with *pianissimo* phrases to Bb3.
The singing of Amneris is important to the scene but not difficult.
The chorus of priests (SATTBB) may be sung offstage.

Radamès, believing himself to be alone in the tomb, turns his
thoughts to his beloved Aïda. Almost immediately he discovers
that Aïda is with him; she has come to die with her lover. As
Radamès and Aïda join in a tender farewell to the world, Amneris,
in deep mourning, offers a prayer in the temple above the tomb.

ALBERT HERRING

Benjamin Britten (1913-1976)

An English Village, About 1900

EXCERPT 1   B&H   e   pp. 1-91/1/1   25 min.

A lively and exacting ensemble scene with solo lines for each of
the six principals, especially Lady Billows, soprano, a domineer-
ing village matriarch. Included are Florence Pike, Lady Billows's
housekeeper-secretary, low mezzo-soprano; Miss Wordsworth,
schoolteacher, lyric-coloratura soprano to C5; the Mayor, tenor;
the Vicar, high lyric baritone; and Police Superintendent Budd,
bass (F1-E3). Each character must be sharply defined to indicate
age and occupation within the framework of typical Victorian
English society.

Lady Billows has called the members of the town committee to
her home for a meeting to select a May Queen. As the meeting
progresses and they find none of the village girls virtuous enough
to be worthy of the title, they decide instead to crown Albert
Herring as King of the May.

EXCERPT 2   B&H   e   pp. 247-78/3/5   15 min.

This scene contains two monologues for the youthful Albert
Herring who needs a lyric tenor voice with flexibility and a Bb3.
Nancy and Sid, mezzo-soprano and baritone respectively, should
also be youthful in appearance.

Albert Herring has returned to his mother's greengrocery shop
from his coronation as King of the May (see excerpt 1), unaware
that Sid has spiked his lemonade with rum. When Nancy and Sid
pass by outside the shop, singing of their romantic adventures and
poking fun at Albert who has always led a sheltered life, Albert
resolves to leave home and, for the first time in his life, seek a
night out on the town.

AMAHL AND THE NIGHT VISITORS

Gian-Carlo Menotti (1911-)

Near Bethlehem at the Time of the Birth of Christ

EXCERPT 1   GS   e   pp. 28-33/1/3   4 min.

In this scene the four adult principals are alone onstage: Amahl's mother, mezzo-soprano or soprano who can sustain an A4; King Kaspar, tenor (E2-F3); Melchior, baritone (B1-D3); and Balthazar, bass (G#1-A2). The music is not demanding and lies in the middle register of the voices.

A poor widow has sent her son Amahl out to call the shepherds of the village to bring offerings to three kings who are following the star of Bethlehem and have stopped at her humble cottage to rest. While Amahl is away, his mother admires the rich gifts the kings have with them. When she is told that these are gifts for the newborn child, she can think only of her own child—crippled, hungry, and cold.

ANDREA CHÉNIER

Umberto Giordano (1867-1948)

France, 1789-1794

EXCERPT 1   Int/SZ   i, e   pp. 114/2/1-31/1/3   7 min.

Duet for Chénier, tenor, and Maddalena, soprano, requires sensitive personalities capable of projecting emotion. Both voices need strong middle range up to high A. Optional *pianissimo* Bb3 for Chénier.

In 1793 the first phase of the French Revolution is over. Andrea Chénier, a poet and revolutionary, has been receiving anonymous letters from a woman whom he is now waiting to meet at the Café Hottot in Paris. When she arrives it is some minutes before Chénier recognizes her as Maddalena, daughter of the Countess of Coigny at whose party Chénier recited his poetry some four years earlier.

She asks his help in her loneliness; enchanted, Chénier declares his love for her and they join in a passionate duet.

EXCERPT 2   Int/SZ   i, e   pp. 139-93   28 min.

Two well-known arias are included in this scene. Gérard's "Nemico della patria" demands a strong baritone voice capable of sustaining an F#3; Maddalena's aria "La mamma morta" is for a dramatic soprano whose range extends to B4. Madelon, mezzo-soprano (D2-G4), has a short narrative. Others are Mathieu, bass (B1-E3), and L'Incredibile, tenor (E2-G3). Silent roles of Clerk and the Young Man, and a chorus (women onstage, men offstage) complete the scene.

Gérard appears before a revolutionary tribunal with a fervent plea for money for France. A collection is taken and jewels are contributed by the women. Madelon, a blind old woman, volunteers her grandson to the defense of France. The spy L'Incredibile reports Chénier's arrest to Gérard who thus has a chance to dispose of his rival in love and win Maddalena for himself. When Maddalena learns of her lover's arrest, she offers herself to Gérard in exchange for Chénier's freedom.

EXCERPT 2a   Int/SZ   i, e   pp. 163-71/1/1;   15 min.
                                      172/2/2-93

The portion of excerpt 2 for Gérard and Maddalena only, includes both arias.

EXCERPT 3   Int/SZ   i, e   pp. 220-45   13½ min.

This scene contains a vocally demanding duet for Maddalena and Chénier, and Chénier's aria "Come un bel dì di maggio." Supporting roles in this excerpt are Roucher and Gérard, baritones; Schmidt and Mathieu (offstage), basses.

In his cell in the prison of Saint-Lazare, Chénier, awaiting execution, writes his last poem. Maddalena enters and bribes the jailer to substitute her name for that of another woman in order that she may die with her lover. A passionate love duet concludes the scene.

EXCERPT 3a   Int/SZ   i, e   pp. 232-45   7 min.
                          (If desired, this could be combined
                          with Chénier's aria, pp. 221/2/2-
                          25/3/3, for a total of 10 min.)

The duet between Maddalena and Chénier only, with Schmidt's
two spoken lines.

ARIADNE AUF NAXOS

(Ariadne on Naxos)

Richard Strauss (1874-1949)

Prologue: *Eighteenth-Century Vienna*

Opera: *Ancient Greece*

EXCERPT 1   B&H   g   pp. 65/3/2-77/2/1   6 min.

From the Prologue, the duet between the young composer and
the *commedia dell'arte* actress Zerbinetta can be extracted. The
Composer is played by a lyric or dramatic soprano, or mezzo-
soprano, dressed as a young man of eighteenth-century Vienna.
She should be boyish in appearance and have a strong vocal range
from C#3 to Bb4. Zerbinetta is a lyric-coloratura (D3-B#4) role
with a high tessitura. Her four partners, who have no singing in
this scene, may be imagined to be standing in the wings and Zerbinetta may begin by singing in that direction.
   At the home of a Viennese nouveau riche, preparations are being made for the first performance of an opera commissioned for
the occasion. The Composer, asked to make cuts in his precious
score, is momentarily diverted by the attentions of Zerbinetta.

EXCERPT 2   B&H   g   pp. 93/2/1-105/1/3;   17½ min.
                          106-12; 117/3/2-24

Ariadne, dramatic soprano (G2-Bb4) is attended by three
nymphs: Najade, lyric-coloratura soprano (to D5); Echo, light
lyric soprano; and Dryade, mezzo-soprano. Cuts have been made

to limit the scene to the four women. Further cuts could be made in Ariadne's monologue.

The scene opens with a beautiful but difficult trio sung by the three nymphs who have found the sleeping Ariadne. This is followed by Ariadne's demanding monologue lamenting her desertion by the God Theseus and welcoming death.

EXCERPT 2a   B&H   g   pp. 93/2/1-102/1/5   4 min.

The opening trio only from excerpt 2.

EXCERPT 3   B&H   g   pp. 124/4/3-94/1/1   22½ min.

The five characters in this scene must be good musicians and must be trained in *commedia dell'arte* acting style. The men are Brighella, light lyric tenor to C4; Scaramuccio, second tenor; Harlekin, lyric baritone; and Truffaldin, bass. Zerbinetta has a long, very difficult coloratura aria in this scene which should be attempted only by an experienced singer who can soar to E5 with ease.

Ariadne (see excerpt 2) does not sing in this excerpt and her presence may be merely implied. After the five commedians have tried to cheer the melancholy Ariadne, Zerbinetta appeals to the Princess as woman to woman. In a display of vocal fireworks Zerbinetta assures Ariadne that she is neither the first nor the last to be deserted by her lover. Then Zerbinetta encourages and eludes the commedians who have returned to the stage until she disappears with Harlekin, to the chagrin of the other three.

EXCERPT 3a   B&H   g   pp. 124/4/3-64/2/3   14 min.

A shorter version of excerpt 3, concluding with Zerbinetta's aria.

THE BALLAD OF BABY DOE

Douglas Moore (1893-1969)

Leadville and Denver, Colorado; Washington, D.C.; California; 1880-1899

EXCERPT 1   Chap   e   pp. 38/2/1-50   8 min.

This is the first meeting of Elizabeth (Baby) Doe, lyric-coloratura soprano who must sustain a D5 in her "Willow Song," and Horace Tabor, baritone (B1-B3). Augusta Tabor, mezzo-soprano, is heard briefly offstage.

Through a window in the Clarendon Hotel, Tabor, standing outside, hears Baby Doe singing a sentimental ballad. He applauds; she comes to the window and he sings tenderly to her. As he is about to kiss her hand, his wife Augusta calls him from her own hotel room (offstage) and he obediently retires.

EXCERPT 2   Chap   e   pp. 51-70   10½ min.

This is a confrontation scene between Augusta Tabor, mezzo-soprano who should display a mature, intense vocal quality to an A4, and her husband Horace, baritone. There is also a small mezzo-soprano part for Samantha, the maid.

Augusta, cleaning Horace's desk, finds a check made out for the purchase of the Matchless Mine. She is dismayed. Her discovery of a pair of white gloves momentarily pleases her until her maid shows her the gift card with sentimental verses addressed to Baby Doe. When Horace comes home, Augusta upbraids him and resolves to drive Baby Doe out of town.

EXCERPT 3   Chap   e   pp. 71-93   13 min.

This includes the "Letter Song" for Baby Doe (C#5 with opt. D#5), her confrontation scene with Augusta Tabor, and a short love duet between Baby Doe and Horace Tabor. The roles of Horace and Augusta in this excerpt are not difficult but require mature vocal qualities. A clerk, tenor, and a bellboy, baritone, appear briefly at the beginning of the scene as do a stodgy elderly couple (silent).

Baby Doe sits at a desk in the Clarendon Hotel lobby writing to her mother and telling her of her plans to leave Leadville where she has found the right man but cannot bring herself to interfere with his marriage. Augusta enters and warns Baby Doe to give up Horace. Baby Doe responds that she plans to do so and Augusta bids her a polite good-bye. Irritated by Augusta's actions, Baby Doe changes her mind and decides to stay in Leadville. When Horace comes she tells him of her decision and they vow never to leave each other.

EXCERPT 3a   Chap e   pp. 75/2/4-93   11 min.

The same as excerpt 3 without bellboy, clerk, and elderly couple.

EXCERPT 3b   Chap e   pp. 75/2/4-88/2/1   8½ min.

The portion of excerpt 3 with Baby Doe and Augusta only.

EXCERPT 4   Chap e   pp. 94-105   5 min.

Augusta Tabor, mezzo-soprano, must be capable of sustaining an Ab4 in this scene in which she is the central figure. Her four friends, Sarah, Mary, Emily, and Effie are a women's quartet with precise ensemble singing.

The Tabors have moved to a large house in Denver but Horace has left Augusta and is now keeping Baby Doe in a hotel. As Augusta's friends gather for tea, they urge her to tell the truth to the newspapers in a way that will hurt Horace's political ambitions. She does not become vengeful until her friends imply that her husband plans to divorce her.

EXCERPT 5   Chap e   pp. 146/3/2-68   12 min.

Baby Doe, coloratura soprano; Augusta, mezzo-soprano; Horace, baritone; Mama McCourt, Baby's mother, low mezzo-soprano; a butler; and other silent characters appear in this scene.

During a ball at the Windsor Hotel in Denver in 1893, Baby Doe, Horace Tabor's new wife, and her mother appear on the balcony. Quite unexpectedly Augusta is announced and Mama rushes off to find Horace. Augusta advises Baby Doe that Horace may be suffering financial setbacks. When Horace arrives on the scene, he berates Augusta for her visit and when she leaves, he is assured by Baby Doe that she will never give up the Matchless Mine.

EXCERPT 6   Chap e   pp. 169-85   7 min.

Horace Tabor, baritone, needs dramatic intensity and vocal strength for this scene with his four cronies: Sam, Bushy, Barney, and Jacob, a men's quartet with difficult ensembles and considerable rhythmic speech.

At the poker table the four men deride Tabor's political ambitions. When Tabor joins them he asks them to back him in his "Free Silver" platform and in his wish to risk everything to hold on to the Matchless Mine. They give excuses and completely turn on him at the mention of William Jennings Bryan, the Free Silver candidate for president. Tabor ends the scene with a soliloquy expressing contempt for the cowardice of his friends.

EXCERPT 7   Chap e   pp. 206/4/1-17   8 min.

This scene calls for two mezzo-sopranos: Augusta, who sings an intense dramatic aria with a sustained Ab4; and Mama McCourt, a rather unrefined character who sings in a lower range.

Augusta alone in her California home is shaken by Bryan's defeat in the 1896 election. Baby Doe's mother arrives pleading with Augusta to give financial aid to Tabor now ruined by the defeat of the silver standard. Augusta refuses, recalling Tabor's earlier rejection of her kindness. In a long soliloquy she recalls her love for her former husband and her regret that it is impossible for her to return to him now no matter how much he might need her.

UN BALLO IN MASCHERA

(A Masked Ball)

Giuseppe Verdi (1813-1901)

Stockholm 1792, or Colonial Boston

EXCERPT 1   GS   i, e   pp. 47-72   14½ min.
                 Kal/Int   i, e   pp. 49-80
                 Ric   i   pp. 49-80

This scene focuses on the sorceress Ulrica, a contralto or dramatic mezzo-soprano, whose aria "Re dell'abisso, affrettati"
ranges from G2 to several G's and Ab's above the staff. Other
principals are Amelia, lyric-spinto soprano (B2-B4), and Riccardo
(King Gustav III), a tenor needing a strong middle range. Also included are a short solo for Silvano, baritone; a Servant, tenor; and
a chorus of women and children.

In the disguise of a fisherman, Riccardo visits the den of Ulrica,
the fortune-teller, where a crowd is hearing Ulrica's prophecies. A
veiled woman enters. She is Amelia, wife of Riccardo's best friend,
who has come to Ulrica for help in overcoming her love for
Riccardo. The latter overhears Ulrica tell Amelia to seek a magic
herb that grows beneath the gallows outside the city. The three
join in a trio with Riccardo resolving, in asides, to meet Amelia at
the gallows at midnight.

EXCERPT 1a   GS   i, e   pp. 47-50; 51/5/5-54; 61-71   10 min.
                 Kal/Int   i, e   pp. 49-53; 55/1/5-58; 66-79/1/7
                 Ric   i   pp. 49-53; 55/1/5-58; 66-79/1/7

With cuts, excerpt 1 may be done with Ulrica, Riccardo and
Amelia only.

EXCERPT 2   GS   i, e   pp. 116-54   20 min.
                 Kal/Int   i, e   pp. 131-76
                 Ric   i, e   pp. 131-76

This scene contains the demanding soprano aria for Amelia,
"Ma dall'arido," with a range from A2 to a sustained C5. Riccardo

joins her in a duet in which he sings Bb3 or an optional C4. Renato, baritone, must have a range from A1 to G3 in the trio that follows.

Amelia goes to a field near the gallows at midnight to pick the magic herb (see excerpt 1). Riccardo finds her and she confesses her love for him but begs him to forget her for the sake of her husband's honor. Just then Amelia's husband Renato arrives to warn Riccardo that his life is in danger. Renato consents to escort the veiled Amelia back to the city without speaking to her or trying to learn her identity.

EXCERPT 2a   GS   i, e   pp. 116-40   15½ min.
                  Kal/Int   i, e   pp. 131-59
                  Ric   i   pp. 131-59

This scene is the same as excerpt 2 with Amelia and Riccardo, but ending before Renato's entrance.

EXCERPT 3   GS   i, e   pp. 176-215   21 min.
                  Int/Kal   i, e   pp. 200-48
                  Ric   i   pp. 200-48

This scene contains demanding arias for Amelia (A2-B4) and Renato (A1-G3), "Morrò, ma prima in grazia" and "Eri tu che macchiavi." The two conspirators are both basses requiring an F3. Oscar, the page, is a trouser role for light lyric-coloratura soprano who needs a trill; she sings below Amelia in the ensembles.

Renato is enraged when he discovers that it is his wife Amelia whom Riccardo met at the gallows, and he calls the conspirators to a secret meeting. Before they arrive in his study, Renato threatens to kill his wife but relents when she pleads with him to let her bid a last farewell to their son. Left alone, Renato gazes at Riccardo's portrait and expresses his anger. When the conspirators arrive and learn that Renato wishes to join their plot, they decide to draw lots for the privilege of killing Riccardo, and when Amelia returns, Renato makes her draw a name from an urn. It is his own. When Oscar arrives with the invitation to a masked ball, all join in a brilliant quintet in which they express their individual feelings about the forthcoming events.

EXCERPT 3a   GS   i, e   pp. 176-88/1/3   11 min.
              Int/Kal   i, e   pp. 200-15
              Ric   i   pp. 200-15

The opening of excerpt 3, including the two arias, can be sung by Amelia and Renato only and conclude before the entrance of Samuel and Tom.

EXCERPT 3b   GS   i, e   pp. 176-201   18 min.
              Int/Kal   i, e   pp. 200-32
              Ric   i   pp. 200-32

The excerpt begins the same as excerpt 3 but ends with the quartet naming Renato as the assassin and does not include Oscar.

IL BARBIERE DI SIVIGLIA

(The Barber of Seville)

Giovanni Paisiello (1740-1816)

Seville, Spain, About 1770

EXCERPT 1   Ric   i   pp. 6-59   27 min.

The characters in this scene are Rosina, light lyric soprano; Count Almaviva, tenor; Figaro, baritone; and Bartolo, comic bass. The role of Dr. Bartolo (Bb1-D3) tends to lie in a high range, but the other roles are all in the middle register and not too difficult.

The Count has arrived in Seville hoping to court Rosina, the ward of Dr. Bartolo. Figaro, barber and jack-of-all-trades, enters; they recognize each other, and Figaro sings of his adventures in an aria, "Scorsi già molti paesi." Rosina appears on the balcony of her house. Dr. Bartolo questions her about a piece of paper she is holding. She tells him it is a new piece of music she is learning, but while the old man is not looking, she throws it down to the Count. Accompanied by Figaro's guitar, the Count serenades Rosina with the new song. The two men then plot how they are going to outwit the old doctor so that the Count may marry Rosina.

EXCERPT 1a   Ric   i   pp. 6-28   11½ min.

The opening section of excerpt 1 with the Count and Figaro only.

EXCERPT 1b   Ric   i   pp. 52/4/4-59   3½ min.

The closing of excerpt 1 with the Count and Figaro only.

EXCERPT 2   Ric   i   pp. 65-77   5 min.

Trio for Bartolo, bass; Svegliato, bass or baritone; and Giovenetto, tenor; all comic roles not vocally demanding.

Bartolo tries to question his two servants about events that have transpired in his house while he was away. Under the influence of medicines administered by Figaro, Svegliato who yawns constantly and Giovinetto (ironically an *old* servant) who does nothing but sneeze all the time, offer little response.

EXCERPT 3   Ric   i   pp. 78-85   4 min.

An aria, "La calunnia," for Don Basilio, bass with several sustained E3's. Bartolo, bass, sings only in the recitative in this scene.

Bartolo enlists Basilio's help in drawing up a contract to marry Rosina. Basilio has seen Count Almaviva in town and Bartolo believes the Count is Rosina's unknown serenader. Basilio suggests overcoming this obstacle by slandering the Count.

EXCERPT 4   Ric   i   pp. 88/3/1-123   17 min.

Rosina, Count Almaviva, and Bartolo, as described in excerpt 1, are in this scene.

Dr. Bartolo questions his ward Rosina about the ink stains on her fingers, the quill pen still wet with ink, and a missing sheet of paper. Having actually written a love note to the Count, Rosina must give false answers. The old man upbraids her in the aria "Veramente ho torto, è vero." The Count arrives disguised as a drunken soldier. While Bartolo is not looking, the Count gives a letter to Rosina. There is a great deal of intrigue over the letter, and finally Bartolo manages to get rid of his unwanted guest. Left alone, Rosina reads the Count's letter and sings the aria "Giusto ciel, che conoscete."

EXCERPT 4a   Ric   i   pp. 97-114   7½ min.

The trio section of excerpt 4 may be used alone.

EXCERPT 5   Ric   i   pp. 124-94   31 min.

A scene for Rosina, light lyric soprano; Count Almaviva, tenor; Figaro, baritone; Bartolo and Basilio, basses.

Count Almaviva again enters the music room of Bartolo's house, this time disguised as a music teacher coming to give Rosina her voice lesson in place of the indisposed Basilio. Soon Figaro arrives to give Dr. Bartolo his shave. Don Basilio's untimely arrival causes some stir, but he is sent home "sick" with "medicine" in the form of money. All goes well until Bartolo overhears a few words between the lovers during their "music lesson." The three conspirators jokingly ridicule the enraged doctor.

EXCERPT 5a   Ric   i   pp. 124-50   17 min.

The opening portion of excerpt 5 with Rosina, the Count and Bartolo only.

EXCERPT 6   Ric   i   pp. 199-237   15½ min.

The finale of the opera. In addition to Rosina, Count Almaviva, Figaro, Bartolo, and Basilio who have been previously described, two new characters are involved: a Notary, baritone, and the Mayor, tenor.

Bartolo shows Rosina a letter the Count has given him and convinces her that her suitor is up to no good. She agrees to marry Bartolo; when Figaro and the Count enter through a window, Rosina greets them with a storm of reproaches. The Count now reveals his true identity and the lovers are united in happiness. When Don Basilio and the Notary arrive, Figaro persuades the Notary to marry Rosina to the Count instead of to Bartolo. Bartolo arrives with the Mayor and orders everyone arrested. When the Mayor, in questioning the parties involved, learns that he is in the presence of Count Almaviva and that the marriage contract has been signed, he and Bartolo have little choice but to give the couple their blessings.

IL BARBIERE DI SIVIGLIA

(The Barber of Seville)

Giocchino Rossini (1792-1868)

Seville, Spain, About 1770

EXCERPT 1   B&H/GS/Kal   i, e   pp. 31/3/1-   20 min.
                    45/3/3; 49/1/2-50/3/1; 51/2/3-71/1/3;
                    73/4/3-74/4/8
              Ric   i, e   pp. 40-100 (trad. cuts in score)

This excerpt centers around the well-known aria "Largo al fac-
totum" for Figaro, baritone (D2-G3, opt. A3) requiring strength
and flexibility in a high tessitura. Also included are the serenade
"Se il mio nome" of Count Almaviva, tenor (E2-A3) capable of
vocal agility in a high tessitura, and the duet "All'idea di quel
metallo." Rosina, mezzo or soprano, and Bartolo, bass, appear
only briefly.

On a street in Seville, Count Almaviva recognizes Figaro, a barber and jack-of-all-trades, who has entry into the homes of many
important people. The Count enlists his service in trying to win
the beautiful Rosina with whom he has fallen in love.

EXCERPT 1a   B&H/GS/Kal   i, e   pp. 54-71/1/3;   9 min.
                    73/4/3-74/4/8
              Ric   i, e   pp. 73-100 (trad. cuts in score)

The duet between Figaro and Count Almaviva.

EXCERPT 2   B&H/GS/Kal   i, e   pp. 75/3/1-   25 min.
                    85/2/3; 86/3/1-93/2/2; 94/2/2-
                    108/3/2; 108/5/4-15/2/3;
                    119/1/5-20/5/2; 122/2/2-23
              Ric   i, e   pp. 102-70 (trad. cuts in score)

This excerpt includes four well-known selections from the
opera. Rosina's "Una voce poco fà" is written for mezzo-soprano
(G#2-B4) with extreme agility for coloratura passages; often taken
by a coloratura soprano (C3-D5 or F5). (Options are found in the

appendices of some scores.) Don Basilio's aria "La calunnia" is usually transposed down a whole step, calling for a bass (B1-E3). There is a duet for Rosina and Figaro, "Dunque io son," and an aria, "A un dottor della mia sorte," for Dr. Bartolo, comic bass (Bb1-Eb3) capable of sustaining a high tessitura in contrast to the deeper bass quality of Basilio.

In her room in Dr. Bartolo's house, his ward Rosina is giving vent to her feelings in an extended coloratura aria while composing a letter to her suitor Lindoro (Count Almaviva in disguise). A visit from Figaro is interrupted by Dr. Bartolo who, with the help of Don Basilio, intends to marry Rosina himself. Bartolo knows Count Almaviva has been in town and concludes that he is Rosina's unknown serenader. Basilio suggests they create a scandal about the Count. After they leave, Figaro, who has overheard, tells Rosina that "Lindoro" awaits a note from her; Rosina produces the note she has written. Bartolo questions Rosina about the ink stains on her finger, the quill pen wet with ink and a missing sheet of paper. She gets a strict but comical upbraiding from the old man.

EXCERPT 2a   B&H/GS/Kal i, e pp. 75/3/1-   13 min.
              83/4/2; 96/3/2-107/2/7
              Ric   i, e pp. 102-12/1/2; 131/1/2-47

Rosina's aria followed by Figaro's entrance. The cut from Figaro: "io voglio" ("I've news for you") to Rosina: "ebbene" ("What news") leads to the duet for Figaro and Rosina.

EXCERPT 2b   B&H/GS/Kal i, e pp. 86/3/1-   5 min.
              93/2/2; 94/2/2-94/5/5
              Ric   i, e pp. 117-28 (trad. cut in score)

Basilio's aria, with Bartolo singing only in recitatives.

EXCERPT 2c   B&H/GS/Kal i, e pp. 75/3/1-   20 min.
              85/1/2; 96/3/2-108/3/2;
              108/5/4-15/2/3; 119/1/5-20/5/2;
              122/2/2-23
              Ric   i, e pp. 102-14/4/1; 131/1/2-70 (trad.
              cuts in score)

Rosina, Figaro, and Bartolo only; includes Rosina's aria, the duet, and Bartolo's aria.

EXCERPT 3   B&H/GS/Kal   i, e   pp. 125-97/1/2-   19 min.
                         200/2/1-201; (other possible cuts
                         163/1/2-65/1/1; 177/1/1-91/2/2)
              Ric   i, e   pp. 173-282/1/2; 289-90; (other
                         possible cuts 220/2/1-22/1/2; 243-71)

In addition to Rosina, Count Almaviva, Figaro, Bartolo, and Basilio, all described in previous excerpts, there appears in this ensemble the housekeeper Berta, usually sung by a mezzo-soprano taking the lower line while Rosina sings the top. If, however, Rosina is sung by a mezzo-soprano with a dark timbre, Berta could be a soprano and sing the top line. A sergeant, baritone (E2-F3), appears with a chorus of soldiers.

Count Almaviva enters Bartolo's house in the guise of a soldier pretending to be drunk. Bartolo, suspicious of the disguise, indignantly resists the order for the quartering of soldiers in his home. The Count manages to slip a note to his beloved Rosina; the arrival of Don Basilio and Berta, and eventually Figaro, heightens the confusion. Finally a group of soldiers arrive to arrest the intruder but when Almaviva secretly reveals his true identity to the officer, the scene concludes with a typical Rossini finale.

EXCERPT 4   B&H/GS/Kal   i, e   pp. 202-16/2/1;   28 min.
                         216/4/2-21/3/3; 223/4/1-55/3/5;
                         257/2/1-57/3/13
              Ric   i, e   pp. 291-373 (trad. cuts in score)

Rosina, Almaviva, Figaro, Bartolo, and Basilio, as described in excerpts 1 and 2, are in this scene. In the music lesson, the aria in the score may be transposed a minor third higher by sopranos, or another selection of the singer's choice may be substituted. (A synopsis of this scene may be found in excerpt 5 of Paisello's *Il Barbiere di Siviglia*, page 15.)

EXCERPT 4a   B&H/GS/Kal   i, e   pp. 202-16/2/1;   15 min.
                         216/4/2-21/3/3;223/4/1-24
               Ric   i, e   pp. 291-321 (trad. cuts in score)

Count Almaviva, Bartolo, and Rosina only; the "lesson scene" to end with Rosina's aria.

EXCERPT 5   B&H/GS/Kal   i, e   pp. 273/6/1-89;   7 min.
                            (possible cuts 275/1/1-275/5/1;
                            281/2/1-83/4/1)
                    Ric   i, e   pp. 395-417 (possible cuts indicated
                            in score)

A trio for Figaro, Count Almaviva, and Rosina.

The Count and Figaro enter Bartolo's house by means of a stolen key. Rosina reproaches them, having been shown a note indicating her lover's deception. But when the Count reveals his true identity, she realizes her mistake; the Count is delighted that she has fallen in love with him not knowing he was wealthy. The lovers exchange romantic phrases as the impatient Figaro tries to speed up the elopement process.

THE BARTERED BRIDE

(Die Verkaufte Braut)

Bedřich Smetana (1824-1884)

A Bohemian Village, About 1850

EXCERPT 1   B&H   e   pp. 32-49   11 min.
                    GS   e   pp. 32-49
                    Kal   e, g   pp. 37-57

Mařenka (Marie) and Jenik (Hans), soprano and tenor respectively, are both roles that can be sung by young, lyric voices. Both should have a high Bb.

Mařenka is unhappy because her parents have arranged a marriage for her while she is in love with Jenik. Alone in the village square, Mařenka and Jenik sing of their love in a tender, lyric duet.

EXCERPT 2   B&H e   pp. 50-81   13 min.
             GS e   pp. 50-81
             Kal e, g pp. 58-92

This scene uses Ludmila, the mother, a mezzo-soprano or soprano (D3-G4); Krušina, the father, a baritone; Kecal, a bass (E1-
E3) who must have rapid articulation; and Mařenka, soprano.

Mařenka's parents are being harangued by Kecal, the marriage
broker. He suggests a suitor, Vašek, son of Micha. Despite the
protests of Mařenka, her father promises that his daughter will
marry no one except Micha's son.

EXCERPT 3   B&H e   pp. 106-22   9 min.
             GS e   pp. 106-22
             Kal e   pp. 120-39

Vašek, a buffo tenor who sings an amusing stuttering aria, and
Marenka are included in this scene.

At the village inn Vašek is heard stuttering about having been
sent off by his mother to seek a bride. Mařenka, arriving on the
scene and realizing that this laughable character is to be her
bridegroom, does not identify herself but encourages Vašek to
take another girl who has become attracted to him.

EXCERPT 4   B&H e   pp. 123-46   13½ min.
             GS e   pp. 123-45
             Kal g, e pp. 140-65

Jenik, tenor, in this scene sings an A3 with an optional B3.
Kecal, bass, needs a wide range.

While the two men are having a drink at the village inn, Kecal
tries to bribe Jenik to renounce Mařenka. Jenik agrees as long as
Mařenka marries the son of Micha. Kecal, satisfied with the bargain, leaves Jenik singing a love song, confident the scheme will
work.

EXCERPT 5   B&H e   pp. 158-78   14 min.
             GS e   pp. 157-76
             Kal g, e pp. 178-200

A lively scene which includes Esmeralda, a circus dancer, light lyric soprano; and Vašek, buffo tenor. Others are the circus-master, tenor; an Indian, bass; and members of the troupe (mimes who perform as clowns and acrobats).

Vašek is seen admiring the beautiful Esmeralda who suggests to the circus-master that Vašek should replace the drunkard who plays the performing bear. In a charming duet in which the tenor line may be sung by either Vašek or the circus-master, Esmeralda teaches Vašek to dance.

EXCERPT 6 B&H e pp. 179-204   16 min.
       GS e pp. 177-202
       Kal g, e pp. 201-30

This is a scene for seven characters: Mařenka, lyric soprano; Ludmila, her mother, soprano or mezzo-soprano; Hata, Vašek's mother, mezzo-soprano; Vašek, tenor; Krušina, Mařenka's father, baritone; Micha, bass; and Kecal, marriage broker, bass with wide range. This excerpt could be combined with Vašek's aria from excerpt 5 if a longer scene is desired.

Vašek's parents urge him to come with them to meet his future bride. Mařenka now appears, heartbroken by the news that Jenik has sold her. She agrees to consider marrying Vašek but asks for time to think about it. The ensemble reflects this contemplative mood which continues through Mařenka's aria.

EXCERPT 7 B&H e pp. 199-212   9 min.
       GS e pp. 197-210
       Kal g, e pp. 224-40

In this excerpt, lyric soprano Mařenka's range is extended to C5. Jenik is a lyric tenor.

Mařenka, after singing her melancholy aria, is greeted by Jenik who appears to be in the best of spirits. He so annoys Mařenka that in the ensuing argument she resolves to marry Vašek.

LA BOHÈME

Giacomo Puccini (1858-1924)

Paris, About 1830

EXCERPT 1   GS i, e pp. 58/2/1-78; 82-87   16 min.
             Kal i, e pp. 40-55; 58/2/1-62
             Ric i   pp. 54/2/1-74; 78-82
             Ric i, e pp. 55/3/1-75; 79-84

The famous love scene for Mimi, lyric soprano, and Rodolfo, tenor. Both should be capable of sustaining a high C even though the tessitura of the roles is not especially high.

Rodolfo, alone is the garret on Christmas Eve, tries to concentrate on his writing when he is interrupted by a knock on the door. It is Mimi asking for a light for her candle. They fall in love at first sight, tell each other about themselves and then sing together the famous love duet after which they leave arm in arm to join the crowd at the Café Momus.

EXCERPT 2   GS i, e pp. 177-236   23 min.
             Kal i, e pp. 133-72
             Ric i   pp. 167-222
             Ric i, e pp. 179-228

Act 3 with Mimi, soprano capable of sustaining phrases with heavily orchestrated accompaniment, and Musetta, soprano, whose vocal timbre should be contrasting to that of Mimi. Rodolfo, lyric tenor, and Marcello, baritone to F3, have important singing and acting roles. In performing the entire act, the small roles of the Customs Officer and the Sergeant (basses) and the Serving Woman (silent) are necessary as is the chorus which appears briefly.

Mimi appears at the Barriére d'Enfer and confides to Marcello how difficult life with Rodolfo has become; then staying out of sight, Mimi hears Rodolfo tell Marcello that she is ill. Mimi and Rodolfo meet and decide to part while Marcello and the fiery Musetta have yet another quarrel. Realizing they cannot separate, Rodolfo and Mimi leave together, their love renewed.

EXCERPT 2a   GS   i, e   pp. 188/2/1-201/3/7   5½ min.
              Kal   i, e   pp. 140/3/1-49/1/1
              Ric   i   pp. 178/2/1-91/3/7
              Ric   i, e   pp. 188/2/1-98

This scene features only the portion of act 3 with Mimi and
Marcello.

EXCERPT 2b   GS   i, e   pp. 188/2/1-236   19 min.
              Kal   i, e   pp. 140/3/1-72
              Ric   i   pp. 178/2/1-222
              Ric   i, e   pp. 188/2/1-228

This excerpt features only the quartet of principals from act 3
and omits the lesser roles and chorus.

EXCERPT 3   GS   i, e   pp. 238-92   27 min.
              Kal   i, e   pp. 173-216
              Ric   i   pp. 223-77
              Ric   i, e   pp. 231-83

Act 4 complete includes the death of Mimi whose music is not
taxing but must be interpreted with sensitivity by an experienced
lyric soprano. Musetta, a contrasting soprano voice, has no difficult singing in this act. Rodolfo, lyric tenor, has dramatic music;
Colline, bass, sings his aria "Vecchia zimarra." Marcello and
Schaunard, baritones, complete the cast for the act.

In the garret, Rodolfo and Marcello sing a nostalgic duet. Spirits are raised when Schaunard and Colline arrive with food and
drink but the merriment is interrupted with the news that Mimi
is dying and wishes to be near Rodolfo. She and Rodolfo sing of
their love while Colline parts with his coat to provide medicine,
and the others seek help for Mimi. It is too late; Rodolfo suddenly
realizes what the others have already seen—Mimi is dead.

EXCERPT 3a   GS   i, e   pp. 238-46/3/1   4 min.
              Kal   i, e   pp. 173-79
              Ric   i   pp. 223-31/3/1
              Ric   i, e   pp. 231-40/2/1

This is the opening duet only of act 4 in which Rodolfo and
Marcello recall their happy days with Mimi and Musetta.

BORIS GODOUNOV

Modest Mussorgsky (1839-1881)

Russia and Poland, 1598-1605

EXCERPT 1	Kal	g, e	pp. 45-64	16½ min.
			(Rimsky-Korsakoff ed.)	
	Kal	r, g	pp. 51-80	20 min.
			(Lamm ed.)	
	Ox	e	pp. 50-79	20 min.

The role of Pimen, an old monk, is written for a bass who can sing an F3. Gregory should be sung by a strong-voiced lyric tenor. There is some incidental offstage music in this scene.

In the cell at the monastery, Pimen is recording the history of Russia. Gregory a novice, suddenly awakens from a nightmare. Pimen narrates the murder of Dimitri, heir to the throne, instigated by Boris Godounov who has just been crowned tsar. Gregory, realizing that he himself is about the same age as the slain heir, determines to spread the rumor that Dimitri still lives. In this way he will avenge the boy's death and claim the throne for himself.

EXCERPT 2	Kal	g, e	pp. 65-97	18½ min.
			(Rimsky-Korsakoff ed.)	
	Kal	r, g	pp. 81-118	20 min.
			(Lamm ed.)	
	Ox	e	pp. 80-117	20 min.

This scene includes the Hostess, low mezzo-soprano; Varlaam, comic bass, to F#3; Missail, light tenor; Gregory, lyric-dramatic tenor to G3; and Guard, bass, with other soldiers who do not sing.

At an inn on the Lithuanian border, the hostess is singing a folk-like ditty when Gregory and two monks, Missail and Varlaam, arrive. Varlaam sings a lively drinking song before falling into a drunken sleep. Soldiers arrive in pursuit of Gregory but in the confusion, they believe Varlaam to be the man for whom they are searching and Gregory escapes.

EXCERPT 3   Kal   g, e   pp. 98-149   28½ min.
                        (Rimsky-Korsakoff ed.)
                  Kal   r, g   pp. 119-57   25½ min.
                        or pp. 158-228   31½ min.
                        (Lamm ed.)
                  Ox   e   pp. 118-56   25½ min.
                        or pp. 157-227   31½ min.

Fyodor can be sung by a boy soprano or a young mezzo-soprano, and his sister Xenia by a light lyric soprano. The Nurse is a mezzo-soprano role with a low tessitura but also an Ab4. Boris is a demanding role for bass or bass-baritone with a dark quality up to Gb3. Shiusky should be sung by a dramatic tenor (D2-A3); a Boyar, a minor role, is also a tenor. A women's off-stage chorus could be omitted.

In the tsar's apartment, Boris's children Fyodor and Xenia are together with their nurse. Xenia is grieving over the death of her fiancé; Fyodor is studying a map of Russia. Boris enters and affirms that his son will someday rule the land. Left alone, Boris sings a magnificent monologue revealing the stress he is feeling. A Boyar asks Boris for an audience on behalf of Prince Shiusky. The Prince enters and informs Boris that the Poles are prepared to back the Pretender. Tortured by the memory of his crime, Boris seems to see the apparition of the real Dimitri and prays to God for mercy.

EXCERPT 3a   Kal   g, e   pp. 98-123/1/2   14 min.
                        (Rimsky-Korsakoff ed.)
                  Kal   r, g   pp. 158-92   14½ min.
                        (Lamm ed.)
                  Ox   e   pp. 157-91   14½ min.

This is the same as excerpt 3, ending with Boris's difficult monologue and omitting Shiusky, the Boyar, and the women's chorus.

EXCERPT 3b   Kal   g, e   pp. 131/4/1-49   10 min.
                        (Rimsky-Korsakoff ed.)
                  Kal   r, g   pp. 205/3/1-28   12 min.
                        (Lamm ed.)
                  Ox   e   pp. 204/3/1-27   12 min.

This scene taken from excerpt 3 uses only Boris, mature bass-baritone, and Shiusky, dramatic tenor, in singing roles. In staging the scene, a director might wish to use Fyodor and the Boyar to clarify the action.

EXCERPT 4 Kal g, e pp. 150-74   13 min.
         (Rimsky-Korsakoff ed.)
      Kal r, g pp. 229-55   13 min.
         (Lamm ed.)
      Ox e pp. 228-54   13 min.

The role of Marina is written for lyric mezzo-soprano and she has a beautiful aria in this scene. Rangoni, baritone, should have strength and facility. The complete scene includes a women's chorus.

Princess Marina, in her boudoir in her castle in Poland, is being entertained by her ladies-in-waiting. Left alone, she sings a mazurkalike aria expressing her royal ambitions. The Jesuit monk Rangoni enters and exhorts her to remember her duty when she ascends the throne—to convert Russia to Roman Catholicism.

EXCERPT 4a Kal g, e pp. 159-74   9 min.
         (Rimsky-Korsakoff ed.)
      Kal r, g pp. 238/4/1-55   9 min.
         (Lamm ed.)
      Ox e pp. 237/4/1-54   9 min.

This is the same scene as excerpt 4 without the opening women's chorus.

EXCERPT 5 Kal g, e pp. 175-90/1/1 9 min.
         (Rimsky-Korsakoff ed.)
      Kal r, g pp. 256-70   9 min.
         (Lamm ed.)
      Ox e pp. 255-69   9 min.

Gregory, now known as the false Dimitri, the Pretender, is a lyric-dramatic tenor; Rangoni, a baritone, Both require mature vocal qualities, but neither has extremes in range.

In the garden of the Polish Palace, Rangoni informs Dimitri that

Marina loves him passionately. Rangoni encourages the union between the two.

EXCERPT 6   Kal   g, e   pp. 200-20   11½ min.
                        (Rimsky-Korsakoff ed.)
              Kal   r, g   pp. 283-305   12 min.
                        (Lamm ed.)
              Ox   e   pp. 282-304   12 min.

Marina and Dimitri, the Pretender, meet in the garden of the Polish Palace. Marina taunts Dimitri for his lack of ambition until he finally succumbs and agrees to lead an attack against Moscow, seize the throne from Boris, and make Marina his queen.

CARMEN

Georges Bizet (1838-1875)

Seville, Spain, 1820

EXCERPT 1   Al   f, g   pp. 5-18   5½ min.
              B&H/GS/Kal   f, e   pp. 5-20
              Chou   f   pp. 5-19

The roles of Micaëla, soprano, and Morales, baritone (to F#3), can both be sung by young, lyric voices. A men's chorus completes the scene.

Commanding officer Morales and his soldiers are near the guardhouse of a public square. Micaëla, a peasant girl, comes in asking for Don José. Morales informs her that Don José will arrive with the changing of the guard, and offers the girl shelter in the guardhouse. She politely refuses the soldiers' advances and runs off, saying she will return later.

EXCERPT 2   Al   f, g   pp. 34-59   9½ min.
              B&H/GS/Kal   f, e   pp. 33-57
              Chou   f   pp. 31-56

This excerpt is included because of Carmen's famous

"Habanera," written for mezzo-soprano with a range from D3 to
F#4. She is accompanied by a chorus of cigarette girls (S-A with
divisi ending), townspeople, and soldiers (SATTB). At the end of
the scene she throws a flower at Don José, who has been ignoring
her and who does not sing in this excerpt.

EXCERPT 3   Al   f, g   pp. 60 or 61-77   8 min.
                   B&H/GS/Kal   f, e   pp. 58-73
                   Chou   f   pp. 57-73

This excerpt is the duet between Micaëla, lyric soprano, and
Don José, tenor. Neither role presents any particular vocal demands in this excerpt.
     In a public square, Don José has been thrown a flower by the
gypsy girl Carmen. He quickly hides it as he sees his village sweetheart, Micaëla, entering the square. She brings Don José news
from home and they join in a nostalgic duet.

EXCERPT 4   Al   f, g   pp. 82-125   11½ min.
                   B&H/GS/Kal   f, e   pp. 76-109
                   Chou   f   pp. 76-108

The characters in this excerpt are Carmen, mezzo-soprano, who
sings her "Séguedille;" Don José, tenor, who must sustain an A#3;
and Zuniga, bass. The two-part chorus of cigarette girls is crucial
to the completion of this scene.
     Don José is about to throw away the flower Carmen has given
him when he hears a noise from the cigarette factory. There has
been a fight; Carmen has wounded one of the girls. Carmen defiantly avoids answering the questions of Captain Zuniga who finally leaves her in Don José's charge. She then mocks Don José and
flirts with him until he agrees to let her go free if she will meet
him later at Lillas Pastia's Inn. She draws her hands free of the
rope and runs away.

EXCERPT 4a   Al   f, g   pp. 108 or 109-21   6 min.
                    B&H/GS/Kal   f, e   pp. 93-105
                    Chou   f   pp. 93/2/1-104

The portion of excerpt 4 with Carmen and Don José only.

EXCERPT 5   Al   f, g   pp. 128-171   12 min.
              B&H/GS/Kal   f, e   pp. 113-53
              Chou   f   pp. 112-47/2/5

This scene is included for its two familiar arias with chorus, the
"Gypsy Song" and the "Toreador Song." The former, sung by
Carmen, mezzo-soprano, requires flexibility and a range from B2-
G#4. The latter, sung by Escamillo, baritone, requires a strong,
low register as well as a *fortissimo* F3. Other characters are
Frasquita, soprano; Mercedes, soprano or mezzo-soprano; Morales,
baritone; Zuniga, bass; and a substantial chorus. In the original
opéra-comique version, there is a speaking part for Lillas Pastia.

In Lillas Pastia's Inn, Carmen, Frasquita and Mercedes are entertaining the soldiers and gypsy men. Just as the Inn is about to
close, Escamillo, the famous bullfighter, arrives, followed by some
admirers. Before the close of this scene, Escamillo notices Carmen
and makes known his attraction to her.

EXCERPT 6   Al   f, g   pp. 172 or 173-99   4½ min.
              B&H/GS/Kal   f, e   pp. 154-83
              Chou   f   pp. 147/3/1-75

This is the famous smugglers' quintet, a lively, exacting ensemble which calls for precise movement in keeping with the music.
The quintet is Frasquita, soprano (Db3-Bb4); Mercedes, light
mezzo-soprano or soprano (Bb3-Ab4); Carmen, mezzo-soprano
(Db3-Bb4); Remendado, tenor (Bb2-Ab3) and Dancairo, baritone
or second tenor (Bb2-F3).

When everyone else has left Lillas Pastia's Inn, the two smugglers try to persuade the women to join them on their forthcoming
missions, claiming that feminine charm will make it easier to smug-
gle goods past the guards. Carmen is the only one who resists, telling the others she is awaiting the arrival of Don José with whom
she is in love. After the others tease her and plead with her, she
finally assents.

EXCERPT 7   Al   f, g   pp. 205/3/1-34   12 min.
              B&H/GS/Kal   f, e   pp. 186/3/1-212
              Chou   f   pp. 176/3/1-202

This scene occurs between Carmen, mezzo-soprano, who should

be able to dance and play castanets; and Don José, who sings the famous tenor aria "La fleur que tu m'avais jetée."

Don José finally arrives at Lillas Pastias's tavern after serving a prison term for having let Carmen go free. Alone with him, Carmen begins her dance, but he interrupts her when he hears the sound of the retreat. She then taunts him with the thought that he is placing duty above his love for her. He shows her the flower she gave him, which he has kept while in prison, and sings of his love for her. Carmen tries to persuade him to come with her and the smugglers to the mountains.

EXCERPT 8   Al f, g pp. 286-301   6 min.
                    B&H/GS/Kal f, e pp. 262-78
                    Chou f pp. 247-61

This is the famous "Card Scene." Frasquita, soprano; Mercedes, mezzo-soprano or soprano; and Carmen are included. Carmen's part lies low in this excerpt and should be sung by a voice with a dark timbre. Frasquita and Mercedes may interchange lines when necessary to best accommodate the two voices.

Frasquita and Mercedes read their fortunes with cards. As one sees the inheritance of wealth, and the other, a passionate love affair, Carmen decides to try her luck. She finds in her cards only death.

EXCERPT 9   Al f, g pp. 396-414   7 min.
                    B&H/GS/Kal f, e pp. 373-91
                    Chou f pp. 346-63

This is the most dramatic scene in the opera for Carmen, mezzo-soprano, and Don José, tenor. It requires the intense and believable staging of Don José's stabbing of Carmen. If a chorus is not available, the offstage chorus music could be played in the accompaniment.

Carmen, in love with the bullfighter Escamillo, remains in the square while Escamillo enters the arena to prepare for the bullfight. Don José finds her there and begs her to come with him to begin a new life. She defiantly refuses, saying she will always be free. Don José's anger mounts, and amid cries of victory from the arena, he plunges his knife into Carmen's body and falls to the ground beside her.

CAVALLERIA RUSTICANA

Pietro Mascagni (1853-1945)

A Sicilian Village, Easter 1890

EXCERPT 1   GS   i, e   pp. 24-28; 70-76/2/4   9 min.
                 Kal   i, e   pp. 27-32/4/4; 74-81
                 SZ   i   pp. 25-30/2/4; 70-77

This scene includes the first recitative of the opera and then cuts
to the aria "Voi lo sapete." Santuzza, dramatic soprano or mezzo-
soprano, must have a substantial voice with a range from B2 to A4
for this aria. Mamma Lucia, mezzo-soprano (B2-D4), has a lesser
part in this scene.

The young peasant girl Santuzza finds Mamma Lucia outside
her tavern. Santuzza asks for news of her ex-lover Turiddu, Lucia's
son. When Lucia says he has gone to Francofonte to get some
wine, Santuzza confesses that she knows Turiddu has abandoned
her because he is still in love with Lola, now Alfio's wife. Santuzza,
sad and forsaken, begs Turiddu's mother to pray for her.

EXCERPT 2   GS   i, e   pp. 76/3/1-100/3/4   11 min.
                 Kal   i, e   pp. 82-112/3/4
                 SZ   i   pp. 78-105

This is the confrontation scene between Santuzza, dramatic
soprano or mezzo-soprano, and Turiddu, a strong lyric or dramatic tenor. Lola, lyric mezzo-soprano, also appears in this scene.

Santuzza, wishing to speak with her former lover Turiddu, is
waiting for him in the village square when he returns to his home.
She upbraids him for having pretended to leave the village when he
was actually visiting Lola. Soon the flirtatious Lola arrives, singing
a ditty and mocking Santuzza. Santuzza sings to Turiddu of her
love and begs him to stay with her. He repulses her, throws her to
the ground, and follows Lola into the church.

EXCERPT 3   GS   i, e   pp. 100/4/1-111/2/4   4 min.
                 Kal   i, e   pp. 112/4/1-24
                 SZ   i   pp. 106-117

This scene is a short but powerful duet between Santuzza and Alfio, baritone, both parts calling for strong, dramatic voices.

After being repulsed by her former lover Turiddu, Santuzza sees Alfio and proceeds to tell him that his wife Lola has been unfaithful to him and loves Turiddu. While Alfio swears vengeance, Santuzza expresses her guilt for having scandalized the man whom she still loves.

LA CENERENTOLA

(Cinderella)

Gioacchino Rossini (1792-1868)

Once upon a Time

EXCERPT 1 Kal i, e pp. 11-58/3/4 15½ min.
Ric i pp. 11-58/3/4
Ric i, e pp. 10-60

A lively and amusing scene featuring Clorinda, light soprano (C3-B4), and Thisbe, mezzo-soprano (B2-G4), in a comic *duettino*. Their stepsister, known as Cenerentola (Cinderella), is sung by a coloratura mezzo-soprano (A2-G#4) with extreme vocal flexibility. Don Magnifico is a comic bass role (D2-E3) with a patter aria requiring rapid articulation. Alidoro can be sung by lyric baritone or bass (B1-Eb3). A men's ensemble of courtiers may be reduced to two if necessary.

At the home of Don Magnifico, Cenerentola is making coffee for her stepsisters. When philosopher Alidoro, disguised as a beggar, comes to the door, only Cenerentola is kind to him. The men of Prince Ramiro's court arrive to invite Clorinda and Thisbe to a ball where the Prince will choose a bride. The hubbub of the girls making ready for the ball causes their father Don Magnifico to appear, awakened from a symbolic dream in which an ass (Don Magnifico himself) sprouted wings (his two daughters), flew to the top of a belfry (rose to a royal position), whereupon bells (wedding bells) began to ring wildly.

EXCERPT 1a   Kal   i, e   pp. 11-45   8½ min.
                 Ric   i   pp. 11-45
                 Ric   i, e   pp. 10-41

The same as excerpt 1 without Don Magnifico.

EXCERPT 2   Kal   i, e   pp. 58/4/1-71   9 min.
                 Ric   i   pp. 58/4/1-71
                 Ric   i, e   pp. 61-79

A *bel canto* duet for Cenerentola, coloratura mezzo-soprano
(A2-B4) and Ramiro, *leggiero* tenor (D2-B3). The offstage voices
of Clorinda and Thisbe could be eliminated by making a cut in the
scene.

Prince Ramiro and his servant Dandini have exchanged clothes
as they begin their search for a bride for the Prince—a bride who
will marry for love and not for money and a title. Cenerentola
enters the room and it is love at first sight for her and the disguised Prince who has come to Don Magnifico's house.

EXCERPT 3   Kal   i, e   pp. 74-125   19 min.
                 Ric   i   pp. 74-125
                 Ric   i, e   pp. 83-152

This excerpt contains a very florid aria for Dandini, baritone
(Ab1-F3). Other characters in the scene are Clorinda, light soprano;
Thisbe, mezzo-soprano; Cenerentola, mezzo-soprano; Prince
Ramiro, *leggiero* tenor; Magnifico, bass; and Alidoro, baritone or
bass. The ensemble of courtiers accompanies Dandini.

The Prince's valet Dandini now appears, posing as the Prince.
Clorinda, Thisbe, and Don Manifico make up to Dandini, who
encourages them while whispering asides to the Prince about what
horrible creatures they really are. After the girls are taken to the
ball, Cenerentola remains. When Alidoro appears as the town
clerk inquiring about Don Magnifico's third daughter, the mixed
reactions of the five remaining characters are combined in a rousing quintet.

EXCERPT 3a   Kal   i, e   pp. 92/4/1-125   11 min.
               Ric   i   pp. 92/4/1-125
               Ric   i, e   pp. 111/3/2-52

   The quintet of excerpt 3, without Clorinda, Thisbe and the
courtiers.

EXCERPT 4   Kal   i, e   pp. 133/4/4-36; 153-69   7 min.
               Ric   i   pp. 133/4/4-36; 153-69
               Ric   i, e   pp. 163/2/1-68; 189-213

   A comical quartet for Clorinda, soprano; Thisbe, mezzo-soprano;
Ramiro, tenor; and Dandini, baritone.
   In the palace of the Prince, Dandini, still acting the part of the
Prince, flirts with Clorinda and Thisbe. Then he discusses the ugly
creatures with Ramiro. When the girls return, Dandini tells them
he will marry one and give the other to his servant—an arrangement the girls find unacceptable indeed.

EXCERPT 5   Kal   i, e   pp. 257/3/2-69   6 min.
               Ric   i   pp. 257/3/2-69
               Ric   i, e   pp. 325/4/1-44

   A *buffo* duet for Dandini, baritone (B1-E3), and Don Magnifico,
bass (B1-D3), in which the valet finally reveals his identity to the
fiercely ambitious and disappointed father.

EXCERPT 6   Kal   i, e   pp. 271-74/5/3;   11 min.
                            279-97/1/2; 310-24
               Ric   i   pp. 271-74/5/3; 279-97/1/2; 310-24
               Ric   i, e   pp. 346-52; 357-86; 404-31

   A sextet for Clorinda, soprano; Thisbe, mezzo-soprano; Cenerentola, mezzo-soprano; Ramiro, tenor; Dandini, baritone; and Don
Magnifico, bass.
   Cenerentola, back in her home, muses on the events of the night
before, when she was magically transformed into an elegantly
dressed beauty and captured the Prince's heart at the ball. Prince
Ramiro and Dandini, in their rightful guises, come to the house;
Ramiro realizes that Cenerentola is indeed the one he loves, and
proposes marriage. Their happiness, contrasted with the indignance

of Don Magnifico and the stepsisters, provides the basis for a
lengthy, difficult ensemble.

EXCERPT 6a   Kal   i, e   pp. 271-74/5/3;   17 min.
                                279-97/1/2; 337/3/1-54
                Ric   i   pp. 271-74/5/3; 279-97/1/2;
                                337/3/1-54
                Ric   i, e   pp. 346-52; 357-86; 449-73

The same as excerpt 6 but with a different ending. The cut skips
to Cenerentola's *rondo* "Non più mesta," the best-known number
in the score, in which all is forgiven and everyone lives happily
ever after.

LE COMTE ORY

(Il Conte Ory) (Count Ory)

Gioacchino Rossini (1792-1868)

Touraine, Early Thirteenth Century

EXCERPT 1   Ric   e   pp. 51/2/1-93   20 min.
               Ric   i   pp. 47-82

A scene for Isolier, trouser role for mezzo-soprano (C3-B4) requiring flexibility throughout the range; Count Ory, high lyric
tenor with several C#4's; and the Tutor, bass-baritone (F1-F3),
who sings a difficult aria. The supporting role of Alice, soprano,
and a chorus of peasant girls (SSAA) complete the scene.
    Count Ory has been missing for a week. His page Isolier and the
Tutor are approaching Countess Adele's castle when they come
upon a hermit with a group of village girls. The hermit is really
Count Ory in disguise. Not recognizing his master, Isolier consults
the hermit on the matter of his love for Countess Adele. Thus the
Count learns that his own page is his rival for the Countess's love.

EXCERPT 1a   Ric   e   pp. 77/4/1-93   8 min.
               Ric   i   pp. 70-82

The duet between Isolier and Count Ory only.

EXCERPT 2   Ric   e   pp. 94-172   22 min.
               Ric   i   pp. 83-151

The Countess, soprano (Bb2-C5), sings a beautiful florid aria;
Ragonde is a low mezzo-soprano (A2-F4), and Robert, a baritone
(G#1-G3). The roles of Alice, Isolier, the Count, and the Tutor are
described in excerpt 1. A chorus of ladies-in-waiting, villagers, and
servants complete the scene.

The Countess Adele approaches the hermit (Count Ory in disguise) and confides in him that she seeks release from her vow of
widowhood so that she can return Isolier's love. This delights
Isolier, but the Count intends to win the Countess for himself be-
for her brother and his soldiers return from the Crusades. The
Tutor, seeing the Count's friend Robert, exposes the Count's disguise, providing the basis for an extended Rossini finale.

EXCERPT 3   Ric   e   pp. 173-224/2/6   23 min.
               Ric   i   pp. 152-202

A scene for the Countess, soprano; her companion Ragonde,
mezzo-soprano; with a chorus of ladies; and Count Ory, tenor.
Singing in four-part harmony with the Count offstage are a Cavalier, second tenor; Robert, baritone; and the Tutor, bass.

In the Countess's bedroom, the Countess and her female companions feel safe from the scheming Count Ory. During a storm, a
group of nuns seek shelter—none other then the Count Ory and
his friends in disguise. They are received by the women. The
Count strikes up a conversation with the Countess, thereby hoping
to win her love.

EXCERPT 3a   Ric   e   pp. 205/2/4-24/2/6   9½ min.
               Ric   i   pp. 186/5/1-202

The duet between the Count and the Countess from excerpt 3.

EXCERPT 4   Ric   e   pp. 225/3/2-76   15 min.
                 Ric   i   pp. 203/4/3-49

A scene for the Count, tenor; the Tutor, bass; a Cavalier, second
tenor; and Robert, baritone; joined by a chorus of men (optional).

Left alone, the four men who have disguised themselves as nuns
are joined by their companions in a rousing song. Robert has discovered the wine cellar of the castle; thus the song becomes mer-
rier as it progresses.

EXCERPT 5   Ric   e   pp. 278/5/1-312   15 min.
                 Ric   i   pp. 251/3/2-79

A trio for the Countess, soprano; the Count, tenor; and Isolier,
mezzo-soprano. A Lady and Ragonde, both mezzo-sopranos, have
small parts.

In the darkness, the Count, still disguised as a nun, thinks Isolier
is the Countess and proceeds to embrace him and sing passionately
to him. Isolier plays along with this, and an amusing trio develops
as Isolier, at the same time, takes the hand of the Countess and
sings to her.

THE CONSUL

Gian-Carlo Menotti (1911-)

An Eastern European City, About 1949

EXCERPT 1   GS   e   pp. 1-51/1/1   22 min.

The principal characters are Magda Sorel, a dramatic soprano
(B2-Ab4) with a strong personality; John Sorel, baritone (A1-F3);
and John's mother, low mezzo-soprano or contralto (A2-Ab4). A
secret police agent, bass (C2-F3), appears in this scene, as well as
two plainclothesmen (silent). A voice on a record (soprano or
mezzo-soprano) is heard at the beginning, coming from a nearby
café.

John stumbles into his apartment, wounded. His mother and
his wife Magda rush in to bandage his leg. The secret agent and

plainclothesmen arrive to search the apartment while John hides and Magda claims she has not seen her husband recently. After the police leave, John tells his wife and his mother that he must cross the frontier that night. They sing a tender farewell in the trio "Now, o lips, say goodbye."

EXCERPT 1a   GS   e   pp. 29/4/1-51/1/1   9½ min.

The portion of excerpt 1 starting after the police have left. Magda, John and his mother are the only persons involved.

EXCERPT 2   GS   e   pp. 54-104   17 min.

Seven characters are included in this scene: Magda, dramatic soprano (C3-A4); the Secretary, lyric mezzo-soprano (C3-G4); the Magician, tenor (E2-Ab3), who should be a character actor capable of learning some magic tricks; and Mr. Kofner, bass (G1-Eb3). Lesser characters in the ensemble are Anna Gomez, soprano; Vera Boronel, mezzo-soprano; and a Foreign Woman, soprano. Contrasting characterizations are important in the canonic quintet.

In the waiting room of the consulate, visa applicants are waiting for help while Mr. Kofner is translating for the Foreign Woman. Magda Sorel enters demanding to speak to the Consul. The Secretary replies that the Consul is busy and hands Magda more forms to be filled out. Nika Magadoff does some magic tricks to entertain those who are waiting. The scene ends with everyone except the Foreign Woman and the Secretary expressing the frustrations of waiting daily at the consulate.

EXCERPT 3   GS   e   pp. 105-15/4/1   7 min.

This scene centers around the Mother's well-known "Lullaby," for a mezzo-soprano or contralto voice with a low F2. Magda, soprano, appears briefly, and the Voice on the Record (see excerpt 1) is heard at the opening.

In the Sorel home, Magda and the Mother are discussing the possibility of getting a visa. Magda and John's baby is ill; his grandmother tries first to cheer him, and then she sings the lullaby.

EXCERPT 4   GS   e   pp. 150/4/4-216   23 min.

A scene for the seven characters described in excerpt 2. Magda's dramatic monologue "To this we've come" occurs in this excerpt. The Secret Police Agent appears at the end of the scene but is silent.

The same people seen in excerpt 2 are again waiting at the consulate. Unable to get a visa, the Magician proves his right to the title of artist by making a watch disappear. He then hypnotizes everyone in the room. After everyone wakes up, it is Magda's turn to speak with the Secretary. As Magda's doubts and anxieties grow stronger, she screams "Liar!" and hurls endless papers about the room. Finally the Secretary tells her that she may see the Consul as soon as his present visitor leaves. The visitor turns out to be the Secret Police Agent; as he and Magda recognize each other, Magda falls in a faint.

EXCERPT 4a   GS   e   pp. 190/3/5-216   11½ min.

Magda's aria and her dialogue with the Secretary. The incidental ensemble of Anna Gomez, Vera Boronel, and Mr. Kofner, doubling the accompaniment, may be omitted; the Secret Police Agent is silent at the end of the scene.

LES CONTES D'HOFFMANN

(The Tales of Hoffmann)

Jacques Offenbach (1819-1880)

Nuremberg; Venice; Munich, About 1800

EXCERPT 1   Chou f   pp. 79-97/3/3;   15½ min.
                          117-25/1/3; 131-37
               GS   f, e pp. 74-90/4/1; 110-18/1/3;
                          124-30/4/1
               Kal   f, e pp. 73-89/3/3; 109-17/1/3;
                          123-29/3/2

The role of Olympia calls for a light coloratura soprano capable of singing up to an Eb5; she should resemble a mechanical doll in appearance and movement. Nicklausse is a trouser role for mezzo-soprano (Bb2-G4); Hoffmann, a strong lyric tenor (F2-B3) role with rather high tessitura. Coppélius is sung by a bass (Bb1-Eb3) who should be a good actor.

The poet Hoffmann has become attracted to a girl who is actually a mechanical doll invented by Spalanzani. Coppélius persuades Hoffman to wear a pair of spectacles to make the doll appear human. Despite sarcastic comments from his friend Nicklausse, the lovesick Hoffmann is enchanted by Olympia's song "Les oiseaux dans la chàrmille."

EXCERPT 2   Chou   f   pp. 160-68/4/2;174-75;   15½ min.
                              177-97/3/1; 201-02
              GS   f, e   pp. 152-60/4/2; 166-67; 169-95
                              (trad. cut in score)
              Kal   f, e   pp. 152-59/4/3; 166-67; 169-94
                              (trad. cut in score)

This excerpt includes the best-known music from the Venetian Act: the "Barcarolle," sung by Giulietta, a soprano or mezzo-soprano (B3-Bb4) with voluptuous vocal quality and physique, and Nicklausse, mezzo-soprano (A2-F#4) trouser role; a duet for Hoffmann and Giulietta; and Dapertutto's "Scintille, diamant" (this aria with a high G# is often transposed down one whole step when the role is sung by a bass-baritone). Minor characters in the scene are Pitichinaccio, a dwarf, tenor; and Schlemil, baritone or bass.

In the gallery of Giulietta's palace, overlooking the Grand Canal of Venice, Nicklausse and Giulietta sing the "Barcarolle." Hoffmann, despite Nicklausse's warnings, becomes fascinated with Giulietta who is really under the spell of Dapertutto, a magician. For him she has stolen the shadow of Schlemil and sets out to steal Hoffmann's shadow as well. She succeeds in doing so in the duet.

EXCERPT 3   Chou   f   pp. 224-308   36½ min.
              GS   f, e pp. 218-99
              Kal   f, e pp. 214-98

Act 3, the Antonia scene, may be done uncut requiring a total of seven characters. One of them, Nicklausse, mezzo-soprano, appears very briefly and sings one short line which could conceivably be omitted. Another mezzo-soprano (D3-G#4), the Voice of the Mother, is used to represent a voice coming from a picture on the wall. The complete role of Antonia, lyric soprano, requiring a trill and high D, is found in this act. Other characters are Dr. Miracle, bass-baritone (A1-F#3); Crespel, bass (A1-E3); and Frantz, *buffo* tenor (D2-A3). Hoffmann's tenor role is more lyric and less demanding in this scene but he must be capable of singing a B3.

Hoffmann has come to Munich where he has fallen in love with the frail young singer Antonia, daughter of Crespel. Antonia is consumptive and has been forbidden to sing, but Dr. Miracle, by bringing her mother's picture to life, forces her to sing and thus brings about her death. The amusing song-and-dance aria of Crespel's deaf and inefficient servant, Frantz, and the nostalgic love duet for Hoffmann and Antonia are two of the highlights of act 3.

EXCERPT 3a	Chou	f	pp. 224-54	15½ min.
	GS	f, e	pp. 218-47	
	Kal	f, e	pp. 214-44	

The same as excerpt 3, using only Antonia (D3-Bb4), Hoffmann, Frantz, and Crespel.

EXCERPT 3b	Chou	f	pp. (224-29) 242-54	5-9 min.
	GS	f, e	pp. (218-22) 234-47 .	
	Kal	f, e	pp. (214-18) 231-44	

The same as excerpt 3, using the Antonia-Hoffmann duet only, or including the Antonia aria.

EXCERPT 3c	Chou	f	pp. 242-82	16 min.
	GS	f, e	pp. 234-73	
	Kal	f, e	pp. 231-72	

The same as excerpt 3, using Antonia, Hoffmann, Dr. Miracle, Crespel. Frantz has only two lines in this excerpt; they could be omitted.

EXCERPT 3d   Chou   f   pp. 282-308   8 min.
               GS   f, e pp. 274-94
               Kal   f, e pp. 273-94

The same as excerpt 3, using Antonia, the Voice of the Mother, and Dr. Miracle only.

COSÌ FAN TUTTE

(Women Are Like That)

Wolfgang Amadeus Mozart (1756-1791)

Naples, Eighteenth Century

EXCERPT 1   B&H   i, e   pp. 6-25   7 min.
              GS/Int   i, e   pp. 11-29/4/5
              Kal   i, e   pp. 7-24

A series of trios for the three male principals—Ferrando, lyric tenor with vocal agility; Guglielmo, baritone (B1-E3), also requiring vocal strength and agility; Don Alfonso, baritone or bass-baritone (C2-D3) who must portray an older character. It is customary for Guglielmo and Don Alfonso to exchange parts in the ensembles where they sing the same text.

On the terrace of a café, the two young officers Ferrando and Guglielmo are defending the constancy of their sweethearts Dorabella and Fiordiligi, in the face of the cynicism of Don Alfonso, an old bachelor. It is not long before the two young men place a bet with the old gentleman that their sweethearts would never be unfaithful. To prove them wrong, Don Alfonso insists that the men do exactly as he prescribes. They agree to do this for twenty-four hours and the three drink a toast to the wager.

EXCERPT 2   B&H   i, e   pp. 26-32/3/2; 33/3/3-49;   20 min.
                              53/1/1-68
              GS/Int   i, e   pp. 29/4/1-37/1/1; 37/4/1-52;
                              56/3/1-71/1/3
              Kal   i, e   pp. 25-31/3/1; 32/2/1-47; 51/2/1-68

The scene opens with a duet for Fiordiligi, lyric-spinto soprano (A2-A4), whose music is noted for its wide skips and passages down to A2, and her sister Dorabella, mezzo-soprano (D3-G#4) whose music is often florid with a high tessitura. They are joined by the three men (see excerpt 1 for description). A chorus appears briefly but it could be eliminated or sung offstage.

The two sisters are in their garden, admiring the medallions of their lovers, which they wear around their necks. Don Alfonso rushes in with word that the girls' lovers have been called off to the wars. Ferrando and Guglielmo appear and bid farewell to the unhappy sisters. A drum roll and military song signal the departure of the officers' ship. Don Alfonso attempts to console the ladies as he joins them in a prayer for a safe journey.

EXCERPT 2a   B&H   i, e   pp. 26-31/3/7   4 min.
              GS/Int i, e   pp. 29/5/1-36/2/6
              Kal   i, e   pp. 25-30

From excerpt 2, this is only the duet for Fiordiligi and Dorabella.

EXCERPT 2b   B&H   i, e   pp. 26-32/3/2;   18 min.
                    33/3/3-79; 56-68
              GS/Int i, e   pp. 29/5/1-37/1/1; 37/4/1-52;
                    59/2/1-71/1/3
              Kal   i, e   pp. 25-31/3/1; 32/2/1-47; 55-68

The same as excerpt 2 but with the principals only, no chorus necessary.

EXCERPT 2c   B&H   i, e   pp. 63-68   3 min.
              GS/Int i, e   pp. 66-71/1/3
              Kal   i, e   pp. 63-68

Only the final trio of excerpt 2, sung by Fiordiligi, Dorabella, and Don Alfonso.

EXCERPT 3   B&H   i, e   pp. 71-136/2/6   28 min.
              GS/Int i, e   pp. 73-137/2/6
              Kal   i, e   pp. 71-134

All six principals appear in this scene. Despina, the ladies' chambermaid is a typical soubrette, a light lyric soprano who seldom sings above A4 and often has the lower line in ensembles. Here Fiordiligi has a *bravura* aria, "Come scoglio," with leaps and runs in a range from A2 to C5. Dorabella's aria lies in a high range for a mezzo-soprano and is the only portion of her role that borders on the dramatic rather than the lyric. Don Alfonso, Ferrando and Guglielmo, described in excerpt 1, are in this scene; Ferrando and Guglielmo each have an aria.

Inside Fiordiligi's and Dorabella's house, Despina is preparing breakfast for the ladies and complaining of her servitude. The ladies arrive with a somewhat exaggerated show of grief and almost immediately Dorabella vents her rage in the aria "Smanie implacabili." When Despina finally learns that the ladies' boyfriends have gone off to war, she encourages the girls to have fun, which is probably what their heroes are doing. While she sings a bouncy aria expressing contempt for philandering males, her two mistresses indignantly leave the room. Then Don Alfonso proceeds to bribe Despina into assisting him in his little scheme. He introduces her to two "Albanians" who are really Ferrando and Guglielmo in disguise. The "Albanians" set out to woo each other's sweethearts, receiving nothing but negative responses. They laugh at Don Alfonso who reminds them that he has twenty-four hours to win the wager. Ferrando closes with the romantic aria "Un'aura amorosa."

EXCERPT 3a   B&H   i, e   pp. 71-87   8 min.
                GS/Int   i, e   pp. 73-88/3/5
                Kal   i, e   pp. 71-87/2/5

The portion of excerpt 3 with the female characters only, including Despina's and Dorabella's arias but not Fiordiligi's.

EXCERPT 4   B&H   i, e   pp. 143-95   17 min.
               GS/Int   i, e   pp. 142/4/1-99
               Kal   i, e   pp. 139-96

This scene is a through-composed ensemble using the six characters as described in previous scenes. The two leading men and women sing in pairs and Despina has an impersonation of a doctor usually involving an affectation of vocal quality.

Fiordiligi and Dorabella begin this act 1 finale with a melancholy *duettino*. They are soon interrupted by the desperate cries of Ferrando and Guglielmo who have taken "poison" because of their unrequited love. When Despina is asked to fetch a doctor, she returns disguised as the doctor herself and proceeds to "cure" the men of their poisoning. As the men revive, the sisters are urged by Despina and Don Alfonso to take pity on the men and yield to their embraces. The ladies vehemently rebel and act 1 ends in a rousing sextet.

EXCERPT 5   B&H   i, e   pp. 196-97/4/1;   8 min.
                      202/4/1-16/2/4
             GS/Int   i, e   pp. 200-201/4/1; 204/5/3-19
             Kal   i, e   pp. 197-98/4/1; 201/5/3-14/2/4

Despina, Fiordiligi and Dorabella as described in excerpts 2 and 3.

In the ladies' house, Despina, in a sprightly aria, lectures Fiordiligi and Dorabella to indulge in a diversion to pass the time until their boyfriends return from military service. After Despina leaves, the sisters discuss the possibility and decide that a discreet frivolity would not be out of line. Their duet reflects the gaiety with which they set about to accomplish this.

EXCERPT 6   B&H   i, e   pp. 228/1/2-/2/2;   6½ min.
                      229/2/2-39/1/6
             GS/Int   i, e   pp. 231/2/1-/2/2; 232/1/3-41/2/6
             Kal   i, e   pp. 226/2/2-/3/3; 227/1/3-35
             (with appropriate cuts in the recitatives of
                      Fiordiligi and Ferrando)

A scene for Dorabella, mezzo-soprano (D3-F4), and Guglielmo, baritone (D2-D4).

In the garden, Guglielmo, in Albanian disguise, woos Dorabella who is really Ferrando's sweetheart. In this tender lyric duet, Guglielmo gives Dorabella a heart-shaped locket, removing the miniature of Ferrando that she has been wearing.

EXCERPT 7   B&H   i, e   pp. 278-79/3/1; 282/4/3-   8½ min.
                83/4/1; 290/1/2-91/3/2; 294/4/1-
                96/5/3; 297/4/3-300/1/1; 300/3/2-
                302/1/4
               GS/Int   i, e   pp. 281/2/1-82/2/2; 285/2/1-/5/1;
                292/5/1-93/5/2; 295/5/2-98/2/4;
                299/3/2-301/2/1; 303/1/2-304
               Kal   i, e   pp. 273/3/1-74/5/1; 277/2/1-/5/1;
                284/2/2-85/2/3; 287/2/2-89;
                290/4/5-93/8/1; 294/1/3-95

Fiordiligi, soprano (E3-A4), and Ferrando, tenor (F#2-A3), sing
a florid duet in this scene while Dorabella, mezzo-soprano, and
Despina, soprano, sing only in the recitatives.

Dorabella receives congratulations from Despina on her sensible
behavior. An indignant Fiordiligi declares that the only way she
and her sister can retain their honor is by joining the men at the
battlefront. No sooner has she sent Dorabella and Despina off to
fetch some old uniforms than Ferrando, still in Albanian garb, arrives in a final attempt to win Fiordiligi. In the middle of an extended duet, the music speaks for her as her heart is conquered by
the new love.

EXCERPT 7a   B&H   i, e   pp. 290/3/2-91/3/2;   7½ min.
                294/4/1-96/5/3; 297/4/3-300/1/1;
                300/3/2-2/1/4
               GS/Int   i, e   pp. 292/6/3-93/5/2; 295/5/2-
                98/2/4; 299/3/2-302/2/1; 303/1/2-4
               Kal   i, e   pp. 284/3/3-85/2/3; 287/2/2-89;
                290/4/5-93/3/1; 294/1/3-95

Excerpt 7 omitting Dorabella.

EXCERPT 8   B&H   i, e   pp. 309/3/1-63   18½ min.
               GS/Int   i, e   pp. 311-66
               Kal   i, e   pp. 302-57

All six characters as described in earlier excerpts appear for a
complicated finale with a chorus of servants and wedding guests.

Ferrando and Guglielmo, having lost the bet with Don Alfonso,
are persuaded by him to marry their "new" sweethearts, who are

actually each other's former sweethearts. Likewise, the girls have
made up their minds to marry their "Albanian" suitors. Don Alfonso and Despina prepare an elaborate wedding feast. As the two
couples are toasting their happiness, Despina has cleverly disguised
herself as a notary and enters with the marriage contract. Just as
the contract is signed, the military drums are heard; it is the officers Ferrando and Guglielmo returning from the war. In the midst
of tremendous confusion, the bridegrooms "hide" but actually
return in their military uniforms. Eventually the truth is revealed,
all is forgiven and the opera ends with a rousing finale.

EXCERPT 8a   B&H   i, e   pp. 309/3/1-11/2/1;   15 min.
                       312/2/2-14; 324/2/4-63
                GS/Int   i, e   pp. 311-12; 313/3/3-16/1/3;
                       324/3/4-66
                Kal   i, e   pp. 302-3; 304/3/3-6; 314/3/1-57

This scene is the same as excerpt 8 but without the chorus.

THE CRUCIBLE

Robert Ward (1917-)

Salem, Massachusetts, 1692

EXCERPT 1   Gal   e, g   pp. 7-109   28 min.

    Act 1 complete is an ensemble scene requiring many individual
characterizations. Abigail Williams, a young servant girl, is a high
lyric soprano (B2-B4); Ann Putnam, a dramatic soprano (C#3-
Bb4). Betty Parris, mezzo-soprano, is primarily an acting role; she
sings only in the ensemble. Rebecca Nurse, an old woman, is an
important mezzo-soprano or contralto role (G#2-F4), as is Tituba
(B2-F#4), a West Indian slave. Giles Corey and Rev. Samuel Parris
are both tenors, Parris requiring a C4. John Proctor and Thomas
Putnam are high dramatic baritones both requiring an F#4. The
major bass role is the Reverend Mr. Hale (F#1-E3); Francis Nurse
is a lesser bass role.

The scene takes place in the Parris home with Betty's room on a different level from the entrance and the parlor. Parris is kneeling at the bedside of his daughter Betty. There has been speculation that her illness might be from unnatural causes, as there has been talk of witchcraft in the town. The men of the community quarrel about this and later the neighbors begin a psalm, praying for God's help, at which point Betty begins writhing and screaming.

Hale, known for his skill in discovering witches, arrives. He soon learns that the slave Tituba has played an important role in what is happening and that she knows conjuring. She is sent for and finally confesses that she has been in communication with the devil but has refused to do anything evil. With this confession the spell over Betty is broken and all rejoice in a hymn of thanksgiving.

EXCERPT 1a Gal e, g pp. 55/2/1-109   12½ min.

The second half of act 1, omitting the roles of John Proctor and Giles Corey.

EXCERPT 2 Gal e, g pp. 110-67   25½ min.

The complete act 2 features John Proctor, a dramatic baritone (G1-G#3) singing in a high tessitura, and his wife Elizabeth, dramatic mezzo-soprano (A2-A4). Mary Warren, lyric soprano (C3-Bb4), sings mostly in the middle range; Cheever, tenor (C2-B3), and Hale, bass (A1-E3), complete the scene.

John Proctor returns home after a day's planting on his farm. Elizabeth has discharged the servant Abigail Williams, suspecting that she has seduced John. Abigail now appears to be at the center of some trouble concerning witchcraft. When John is reluctant to expose the girl, Elizabeth warns him to tear the last feelings for Abby from his heart.

Mary Warren, their current servant, returns from court and reports that many have been arrested. Hale and Cheever enter with a warrant for Elizabeth's arrest. Abby has accused Elizabeth of using a witch's poppet (doll) to try to kill her. John knows that Mary made the poppet; he prevails upon her to go to the court and tell her story.

EXCERPT 2a   Gal   e, g   pp. 110-37/2/1   14 min.

This is the opening of excerpt 2 in which Elizabeth and John
Proctor have a confrontation.

EXCERPT 3   Gal   e, g   pp. 168-79/2/2   6 min.

A scene between Abigail Williams, a soprano (D3-B4) needing
sustained lyricism, and John Proctor (see excerpts 1-2).
John meets the youthful Abigail Williams in the woods. She
tries to persuade him to leave his wife Elizabeth and to join her in
the holy work of cleansing the corrupt town. Instead, he pleads
that she free the town from her foolishness; he threatens to expose
her fraud. She defies him, saying that anything that happens to
Elizabeth now is of his doing.

EXCERPT 4   Gal   e, g   pp. 179/2/3-241   18½ min.

The characters in this scene, all described previously, are Abigail Williams, Mary Warren, Ann Putnam, sopranos; in a brief part,
Elizabeth Proctor, mezzo-soprano; Parris, Giles, and Cheever,
tenors; John Proctor and Thomas Putnam, baritones; Hale and
Francis Nurse, basses. In addition, Judge Danforth, a dramatic
tenor, and an ensemble of six girls (SSA) are in this ensemble
scene demanding strong individual characterizations.
As the court opens, Giles Corey accuses Thomas Putnam of
charging witchcraft out of greed for his neighbors' land. The judge
sentences Corey to jail. John Proctor presents Mary Warren's
statement that Abigail is continuing her witches' fraud to dispose
of John's wife, Elizabeth. In an attempt to clear his wife, John
confesses to adultery with Abigail. Elizabeth is brought in but
fails to confirm John's confession. All but the Reverend Mr. Hale
close in on John Proctor with sadistic vindictiveness.

THE DEVIL AND DANIEL WEBSTER

Douglas Moore (1893-1969)

Cross Corners, New Hampshire, 1840s

EXCERPT 1   B&H   e   pp. 36/2/1-56   13½ min.

The characters in this scene are: Mary Stone, mezzo-soprano (C3-A4), Jabez Stone, bass (F#1-D3), both singing primarily in the middle range; and Daniel Webster, dramatic baritone (Bb1-Gb3).

Jabez Stone, a newly married farmer, has sold his soul to the devil in order to obtain material wealth. The devil in the form of Mr. Scratch, a Boston lawyer, has appeared at the wedding celebration to claim Jabez's soul. The neighbors denounce him and leave the couple alone. Jabez proceeds to tell his bride Mary how he came to make his bargain. They appeal to Daniel Webster, secretary of state, who witnessed the events at the wedding reception; he promises to help them. The scene closes with Mary's simple but effective prayer.

LES DIALOGUES DES CARMÉLITES

(The Dialogues of the Carmelites)

Francis Poulenc (1899-1963)

Paris and Compiègne, France, 1789

EXCERPT 1   Ric   f, e   pp. 1-31   17 min.

Blanche de la Force, a lyric soprano (C#3-A4) requiring subtlety, is heard in this scene with her brother the Chevalier de la Force, a tenor who sings mostly in the middle register but must have a Bb3. Their father the Marquis, baritone, is a strong character. A Servant, baritone, appears briefly.

The Marquis de la Force is sitting in his study when his son bursts in with the news that Blanche has not returned from church and he has heard that her carriage has been surrounded by

a revolutionary mob. Blanche, hiding her fears, decides in the
course of this scene to enter the Carmelite order—a decision to
which her father can offer little resistance.

EXCERPT 2   Ric   f, e   pp. 32-47   9½ min.

Blanche, described in excerpt 1, has an interview with the Prioress, a mezzo-soprano (B2-F4) who must give the impression of
being elderly.

In the parlor of the Carmelite convent, Blanche, separated from
the Prioress by a grille, discusses her reason for wishing to join the
Carmelites; the Prioress in turn explains to the young girl the rules
of the order. Blanche chooses for herself the name Sister Blanche
of the Agony of Christ, and the Prioress blesses her.

EXCERPT 3   Ric   f, e   pp. 48-64   9 min.

This is a scene between Blanche, lyric soprano (E#3-B4), and
Sister Constance, a light lyric soprano who sings in a high register.

In a workroom of the convent, the young Sister Constance is
chattering about things which have amused her. Blanche rebukes
her for speaking lightly while the old Prioress is dying. When Constance says that she finds death amusing and confides in Blanche
that it would be a good thing for the two girls to die together,
Blanche forbids her to go on. Constance is apologetic and bewildered.

EXCERPT 4   Ric   f, e   pp. 65-97   17 min.

Mother Marie should be a high mezzo-soprano (Cb3-Bb4) of
lighter timbre but no less authoritative than the Prioress who is
very feeble at this point. Blanche, soprano, has little singing but an
important acting role; a Doctor, baritone, appears briefly.

The Prioress is on her deathbed, confiding in her friend Mother
Marie to whom she entrusts the spiritual care of the novice
Blanche. She gives some final words of wisdom to Blanche. After
becoming delirious, the Prioress wishes to speak to Blanche once
more but dies before she can begin.

EXCERPT 5   Ric   f, e   pp. 98-111   9 min.

The three characters in this scene—Blanche, Constance, and
Mother Marie—are described in excerpts 1, 3, and 4.

Sisters Blanche and Constance are completing their vigil over
the body of their Prioress. Constance goes to fetch the next pair
of sisters. Blanche, frightened, goes to the door and leaves the
body unattended. Mother Marie, discovering this, at first reprimands Blanche, then comforts her in her fears.

EXCERPT 6   Ric   f, e   pp. 112-24   8½ min.

Scene with Madame Lidoine, dramatic soprano requiring vocal
strength up to a Bb4, who is the new Prioress; Mother Marie,
mezzo-soprano; and the chorus of sisters in an unaccompanied
"Ave Maria."

The new Prioress, Madame Lidoine, addresses the members of
the order and after a few words from Mother Marie, the chorus
sings the "Ave Maria."

EXCERPT 7   Ric   f, e   pp. 125-46   11 min.

The scene includes Sister Constance, Sister Blanche, and the
new Prioress, three sopranos of different timbres; the Chevalier,
tenor; and Mother Marie, mezzo-soprano. (See excerpts 1-6 for
detailed descriptions.)

The Chevalier urges Sister Blanche to return to the family home.
He is distraught at her stubborn refusal. Mother Marie comforts
the young woman who fears she may have acted too proudly.

EXCERPT 7a   Ric   f, e   pp. 130-44/4/2   8 min.

The same as excerpt 7 with only Blanche and the Chevalier.

EXCERPT 8   Ric   f, e   pp. 194-204   5 min.

Blanche, soprano, and Mother Marie, mezzo-soprano, as described in excerpts 1-4, are involved in this dramatic excerpt.

Blanche is living in her family home, now ravaged by the mob,
as a servant to some revolutionaries. Mother Marie bursts in
dressed as a civilian, demanding that Blanche come with her to a
safer place. Blanche refuses.

EXCERPT 9   Ric   f, e   pp. 227-42   6½ min.

In the final scene of the opera, the chorus of nuns must number exactly fourteen (seven sopranos and seven altos) plus Sister Constance, light lyric soprano, and Blanche, lyric soprano. A mixed chorus represents the crowd; some soldiers and the Father Confessor should be included if the scene is staged.

As the crowd gathers (the orchestral interlude can be used for this action although it is not included in the piano-vocal score), the nuns who have been condemned to death are brought to the square. In the crowd the Father Confessor dressed in civilian clothes and wearing a Cap of Liberty, murmurs the absolution and makes a furtive sign of the cross as the Carmelites ascend the scaffold singing "Salve Regina." Their chorus diminishes one by one as the thumps of the guillotine are heard offstage. Sister Constance is the last and her face beams as she sees Blanche making her way through the crowd to join the others in death. Blanche mounts the steps and sings, but her voice is silenced by the final thump of the guillotine.

DIDO AND AENEAS

Henry Purcell (1659-1695)

Ancient Carthage

EXCERPT 1   B&H   e, g   pp. 3-23   12½ min.
               Br   e   pp. 4-32
               Kal/Nov   e   pp. 3-25/3/5
               Ox   e, g   pp. 2-30/3/7

The opening scene of the opera contains important passages for Belinda, light lyric soprano (D3-G4), and Dido, mezzo-soprano or soprano (C3-G4). The role of Aeneas is scored for a tenor (D2-E3) but is more often sung by a baritone. A Second Woman, soprano or mezzo-soprano, sings the harmony with Belinda. A chorus of men and women completes the scene.

Dido, the tragic Queen of Carthage, is urged by Belinda to lighten her mood and marry her suitor, the Trojan Prince Aeneas.

EXCERPT 1a   B&H   e, g   pp. 3-14/3/8   8 min.
Br   e   pp. 4-18
Kal/Nov   e   pp. 3-15
Ox   e, g   pp. 2-18/1/8

Same as excerpt 1 without Aeneas.

EXCERPT 2   B&H   e, g   pp. 24-34   8½ min.
Br   e   pp. 33-49
Kal/Nov   e   pp. 25/4/1-37
Ox   e, g   pp. 30/4/1-48

This scene calls for a Sorceress, dramatic mezzo-soprano (C3-F4), and two Witches, soprano and mezzo-soprano, with a mixed chorus. The Echo Chorus and/or the Dance of the Furies at the close of the scene may be cut if necessary.

The Sorceress, with her attending witches, plots the ruin of Carthage and Queen Dido.

EXCERPT 3   B&H   e, g   pp. 61-71   13½ min.
Br   e   pp. 78-89
Kal/Nov   e   pp. 48-66
Ox   e, g   pp. 76-87

This scene includes Dido's lament 'When I am laid in earth." The roles of Dido, Aeneas (with an F3 and optional G3), and Belinda are described in excerpt 1. Again the chorus plays an important part.

Aeneas has been warned by a messenger of the gods (actually an ally of the Sorceress in disguise) that he must leave Carthage to fulfill his destiny in Rome. He tries to tell Dido that the gods are responsible for his desertion; she scornfully rejects his explanation and rejects him, too, when he promises to defy the gods and stay. Left alone, Dido laments her fate and welcomes death.

DON CARLOS

Giuseppe Verdi (1813-1901)

Madrid, Mid-Sixteenth Century

EXCERPT 1   GS   i, e   pp. 7/3/2-11; 13/3/1-   8½ min.
                           24/1/1; 28
                 Int i, e   pp. 6/2/2-10/2/3; 12/2/1-22;
                           27/2/1-27/5/3
                 Kal/Ric (4-act)   i   pp. 7/3/2-11; 13/3/1-
                           24/1/1; 28

The roles of Don Carlos, tenor, and Rodrigo, baritone, are both
written for lyric voices bordering on the dramatic, with solid vocal
techniques.

In this scene, Don Carlos has come to the tomb of his grandfather, Carlos V, in the Monastery of San Giusto, to forget his
troubles, particularly his love for Elisabeth de Valois who for political reasons only, has married his father. He welcomes his friend
Rodrigo who urges Carlos to liberate Flanders. The two men
swear eternal friendship.

EXCERPT 2   GS   i, e   pp. 29-100   38 min.
                 Int i, e   pp. 28-102
                 Kal/Ric (4-act)   i   pp. 29-100

All of the major characters appear in this scene. Queen Elisabeth's soprano singing is primarily in the middle register but requires subtlety and consistency from Bb2-Bb4. Princess Eboli, high
dramatic mezzo-soprano, has a *bravura* aria in this scene with coloratura passages and several A4's. Tebaldo, trouser role for light
mezzo-soprano, is considerably less demanding. Others are King
Philip II, a *basso cantante* capable of sustaining a heavy quality in
the upper register; and Don Carlos and Rodrigo (see excerpt 1).
The women of the chorus are important in this scene; the men,
less important, could be omitted. The crucial role of the Countess
of Aremberg is silent.

In a garden Princess Eboli awaits the Queen. With Tebaldo, the
Queen's page, she entertains the court with a Moorish lovesong.

Elisabeth enters and Rodrigo hands her a message from Carlos. She agrees to see Carlos, who again declares his love for her; but she reminds him of his duty to his father. Philip, finding the Queen unattended, is furious, and banishes the Countess of Aremberg, her lady-in-waiting, from the court. After the Queen withdraws, Philip bids Rodrigo stay behind. In a long duet, Rodrigo begs relief for Flanders. The King argues against this and expresses his misgivings about Carlos and Elisabeth.

EXCERPT 2a	GS	i, e	pp. 29-46	7½ min.
	Int	i, e	pp. 28-45	
	Kal/Ric (4-act)	i	pp. 29-46	

This is the opening section of excerpt 2 using Eboli, Tebaldo, and the women's chorus. It ends with the Moorish romance.

EXCERPT 2b	GS	i, e	pp. 60-73	9 min.
	Int	i, e	pp. 61-76	
	Kal/Ric (4-act)	i	pp. 60-73	

From excerpt 2, this is the duet section with Elisabeth and Don Carlos.

EXCERPT 2c	GS	i, e	pp. 82-100	10 min.
	Int	i, e	pp. 85-102	
	Kal/Ric (4-act)	i	pp. 82-100	

This is the final duet from excerpt 2, using King Philip and Rodrigo.

EXCERPT 3	GS	i, e	pp. 101-28	12 min.
	Int	i, e	pp. 103-29	
	Kal/Ric (4-act)	i	pp. 101-27	

Princess Eboli, mezzo-soprano (Bb2-B4), has dramatic singing in this scene. Included are Don Carlos, tenor, and Rodrigo, baritone (see excerpt 1 for description).

In the palace garden, Carlos keeps a rendezvous with a lady he presumes to be Elisabeth. As he meets the masked figure in the dark and pours out his love to her, the lady is revealed to be Eboli. She vows vengeance and determines to expose the love of Carlos and Elisabeth. Even the diplomat Rodrigo cannot calm her fury.

EXCERPT 4   GS   i, e   pp. 194-242   31 min.
                 Int   i, e   pp. 187-253
                 Kal/Ric (4-act)   i   pp. 191-239

This excerpt includes the aforementioned characters of King
Philip, Queen Elisabeth, Rodrigo, and Eboli who have a magnificent quartet during the scene. Philip sings the famous soliloquy
"Ella giammai m'amò" requiring great subtlety. Eboli has the high
dramatic mezzo-soprano aria "O don fatale" with a sustained Cb5.
The Grand Inquisitor appearing in this scene is aged and blind. A
deep bass (opt. E1), he has a stormy dialogue with King Philip,
also a bass. The Count of Lerma, tenor, sings only one line.

Philip is seated alone at the desk in his study, lamenting his
wife's unloving attitude toward him. The Grand Inquisitor is announced; he demands the life of Rodrigo, a threat to the Church.
The King refuses, claiming Rodrigo to be the only man he can
trust. Elisabeth runs in reporting her jewel box missing. The King
replies that it is on his desk, and he asks her to open it. She refuses;
he opens it himself and finds a picture of Don Carlos. His charge
of infidelity causes Elisabeth to faint. Eboli and Rodrigo come to
her aid and convince Philip of his wife's innocence. Left alone
with the Queen, Eboli admits stealing the jewel box and further-
more admits being the King's mistress. The Queen demands that
Eboli go into exile or enter a convent. Left alone, Eboli curses her
beauty and vows to save Don Carlos whose life is in danger.

EXCERPT 4a   GS   i, e   pp. 194-213   17 min.
                  Int   i, e   pp. 187-206
                  Kal/Ric (4-act)   i   pp. 191-210

This is the beginning of excerpt 4 using only the two basses,
King Philip and the Grand Inquisitor, who should have voices of
different timbre. Without Philip's aria, the scene is approximately
9 minutes.

EXCERPT 4b   GS   i, e   pp. (194-201) 214-42   14 min.
                  Int   i, e   pp. (187-94) 207-35
                  Kal/Ric (4-act)   i   pp. (191-98) 211-39

Excerpt 4 beginning with Elisabeth's entrance omits the Grand

Inquisitor. This could be combined with King Philip's opening aria for a scene of approximately 23 minutes.

EXCERPT 5   GS   i, e   pp. 271-99   17 min.
              Int   i, e   pp. 260-88
              Kal/Ric (4-act)   i   pp. 268-96

The final duet between Don Carlos, tenor, and Elisabeth, soprano, both strong, mature lyric voices. Lesser singing for King Philip, a Friar, and the Grand Inquisitor, all basses; and four guards who sing only one line.

Elisabeth, awaiting Don Carlos alone at the Monastery of San Giusto, sings a nostalgic aria reminiscent of happier days. Carlos comes to bid her a last farewell, for now, since the death of Rodrigo, he must go lead the Flemish. The lovers are discovered by the King and the Inquisitor who immediately orders the death of Carlos. But the mysterious Friar, believed to be the ghost of Carlos V, appears to lead the young prince into the safety of the cloister.

DON GIOVANNI

Wolfgang Amadeus Mozart (1756-1791)

Seville, Seventeenth Century

EXCERPT 1   B&H   i, e   pp. 8-31   11 min.
              GS/Kal   i, e   pp. 8-29

The opening scene of Mozart's masterpiece introduces Don Giovanni, a baritone or lyric bass (Bb1-Eb3) with a romantic quality; Leporello, his servant, a *basso buffo* (A1-D3), and the Commendatore, *basso profondo* (D2-D3). The role of Donna Anna calls for a high dramatic or spinto soprano (F3-A4); Don Ottavio is sung by a lyric tenor (F2-G3) with flexibility.

In the courtyard of the Commendatore's palace, Don Giovanni, who has attempted to seduce Donna Anna, is challenged to a duel by her father, the Commendatore. The old man succumbs to Don Giovanni's sword. Don Giovanni and Leporello flee, and the distraught Donna Anna is comforted by her fiancé, Don Ottavio, in a powerful duet in which they both swear vengeance on her father's murderer.

EXCERPT 1a   B&H   i, e   pp. 21/4/1-31   6 min.
              GS/Kal i, e   pp. 20-29

From excerpt 1, this is the duet of Donna Anna and Don Ottavio only.

EXCERPT 2   B&H   i, e   pp. 32-54   12½ min.
             GS/Kal i, e   pp. 30-49

Donna Elvira, sung by a soprano (D3-Bb4) with strength in the middle register, appears in this scene with Don Giovanni and Leporello (see description in excerpt 1). Leporello sings the famous "Catalogue Aria," a patter song requiring humor and flexibility.

In a lonely square Don Giovanni and his servant Leporello spy a woman who appears to be mourning a lost love. As Don Giovanni approaches her she turns around and he recognizes her as Donna Elvira, one of the many women he has seduced and deserted. She launches into a tirade about his deceitfulness. Don Giovanni manages to escape and leave the distraught lady with Leporello. He proceeds to console her by showing her his master's catalogue in which is recorded the numerous philanderings of the Don.

EXCERPT 2a   B&H   i, e   pp. 44/2/2-54/1/5   6 min.
              GS/Kal i, e   pp. 40/6/2-49

This is Donna Elvira's conversation with Leporello and his aria from excerpt 2.

EXCERPT 3   B&H   i, e   pp. 55-72   8 min.
             GS/Kal i, e   pp. 50/5/1-68/1/6

Zerlina, a light lyric soprano who must sing in the middle range of her voice, and Masetto, a youthful bass or baritone, are supported by a chorus of peasants. Don Giovanni, baritone or lyric bass, and Leporello, *basso buffo*, appear. Leporello sings only in the recitatives in this scene and Don Giovanni has his famous lyric duet with Zerlina, "Là ci darem la mano."

In the country, Zerlina and Masetto are celebrating their forthcoming marriage. When Don Giovanni enters and sees Zerlina, he
succeeds in having Leporello take care of Masetto and the peasants
so that he can be alone with her.

EXCERPT 3a   B&H   i, e   pp. 66-72   4½ min.
               GS/Kal   i, e   pp. 61/5/1-68/1/6

From excerpt 3, the duet between Don Giovanni and Zerlina.

EXCERPT 4   B&H   i, e   pp. 66-76/3/6   6½ min.
              GS/Kal   i, e   pp. 61/5/1-71/4/5

This begins with the duet between Don Giovanni and Zerlina
from excerpt 3 and adds Donna Elvira, soprano.

Don Giovanni has almost succeeded in winning Zerlina when
Donna Elvira appears on the scene, scolding Don Giovanni and
singing an aria which warns Zerlina of the falseness of the man
who is wooing her.

EXCERPT 5   B&H   i, e   76/4/1-102   15½ min.
              GS/Kal   i, e   71/5/1-97/2/7

This scene contains a dramatic soprano recitative and aria for
Donna Anna, "Or sai chi l'onore," and Don Ottavio's lyric sustained tenor aria "Dalla sua pace." The voices of Donna Elvira and
Don Giovanni are included in a quartet with the other two (see
vocal descriptions in excerpts 1 and 2).

Donna Anna and Don Ottavio approach their friend Don Giovanni in the countryside, asking him to help them find the murderer of Donna Anna's father. Donna Elvira's accusations, however,
begin to arouse suspicion, and in Don Giovanni's parting words,
Donna Anna recognizes the voice as that of the murderer of her
father. She recounts the horrible events of that evening, again
swearing vengeance.

EXCERPT 6   B&H   i, e   pp. 111-17/4/4   4½ min.
              GS/Kal   i, e   pp. 104/3/1-10

Masetto has only a few lines of recitative to sing in this scene
which includes Zerlina's aria "Batti, batti."

When Masetto upbraids his fiancée for flirting with Don Giovanni, she begs forgiveness.

EXCERPT 7   B&H   i, e   pp. 170-89/3/4   11 min.
               GS/Kal   i, e   pp. 159-75

This excerpt has the same characters as excerpt 2: Leporello, Don Giovanni, and Donna Elvira.

On a street in front of Donna Elvira's dwelling, Don Giovanni plots his conquest of Donna Elvira's maid. Donna Elvira suddenly appears at the balcony window with protestations of love for the Don. Don Giovanni exchanges cloaks with Leporello, and with the help of darkness, induces Leporello to lure away Donna Elvira. Don Giovanni then serenades the maid.

EXCERPT 8   B&H   i, e   pp. 187/4/1-202   11 min.
               GS/Kal   i, e   pp. 174-87/3/8

This excerpt uses the same characters as excerpt 3 with the addition of a few peasant men (silent). Masetto sings only recitatives in this scene.

Don Giovanni serenades Donna Elvira's maid (see excerpt 7). As Masetto approaoches, the Don assumes the manner of his servant Leporello and Masetto's friends dash off in search of the Don. When they have left he gives Masetto a sound thrashing. Zerlina enters to find Masetto in a battered condition and she prescribes her own personal cure for him in the engaging aria "Vedrai, carino."

EXCERPT 8a   B&H   i, e   pp. 198-202   4½ min.
                GS/Kal   i, e   pp. 183/4/1-87/3/8

This is the scene with Zerlina and Masetto only from excerpt 8.

EXCERPT 9   B&H   i, e   pp. 198-240   19-24 min.
               GS/Kal   i, e   pp. 183/4/1-222; 234-39

In the garden of the Commendatore's palace, an intriguing sextet occurs involving the pairs of Leporello and Elvira, Anna and Ottavio, Zerlina and Masetto (see vocal descriptions excerpts 1-3).

The scene begins with Zerlina's aria "Vedrai, carino." Leporello

does so well with his ludicrous impersonation of Don Giovanni
(see excerpt 7) that Donna Elvira will not let go of him; the other
four principals, also mistaking him for the Don, seek revenge.
Donna Elvira defends him, but eventually he is forced to reveal his
true identity. The scene continues through Don Ottavio's "Il mio
tesoro," and Donna Elvira's aria "Mi tradí."

EXCERPT 9a   B&H   i, e   pp. 203-24/2/6   8 min.
                  GS/Kal   i, e   pp. 187/4/1-212

Using the same characters as excerpt 9, this is the sextet portion
only.

DON PASQUALE

Gaetano Donizetti (1797-1848)

Rome, Early Nineteenth Century

EXCERPT 1   Kal   i, e   pp. 9-22   8 min.
                  Ric   i, e   pp. 8-23

Don Pasquale, an aging bachelor, is sung by a comic bass (Ab1-
Eb3); Dr. Malatesta, his friend, by a lyric baritone (C2-F3) who
can sustain a high tessitura.

Don Pasquale has expressed his desire to marry and wishes to
disinherit his nephew. Dr. Malatesta comes to visit Pasquale's home
and describes in his aria "Bella siccome un'angelo" the bride he has
picked out for Pasquale. Malatesta says she is his "sister." Pasquale,
full of enthusiasm, ends the excerpt with a lively song.

EXCERPT 2   Kal   i, e   pp. 23-39   8 min.
                  Ric   i, e   pp. 24-43

This scene is between Don Pasquale, comic bass, and his nephew
Ernesto, light lyric tenor (F-Bb3), who can sustain a high tessitura.

When Ernesto appears in Pasquale's living room, Pasquale informs him of his decision to marry. Ernesto is irate, especially
when he discovers that Malatesta is backing the plan and that he,
Ernesto, will be disinherited.

EXCERPT 3   Kal   i, e   pp. 40-45/1/3; 45/4/4-   13½ min.
                              46/2/4; 47/5/1-61/3/2; 65/3/3-66
              Ric   i, e   pp. 44-49/2/3; 50/1/3-50/4/4;
                              52/4/1-68/2/3; 73/2/3-74

An excerpt using Norina, lyric-coloratura soprano (C3-C5), in
an important comic aria and Dr. Malatesta, baritone, whose voice
must have flexibility.

Norina is alone in her boudoir reading a romantic novel. She is
in love with Ernesto from whom she receives a farewell note. When
Malatesta arrives, he explains that he plans to trick old Pasquale so
Norina can eventually marry her Ernesto. Together they rehearse
her role in the farce as "Malatesta's sister, the future bride of Don
Pasquale."

EXCERPT 4   Kal   i, e   pp. 76-116; 118/2/2-   21 min.
                              30/2/4; 131/2/1-33/1/5; 135/2/4-36
              Ric   i, e   pp. 84-126/2/4; 128/2/2-44/1/4;
                              145-47/1/3; 149/2/3-50

The major portion of act 2, with Norina, Malatesta, Don Pasquale, and Ernesto (see vocal descriptions in excerpts 1-3). The
supporting roles of a Notary, comic bass or tenor, and a Majordomo, silent, complete the scene.

Don Pasquale eagerly awaits his bride who appears, heavily
veiled, escorted by Malatesta. She is exceedingly shy and coy, and
after some time, accepts the Don's proposal of marriage. A quack
Notary is brought in. At the point where a second witness is required, Ernesto, who has recognized the bride as his own Norina,
is persuaded to restrain his anger and act as a witness to the marriage contract. As soon as the contract is signed, Norina begins to
act as boss in Pasquale's house. Her temperamental ravings, Ernesto's laughter, and Malatesta's attempts to console the bewildered
Pasquale set off a brilliant quartet.

EXCERPT 5   Kal   i, e   pp. 141-52/2/5;   9½ min.
                              155/2/1-57
              Ric   i, e   pp. 155-67/2/6; 170/2/1-72

A scene between Don Pasquale, comic bass, and Norina, lyric
coloratura soprano.

In an amusing duet, Norina insists upon going out to the theatre while old Pasquale must retire early. When he protests, she slaps him in the face.

EXCERPT 6   Kal   i, e   pp. 171/3/2-89   7 min.
              Ric   i, e   pp. 187-205

This is a patter duet for Don Pasquale, comic bass, and Dr. Malatesta, baritone.

In the preceding scene, Pasquale's new "bride" has purposely dropped a note from her "lover," arousing Pasquale's fury. Pasquale calls his friend Malatesta to his home, little suspecting that he is the mastermind behind the plot to trick Pasquale. Malatesta, amused at the turn of events, agrees to help Pasquale capture the illicit lovers.

EXCERPT 7   Kal   i, e   pp. 190-98   7½ min.
              Ric   i, e   pp. 206-16

Ernesto's tenor aria "Come' è gentil," with its high B's and C's, and his duet with Norina, "Tornami a dir," are included in this scene.

Ernesto, in love with Norina, arrives in the garden and sings a serenade to the accompaniment of a mandolin; Norina appears. The lovers are alone for the first time in the opera and share a quiet moment of romantic bliss.

L'ELISIR D'AMORE

(The Elixir of Love)

Gaetano Donizetti (1797-1848)

Italy, Nineteenth Century

EXCERPT 1   GS   i, e   pp. 70/2/1-85/3/3   9 min.
                           (opt. cut 80/2/2-84/2/2)
              Kal   i, e   pp. 48/3/1-58/2/4
                           (opt. cut 55/1/1-57/4/1)

Ric   i   pp. 46/4/1-56/2/4 (opt. cut
53/1/1-55/4/1)

Duet scene with Nemorino, lyric tenor (D2-Ab3), and Adina, lyric or lyric-coloratura soprano (D3-Bb4) requiring flexibility.

Nemorino, a young peasant, is desperately trying to woo Adina. Adina has just seen the handsome Sergeant Belcore and lets Nemorino know that he is rather dull compared to the Sergeant. Adina suggests that Nemorino go visit his sick uncle.

EXCERPT 2   GS   i, e   pp. 85/4/1-88/2/4; 90/1/5-   27 min.
115/1/4; 115/2/6-34/2/1; 138/1/2-
56/3/4; 160/3/5-73
Kal   i, e   pp. 58/3/1-60/2/2; 61/2/4-76/3/7;
77/1/8-90; 94-107/1/3; 109/4/5-17
Ric   i   pp. 56/3/1-58/2/2; 59/2/4-74/3/7;
75/1/8-88; 92-105/3/1; 107/4/5-15

The four major characters of the opera are involved in this scene: Adina, lyric or lyric-coloratura soprano; Nemorino, lyric tenor; Belcore, baritone to F3 with flexibility; and Dr. Dulcamara, comic bass who must be a good actor. A chorus of peasants and villagers completes the scene.

Dulcamara, a quack doctor, arrives on the scene and boasts of his magic potions. Nemorino immediately desires a love potion, hoping to win Adina's affection. The potion is nothing more than Bordeaux wine, and Adina is surprised to see her suitor so merry after swallowing the contents of the bottle. When Belcore returns to woo Adina, she quickly agrees to marry him much to the chagrin of the frustrated Nemorino.

EXCERPT 2a   GS   i, e   pp. 85/4/1-88/2/4; 90/1/5-   9½ min.
115/1/4; 115/2/6-115/3/10
Kal   i, e   pp. 58/3/1-60/2/2; 61/2/4-76/3/7;
77/1/8-77/2/11
Ric   i   pp. 56/3/1-58/2/2; 59/2/4-74/3/7;
75/1/8-75/2/11

The portion of excerpt 2 with Dulcamara and the chorus only.

EXCERPT 2b   GS   i, e   pp. 116-34/2/1; 138/1/2-41   7 min.
               Kal   i, e   pp. 77/3/1-90; 94-96
               Ric   i   pp. 75/3/1-88; 92-94

The scene between Nemorino and Dr. Dulcamara from excerpt 2.

EXCERPT 2c   GS   i, e   pp. 142-56 or 160   7½ min.
               Kal   i, e   pp. 97-107/1/3 or 109
               Ric   i   pp. 95-105/1/3 or 107

Adina and Nemorino's duet from excerpt 2.

EXCERPT 2d   GS   i, e   pp. 142-56/3/4;   10 min.
                               160/2/5-73
               Kal   i, e   pp. 97-107/1/3; 109/4/5-17
               Ric   i   pp. 95-105/1/3; 107/4/5-15

The portion of excerpt 2 with Adina, Nemorino, and Belcore.

EXCERPT 3   GS   i, e   pp. 259-76/2/3;   7½ min.
                               280/2/2-280/4/5
               Kal   i, e   pp. 166-77/2/6; 180/2/3-180/4/5
               Ric   i   pp. 164-75/2/6; 178/2/3-178/4/5

This is the scene between Nemorino, lyric tenor (F2-A3), and Belcore, flexible high baritone (C2-F3).

The love potion given Nemorino by Dr. Dulcamara has not worked and Adina, his sweetheart, is going to marry Belcore. Nemorino lacks the money to buy another bottle of the magic elixir. His rival in love comes along and suggests that Nemorino enlist as a soldier for which he will receive twenty crowns.

EXCERPT 4   GS   i, e   pp. 281-87/2/1; 289/1/3-   18 min.
                               305/2/3; 306/2/3-13/3/2/2;
                               323-49/1/5
               Kal   i, e   pp. 181-85/2/4; 187/1/4-200/1/2;
                               201/1/3-6/1/6; 213/2/1-31/2/7
               Ric   i   pp. 179-83/2/4; 185/1/4-98/1/2;
                               199/1/3-204/1/6; 211/2/1-29/2/7

Nemorino, lyric tenor; Giannetta, soprano or mezzo-soprano;

and a girls' chorus are joined by Adina, lyric or lyric-coloratura soprano; and Dulcamara, comic bass, in this excerpt.

Nemorino has bought a second bottle of "elixir," really wine, and now feels especially happy. The girls have heard that his wealthy uncle has died and they flock around him clamoring for his wealth. Not having heard the news of his inheritance, Nemorino attributes his sudden popularity to the love potion. Adina and Dr. Dulcamara both react with surprise to the strange turn of events.

EXCERPT 4a   GS   i, e   pp. 281-87/2/1;   6½ min.
                       289/1/3-97/1/3
              Kal i, e   pp. 181-85/2/4; 187/1/4-93/2/1
              Ric i   pp. 179-83/2/4; 185/1/4-91/2/1

The portion of excerpt 4 using only Giannetta, Nemorino and the women's chorus.

EXCERPT 5   GS   i, e   pp. 349/2/1-65/3/2;   16 min.
                       370/2/4-/4/6
              Kal i, e   pp. 231/3/1-42/4/3; 246/1/4-/3/6
              Ric i   pp. 229/3/1-40/4/3; 244/1/4-/3/6

The final reconciliation scene between Adina and Nemorino has the most difficult music for Adina (C3-C5); and the important aria "Una furtiva lagrima" for Nemorino.

Adina, deciding she really does prefer Nemorino to Belcore, buys Nemorino's military contract and begs him to stay with her.

DIE ENTFÜHRING AUS DEM SERAIL

(The Abduction from the Seraglio)

Wolfgang Amadeus Mozart (1756-1791)

Turkey, Sixteenth Century

EXCERPT 1   B&H   g, e   pp. 8-36   20 min.
              Int   g, e   pp. 8-37

Kal g, e pp. 7-37/1/3

The leading characters are Belmonte, lyric tenor (G2-A3) with many difficult florid phrases, and Osmin, bass (Eb1-F3). Pedrillo, tenor, has only speaking lines in this scene.

In front of the Pasha Selim's palace, Belmonte is desperately trying to get a glimpse of his beloved Constanza who has been captured by the Pasha. His friend Pedrillo attempts to aid him but the grouchy palace guard Osmin is not obliging.

EXCERPT 1a   B&H g, e pp. 8-21   8 min.
              Int g, e pp. 8-22
              Kal g, e pp. 7-20

The portion of excerpt 1 without Pedrillo and without the difficult arias of Belmonte and Osmin.

EXCERPT 2   B&H g, e pp. 48-56   2 min.
              Int g, e pp. 50-58
              Kal g, e pp. 49-57

A trio for Belmonte, lyric tenor; Osmin, bass; and Pedrillo, tenor, who needs strength in the middle range.

The Pasha has given his permission for Belmonte to enter the palace but Osmin gruffly tries to prevent this. In a lively ensemble, Belmonte and Pedrillo succeed in slipping by Osmin and into the palace.

EXCERPT 3   B&H g, e pp. 57-68   7½ min.
              Int g, e pp. 59-70
              Kal g, e pp. 58-70/2/7

Blonda, light lyric-coloratura soprano to E5, has an aria followed by a duet with Osmin, bass, in which she imitates him with a low Ab2 in chest voice. As difficult as the roles are, they can be handled easily by technically secure young singers as well as seasoned professionals.

In the Pasha's garden, the scene opens with a dialogue in which Osmin is trying to command Blonda to obey his wishes. Blonda cleverly attempts to teach him a more refined form of behavior; when he stubbornly refuses, she demonstrates that he is no match for her in this battle of wits.

EXCERPT 4   B&H   g, e   pp. 93-102   7 min.
                   Int   g, e   pp. 97-107
                   Kal   g, e   pp. 94/4/1-105

An amusing duet between Pedrillo, tenor, and Osmin, bass. If Pedrillo's aria is included, he needs to have a strong B3 even though most of his singing is in a middle tessitura.

Summoning up his courage in a mock-military aria, Pedrillo is determined to give Osmin a sleeping potion so he and Belmonte can get their girls friends out of the palace. A hilarious duet follows: Pedrillo convinces Osmin to try some wine, forbidden by Moslem law, into which Pedrillo has mixed a sleeping potion. Osmin proceeds to get quite drunk and finally falls into a stupor.

EXCERPT 4a   B&H   g, e   pp. 97-102   3 min.
                   Int   g, e   pp. 101-7
                   Kal   g, e   pp. 100-105

The same scene as excerpt 4 without Pedrillo's opening aria.

EXCERPT 5   B&H   g, e   pp. 108-26
                   Int   g, e   pp. 112-32
                   Kal   g, e   pp. 111-30

A quartet for Constanza, high lyric-coloratura soprano (D3-A4); Blonda, light coloratura soprano (D3-A4); Belmonte, lyric tenor capable of singing a florid line; and Pedrillo, tenor, strong in the middle range.

Osmin asleep and out of the way, Belmonte and Pedrillo meet with their girl friends for the first time since the girls were taken into the Pasha's harem. Belmonte suspects Constanza of infidelity; likewise, Pedrillo has his doubts about Blonda. But in the end, all is forgiven, and the four sing in praise of love.

EXCERPT 6   B&H   g, e   pp. 150-60   8½ min.
                          (trad. cuts in score)
                   Int   g, e   pp. 157-61/1/5; 162/4/1-64/2/3;
                                165/2/6-67
                   Kal   g, e   pp. 149-53/3/5; 155/2/1-57/2/6;
                                158/3/4-60

A duet for Constanza, lyric-coloratura soprano (E3-C5), and Belmonte, tenor with a high and flexible voice (F2-G3).

In this lengthy duet, Constanza and Belmonte, when faced with death as punishment for their attempted escape, agree that death together is better than separation.

EUGENE ONEGIN

Peter Ilyitch Tchaikovsky (1840-1893)

Russia, About 1820

EXCERPT 1   GS   e   pp. 1-18; 40-75   22½ min.
              Kal   r, e   pp. 4-17; 30-58

The opening scene of the opera calls for four women and two men, all singing basically in the middle part of their ranges. Tatiana is a lyric-spinto soprano; Mme Larina and Filipievna, both mature mezzo-sopranos; Olga, a young contralto or low lyric mezzo-soprano; Lensky, lyric tenor; and Eugene Onegin, low baritone.

In a garden adjoining Mme Larina's country estate, Olga receives her fiancé Lensky with his rather bored and worldly friend Onegin. Tatiana, Olga's sister, immediately falls in love with Onegin.

EXCERPT 2   GS   e   pp. 76-119   23 min.
              Kal   r, e   pp. 59-97

This excerpt centers around Tatiana's extended letter scene scored for a strong lyric soprano (D3-Bb4) capable of showing great warmth and passion. Filipievna, the old nurse, is sung by a mezzo-soprano (C3-Eb4).

In her room, Tatiana is restless; Filipievna tells her a story. Left alone, Tatiana writes a letter to Onegin candidly expressing her feelings of love for him.

EXCERPT 2a   GS   e   pp. 76-106   18 min.
               Kal   r, e   pp. 59-85

A portion of Excerpt 2, closing at the end of the aria.

EXCERPT 3   GS   e   pp. 120-40   10½ min.
               Kal r, e pp. 98-117

The complete excerpt includes a chorus of girls as well as Tatiana, lyric soprano, and Eugene Onegin, low baritone. In this scene Onegin sings an aria extending upward to an F3.

Onegin meets Tatiana in the garden as she has requested in a letter but spurns her confession of love. Tatiana runs away, dejected and shamed.

EXCERPT 3a   GS   e   pp. 128-38   6½ min.
               Kal r, e pp. 106-15

The same as excerpt 3 without the girls' chorus.

EXCERPT 4   GS   e   pp. 201-18   12 min.
               Kal r, e pp. 173-88

A scene containing a haunting tenor aria for Lensky, going no higher than a G#3, and a duel scene with Onegin, baritone (C2-E3). Their seconds in small roles are Zaretsky, bass, and Gillot, silent.

At a party, Onegin purposely has ignored Tatiana and has flirted with her sister, Lensky's fiancée Olga. Lensky challenges Onegin to a duel. Here they meet at the appointed place near a mill on the banks of a wooded stream and it is Lensky who falls the victim of Onegin's pistol.

EXCERPT 5   GS   e   pp. 252-76   12 min.
               Kal r, e pp. 224-45

The final scene between Tatiana, soprano to B4, and Onegin, baritone to G3, is dramatic and passionate.

Tatiana has married the Prince Gremin, and Onegin has seen her at a royal ball. For the first time Onegin has become interested in her and asks her to meet him. She greets him in the reception hall of the palace. As he kneels at her feet, she reminds him that he rejected her love several years before. For a moment they recall the happiness that could have been theirs but is now out of reach because she is Gremin's wife.

FALSTAFF

Giuseppe Verdi (1813-1901)

Windsor, Early Fifteenth Century

EXCERPT 1   GS/Kal   i, e   pp. 47-126   15 min.
              Int   i, e   pp. 51-130
              Ric   i   pp. 47-126

This ensemble includes all the characters of the opera except
Falstaff himself. It climaxes in a nonet which demands incisive
musicianship as well as individual characterization for each per-
former. The roles are as follows: Alice Ford, soprano (B2-B4) with
strong voice, top line in ensemble; Nannetta, her daughter, lyric
soprano (B2-B4); Meg Page, mezzo-soprano (B2-G4); Dame Quickly, low mezzo-soprano or contralto (G#2-G4) and preferably a
character actress; Fenton, leading lyric tenor (Eb2-B3) with high
tessitura; Dr. Cajus, high tenor (B1-B3) and character actor; Bardolph, *buffo* tenor (B1-G#3), who sings below Fenton and Cajus
in ensemble; Ford, strong leading baritone (B1-E3); Pistol, bass
(F#1-C#3).

In the garden of Ford's house the four women are gossiping
about the identical love letters Meg Page and Alice Ford have received from John Falstaff. While they are plotting against the fat
lecher, the five men enter another part of the garden, all disgusted
with Falstaff for a variety of reasons. Fenton and Nannetta man-
age to steal a few kisses while the others plot revenge.

EXCERPT 1a   GS/Kal   i, e   pp. 47-66; 120/1/2-26   6 min.
              Int   i, e   pp. 51-70; 124/1/2-30
              Ric   i   pp. 47-66; 120/1/2-26

The same scene as above with the women only.

EXCERPT 2   GS/Kal   i, e   pp. 127-90   22 min.
              Int   i, e   pp. 131-94
              Ric   i   pp. 127-90

This scene takes place inside the Garter Inn where Falstaff
spends most of his time. The title role is scored for a baritone

(A1-Gb3) who must be a good actor with a sense of humor. Ford
is also a baritone (Bb1-G3) and should have a high dramatic voice.
Dame Quickly, Bardolph, and Pistol complete the cast (see excerpt
1).

Bardolph and Pistol beg Falstaff's forgiveness for earlier having
turned against him. Dame Quickly is admitted; she brings news
that Mistress Ford would be willing to meet Falstaff when her husband is away. Meg Page regrets that she cannot escape her husband's watchful eye long enough for the rendezvous requested. Unaware of his wife's plan of attack, Ford visits Falstaff under the assumed name of Brook. In order to find out more about Falstaff's
intentions, he asks him to help in Brook's plan to win Alice Ford.
He is outraged to find that Falstaff is planning to visit Alice that
very day. As Falstaff is getting properly dressed for the occasion,
Ford sings a monologue cursing the fickleness of women.

EXCERPT 2a   GS/Kal i, e   pp. 130/3/1-46/2/2   5½ min.
              Int   i, e   pp. 134/3/1-50/2/2
              Ric   i   pp. 130/3/1-46/2/2

The portion of excerpt 2 with only Falstaff and Dame Quickly.

EXCERPT 2b   GS/Kal i, e   pp. 148/2/1-52;   14 min.
                            154-90
              Int   i, e   pp. 152/2/1-56; 158-94
              Ric   i   pp. 148/2/1-52; 154-90

The portion of excerpt 2 with Falstaff and Ford only.

LA FANCIULLA DEL WEST

(The Girl of the Golden West)

Giacomo Puccini (1858-1924)

California, 1849-1850

EXCERPT 1   Ric   i   pp. 82/2/1-91/3/4   6 min.

The role of Minnie, owner of the Polka saloon, calls for a high dramatic soprano (C3-C5). In this scene she is courted by Sheriff Jack Rance, baritone (B1-F#3).

EXCERPT 2   Ric   i   pp. 120/4/1-46   12 min.

A scene with Minnie, dramatic soprano, and Dick Johnson, dramatic tenor (E2-B3), with a lesser part for Nick, tenor.

Minnie and Dick Johnson are left alone in the saloon. Johnson is really the bandit Ramerrez who has come to rob the saloon but, attracted by Minnie's charms, relinquishes his plans and accepts an invitation to supper in her cabin. Nick, the bartender, appears briefly in this scene.

EXCERPT 3   Ric   i   pp. 149-95/2/1   18½ min.

Minnie, dramatic soprano, and Dick Johnson, dramatic tenor to C4 in this scene, are supported by Wowkle, mezzo-soprano, and Billy Jackrabbit, bass.

Wowkle sings a lullaby to her papoose; she and the child's father, Billy, discuss the possibilities of marriage. Johnson arrives to keep his invitation for supper. Minnie persuades him to spend the night in the cabin so he will not get lost in the snowstorm.

EXCERPT 3a   Ric   i   pp. 162-95/2/1   13½ min.

The portion of the scene with Minnie and Dick Johnson and very little singing for Wowkle.

EXCERPT 4   Ric   i   pp. 208-44   16 min.

The three principal characters appear in this scene: Minnie, dramatic soprano; Dick Johnson, dramatic tenor; and Rance, baritone.

Minnie has found out that her guest Dick Johnson is really Ramerrez, the bandit. When he is shot and wounded in an attempt to leave her cabin, he quickly returns to her; she hides him before Jack Rance arrives to question her about the bandit and to try to win her love. Johnson is discovered and Minnie proposes a poker game. If she wins, Johnson is hers; if she loses, the Sheriff may claim the bandit's life. Minnie wins by cheating; Rance politely leaves.

FAUST

Charles Gounod (1818-1893)

Germany, Sixteenth Century

EXCERPT 1   GS/Kal   f, e   pp. 4-30   17 min.

Faust should be sung by a tenor (D2-A4) with a very even range; Mephistopheles by a bass with a wide range (F#1-E3). An off-stage chorus is heard during this scene.

Faust, an aged philosopher, is seated in his study about to take his life by drinking poison when he hears a cheerful offstage chorus. Cursing life and his advanced age, he calls upon Satan to aid him. At that moment Mephistopheles appears in the garb of a cavalier offering Faust wealth and power. Faust wishes for nothing but youth; Mephistopheles agrees to oblige him if he will sign away his soul. Faust hesitates but makes up his mind when he sees a vision of the beautiful Marguerite at the spinning wheel. He is quickly transformed into a young man, and he and Mephistopheles go off in search of pleasure.

EXCERPT 2   GS/Kal   f, e   pp. 103-78   43 min.

The "Garden Scene" involves Faust, tenor (Eb2-C4); Mephistopheles, bass (Ab1-F3); Marguerite, lyric soprano (C3-C5) with a trill; Siebel, mezzo-soprano trouser role (D3-Bb4); and Martha, a deeper mezzo-soprano (C3-F4). Faust needs a C4 for his aria "Salut, demeure" in this scene which includes Marguerite's "Jewel Song."

Siebel, in love with Marguerite, picks a flower only to have it fade as the result of a curse. He solves this problem by dipping his hands in the holy water near the statue of the Madonna. But Mephistopheles has other means for Faust to overcome his rival Siebel. A rich casket of jewels is placed at Marguerite's doorstep and while Mephistopheles flirts with the neighbor woman Martha, Faust is alone with Marguerite. They fall in love and just as Faust is about to bid her goodnight, Mephistopheles works his spell to keep the lovers together throughout the night.

EXCERPT 2a   GS/Kal   f, e   pp. 103-17   10 min.

The portion of excerpt 2 with Siebel and Faust, and Mephistopheles who has limited singing in this excerpt.

EXCERPT 2b   GS/Kal   f, e   pp. 111/3/1-78   39 min.

The portion of excerpt 2 with Marguerite, Martha, Faust, and
Mephistopheles.

EXCERPT 2c   GS/Kal   f, e   pp. 159-73/3/3   9 min.

The duet for Faust and Marguerite from excerpt 2.

EXCERPT 3   GS/Kal   f, e   pp. 275/6/1-99   11½ min.

The final trio of the opera which includes Marguerite, soprano
(C3-B4), singing dramatic passages in a high tessitura; Faust, tenor
(C#2-B3); and Mephistopheles, bass (B1-D#3). An offstage chorus
sings briefly at the end of the scene.

Marguerite, deserted by Faust, has slain their child and is in prison. Faust and the evil genius Mephistopheles arrive; Faust implores Marguerite to escape with him but her mind wanders, flash-
ing back to memories of moments the lovers shared together. When
she sees Mephistopheles, however, she begins to pray to the angels
for salvation and she dies commending her soul to heaven.

LA FAVORITA

(The Favorite)

Gaetano Donizetti (1797-1848)

Spain, 1340

EXCERPT 1   Ric   i   pp. 11-21; 27-31   8 min.

A scene for Fernando, tenor with a C#4, and Baldessare, bass
(F1-E3).

In a gallery of the Monastery of St. James, a young novice, Fernando, confesses his love for an unknown woman. The woman,

Leonora, mistress of King Alfonso of Castile, has arranged a meeting with Fernando who, despite warnings from his superior Baldessare, departs for the Isle of Leon to meet his beloved.

EXCERPT 2   Ric   i   pp. 32-63/3/3; 65/1/4-76   18 min.

A scene for Fernando, tenor; Leonora, mezzo soprano (A2-Ab4) capable of sustaining a florid line; Ines, soprano (C3-Bb4); and a women's chorus.

On the Isle of Leon, Leonora is attended by Ines and the other women. Fernando arrives to keep his meeting with Leonora. Not knowing she is the mistress of King Alfonso, Fernando accepts a commission in the King's army.

EXCERPT 2a   Ric   i   pp. 50/4/2-67   7 min.

The duet for Fernando and Leonora. Ines's one line may be omitted.

EXCERPT 3   Ric   i   pp. 77-86/3/1; 89/3/2-101   14 min.
                          or pp. 77-85; 91/5/3-101   12 min.

A duet for Leonora, mezzo-soprano, and Alfonso, baritone (C2-F3) capable of sustaining a high tessitura. Alfonso sings the aria "Vien, Leonora." Don Gasparo, tenor, and Ines, soprano, appear in supporting roles.

In the Palace of the Alcazar, King Alfonso sings of his love for Leonora. When she appears, she is filled with foreboding about the outcome of her illicit relationship with the King and her love for Fernando. The King soothes her anxiety as they join in a tender duet.

EXCERPT 4   Ric   i   pp. 195-215; 220-21   15 min.

A trio for Leonora, soprano; Fernando, tenor; and Alfonso, baritone; plus Leonora's aria "O mio Fernando." Don Gasparo, tenor, has a brief part. The tenor role of Fernando is not difficult in this scene, going no higher than G3.

Fernando, in reward for his services to the King, asks for Leonora's hand in marriage. Alfonso, astounded, nonetheless gives her to Fernando who is unaware that she has been the King's mistress.

Left alone, Leonora decides she must confess this to Fernando in a letter and let him decide if he still wishes to marry her.

EXCERPT 5   Ric i   pp. 318/2/1-57   23 min.

The final scene with Leonora, mezzo-soprano; Fernando, tenor; and Baldessare, bass. A mixed chorus sings offstage.

Fernando has rejected Leonora at the altar, having heard from other sources that she is the King's mistress. Returning to the monastery, Fernando, before taking his final vows, attempts to banish all thoughts of Leonora from his mind in the aria "Spirto gentil." Leonora, disguised as a novice, appears and tells Fernando of her vain attempt to write him of her past. She rekindles his love, and they decide to flee together but it is too late—Leonora is ill and dies in Fernando's arms.

EXCERPT 5a   Ric i   pp. 326/4/3-57   16 min.

The portion of excerpt 5 which is the duet between Leonora and Fernando with offstage chorus; to this may be added Fernando's aria (4½ minutes).

FIDELIO

Ludwig van Beethoven (1770-1827)

Spain, Eighteenth Century

EXCERPT 1   B&H g, e   pp. 8-50   24 min.
              GS   g, e   pp. 10-58
              Kal g, e   pp. 13-57
              Pet g   pp. 15-56

The opening scene includes a duet for Marzelline, soprano (C3-A4, opt. C5), and Jacquino, light tenor (D2-G3); Marzelline's aria; a quartet for the above; plus Leonore, dramatic soprano (B2-A4); and Rocco, the jailer, bass (Ab1-E3), who sings a short aria. There is also a trio for the two sopranos and Rocco.

In the jailer's quarters of a Spanish prison, Jacquino attempts to court Marzelline, who cleverly puts him off. She has become infatuated with her father Rocco's new assistant "Fidelio" who is really Florestan's wife in disguise. Rocco favors the match, which troubles Leonore because she must continue her disguise until she finds her husband Florestan who has been a political prisoner for two years.

EXCERPT 1a   B&H   g, e   pp. 8-23   8½ min.
                GS   g, e   pp. 10-28
                Kal   g, e   pp. 13-30
                Pet   g   pp. 15-32

The portion of excerpt 1 involving only Marzelline, light soprano, and Jacquino, light tenor.

EXCERPT 1b   B&H   g, e   pp. 31-50   9½ min.
                GS   g, e   pp. 37-58
                Kal   g, e   pp. 38-57
                Pet   g   pp. 38-56

Rocco's aria and the trio from excerpt 1.

EXCERPT 2   B&H   g, e   pp. 51-68   12 min.
                GS   g, e   pp. 59-78
                Kal   g, e   pp. 58-75
                Pet   g   pp. 57-74

This contains a demanding aria for Pizarro, dramatic baritone or bass-baritone (G1-E3), and his duet with Rocco, bass, whose part is not as demanding. A men's chorus also appears in this scene.

Pizarro, governor of the prison, arrives in the prison courtyard and orders Rocco, the jailer, to do away with the most dangerous of prisoners, Florestan. Rocco refuses to commit murder but finally agrees to dig a grave in the prison vaults in order to hide all traces of the crime.

EXCERPT 3   B&H   g, e   pp. 69-121   26½ min.
                GS   g, e   pp. 79-126
                Kal   g, e   pp. 76-116
                Pet   g   pp. 75-115

This excerpt includes Leonore's dramatic *scena* and aria "Abscheulicher! Wo eilst du hin?" requiring the utmost in vocal strength and breath control (B2-B4). Others in the scene include Marzelline, soprano; Jacquino, tenor; Pizarro, baritone or bass-baritone; and Rocco, bass. A chorus of prisoners plays an important part; two prisoners, a tenor and a bass, have short solos.

Having overheard the plot to execute her husband, Leonore vents her emotions in a highly dramatic aria. She then finds out that as "Fidelio," assistant to Rocco, she will be digging her own husband's grave. The prisoners have been allowed to stroll in the garden; when Pizarro hears of this, he angrily puts an end to it. In an emotional finale, each of the characters expresses his or her feelings while the prisoners file back to their cells.

EXCERPT 4   B&H   g, e   pp. 122-72   33 min.
             GS   g, e   pp. 141-95
             Kal   g, e   pp. 117-62
             Pet   g   pp. 116-58

In addition to Leonore, Rocco, and Pizarro, described in excerpts 1-3, Florestan, dramatic tenor (F2-Bb3), appears in this scene and sings the recitative and aria "Gott, welch' dunkel hier."

Florestan believes he sees a vision of his wife Leonore, an angel coming to rescue him. Rocco and Leonore come to dig the prisoner's grave. Pizarro tries to kill Florestan but is prevented by Leonore who interferes, exclaiming, "First kill his wife!" and reveals her identity. Far-off trumpets announce the arrival of Don Fernando, prime minister and friend of Florestan, who interrupts the proceedings. Leonare and Florestan are left alone to reunite their hearts and voices in a rapturous duet.

EXCERPT 4a   B&H   g, e   pp. 122-49   24½ min.
              GS   g, e   pp. 141-69
              Kal   g, e   pp. 117-40
              Pet   g   pp. 116-39

This portion of excerpt 4 involves only Leonore, Florestan, and Rocco.

LA FILLE DU RÉGIMENT

(The Daughter of the Regiment)

(La Figlia del Reggimento)

Gaetano Donizetti (1798-1848)

Tyrolese Mountains, 1815

EXCERPT 1 Int f, e pp. 40-55   7 min.
       Jou f pp. 45-69
       Kal i, e pp. 29/4/1-45
       Ric i pp. 33-50

Marie is a role for a lyric-coloratura soprano (D3-C5 with opt. D5); Sulpice should be a bass-baritone and a comic actor.

Marie has been found and adopted by a French regiment. In this comic duet the Master Sergeant Sulpice and Marie describe her life with the regiment.

EXCERPT 2 Int f, e pp. 78-90   7½ min.
       Jou f pp. 106-25
       Kal i, e pp. 66-79
       Ric i pp. 83-96

Tonio should be a lyric tenor (Eb2-Bb3) in this scene with Marie, lyric-coloratura soprano (C3-Ab5 with opt. Bb4 or Eb5).

Tonio has fallen in love with Marie after having saved her life. He has come to the regimental quarters to find her and here they sing of their love.

EXCERPT 3 Int f, e pp. 137-70   14 min.
       Jou f pp. 203-51
       Kal i, e pp. 128-57
       Ric i pp. 149-82

This excerpt includes Marie, with an optional Eb5; Sulpice, bass-baritone; Marquise of Berkenfeld, mezzo-soprano who should be able to portray a mature, quasi-comic character. Hortensius and the Duchess of Crakentorp, nonsinging roles, can be omitted by making cuts in the dialogue. Chorus TTB sings with Marie in the cabaletta of her aria; this could be omitted if only one verse of the cabaletta is sung.

The Marquise of Berkenfeld, in the salon of her castle, is attempting to give Marie a singing lesson while Sulpice listens. The results are hilarious when Marie, urged by Sulpice, lapses into military airs much to the Marquise's dismay. After the Marquise and Sulpice leave, Marie sings a melancholy aria bemoaning her fate and expressing her loneliness for the companionship of the soldiers in the regiment. In a lively cabaletta, "Salut à la France," she greets the soldiers enthusiastically as they enter the castle to rescue her.

EXCERPT 4	Int	f, e	pp. 171-81	2½ min.
	Jou	f	pp. 252-68	
	Kal	i, e	pp. 160-69	
	Ric	i	pp. 186-97/1/6	

Marie, lyric-coloratura soprano; Tonio, lyric tenor; and Sulpice, bass-baritone sing a sprightly trio when they are finally reunited.

DIE FLEDERMAUS

(The Bat)

Johann Strauss, Jr. (1825-1899)

Bad Ischl, Austria, Late Nineteenth Century

Dialogue is available to accompany Schirmer translation by Ruth and Thomas Martin, or to accompany the Boosey & Hawkes version used by the Metropolitan Opera. The Kalmus score contains complete English and German dialogue.

EXCERPT 1	B&H	g, e	pp. 17-28	3½ min.
	GS	e	pp. 17-27	
	Kal	g, e	pp. 20-30	

The role of Eisenstein, written for a tenor, is sometimes assigned to a high baritone. His wife, Rosalinda, is sung by a lyric soprano with extreme agility. Dr. Blind is a *buffo* tenor taking the lower tenor line in the ensemble.

Gabriel von Eisenstein comes storming into his living room, followed by his lawyer Dr. Blind who has succeeded in getting five days added to his client's jail sentence. Rosalinda tries to calm her distraught husband while helping him get rid of the obnoxious lawyer.

EXCERPT 2   B&H   g, e   pp. 29-35   4 min.
               GS   e   pp. 28-34
               Kal   g, e   pp. 32-39

Eisenstein, tenor or high baritone, and Dr. Falke, baritone (D#2-E3), have a duet in this scene. Dr. Falke sings the lower line.

Falke, knowing that Eisenstein must soon go to jail, lightens his spirits by inviting him to a champagne ball, all part of a practical joke which unfolds as the opera continues.

EXCERPT 3   B&H   g, e   pp. 36-44   5 min.
               GS   e   pp. 35-41
               Kal   g, e   pp. 41-48

This scene includes Rosalinda (C3-C5); Eisenstein (E2-A3); and Adele, a soubrette (B2-E4) whose voice should be lighter than Rosalinda's although she sings below her in the ensemble.

Eisenstein, leaving his home to go to jail, bids his wife Rosalinda farewell with the assistance of the pert chambermaid Adele.

EXCERPT 4   B&H   g, e   pp. 45-66   10 min.
                     (trad. cut in score)
               GS   e   pp. 42-59 (trad. cut 57/3/2-58/2/3)
               Kal   g, e   pp. 49-67 (trad. cut 65/3/2-66/2/3)

Rosalinda (D3-C5); Alfred, flamboyant lyric tenor (F#2-A3), a caricature of operatic tenors; and Frank, prison warden, baritone (D2-F#3), are in this excerpt.

Her husband safely out of the house, Rosalinda receives a visit from her former suitor Alfred. As Rosalinda and Alfred are merrily singing and drinking, Frank arrives to arrest Rosalinda's husband.

To save her honor, she discreetly persuades Alfred to pretend he is her husband and go to prison in Eisenstein's place.

EXCERPT 5   B&H   g, e   pp. 84-95   5 min.
                     (trad. cut in score)
              GS   e   pp. 74-84 (trad. cut 82/1/6-83/3/1)
              Kal   g, e   pp. 89-100 (trad. cut 98/1/6-99/3/1)

A duet scene between Rosalinda and Eisenstein (see excerpt 1 for vocal descriptions).

Rosalinda and her husband, Gabriel von Eisenstein, both arrive at Prince Orlofsky's party under assumed names, the lady concealing her identity behind a mask. Eisenstein is enchanted by her beauty; to pay him back for his philandering, Rosalinda succeeds in taking his jeweled watch to use as evidence.

EXCERPT 6   B&H   g, e   pp. 155-62   6 min.
              GS   e   pp. 136-42
              Kal   g, e   pp. 157-64

Adele has a brilliant coloratura aria in this excerpt demanding a D5. Supporting roles are Frank, baritone, and Ida (Sally), mezzo-soprano.

Having been given Frank's address at the party, the aspiring actress Adele arrives to visit him only to find that he is really a prison warden. Somewhat disillusioned she "auditions" for him anyway in a showpiece in which she portrays three different kinds of characters.

EXCERPT 7   B&H   g, e   pp. 163-85   7 min.
                     (trad. cut in score)
              GS   e   pp. 143-61 (trad. cut 158/2/2-61/1/1)
              Kal   g, e   pp. 167-87 (trad. cut 184/2/2-
                     87/1/1)

A trio with Rosalinda, Alfred, and Eisenstein (see vocal descriptions in excerpts 1-4).

Eisenstein, disguised as a lawyer, visits the jail to find out more about the things that went on between his wife and Alfred in his home the previous night.

DER FLIEGENDE HOLLÄNDER

(The Flying Dutchman)

Richard Wagner (1813-1883)

Norway, Eighteenth Century

EXCERPT 1   GS/Kal   g, e   pp. 29-41/5/5; 42/4/1-   22 min.
                        43/3/1; 45/2/4-63/1/5; 66/2/4-68/2/1
               Pet   g   pp. 34-45/2/4; 45/5/2-46/3/1;
                        48/1/3-63/2/1; 66/2/2-68/3/1

The title role should be sung by a dramatic baritone or bass-baritone with a strong range from G1 to F3. This scene contains his monologue "Die Frist ist um." Daland, also a bass, has speech-like passages from Ab1 to Eb3.

Philip Vanderdecken, the Flying Dutchman, has taken refuge in the same harbor where Daland, a Norwegian sea captain, has anchored his ship. The Dutchman offers Daland riches in exchange for his daughter's hand in marriage.

EXCERPT 2   GS/Kal   g, e   pp. 77-136   27 min.
               Pet   g   pp. 76-128

Senta needs to be a dramatic soprano with a great deal of intensity, especially in the upper register; her suitor Erik, a lyric-dramatic tenor to A3; Mary, the nurse, a mature mezzo-soprano or contralto. In the four-part women's chorus, the second alto part extends downward to an F2.

The girls are all working while Senta gazes at the picture of the Flying Dutchman. When her companions tease her about her daydreams, she sings a ballad telling the story of the mysterious seaman. Erik comes in and attempts to dissuade her from her mad dream.

EXCERPT 2a   GS/Kal   g, e   pp. 77-109/1/3;   16 min.
                        110/4/1-19
               Pet   g   pp. 76-106/5/3; 108/2/1-15

The portion of excerpt 2 using Senta, Mary, and the women's chorus only.

EXCERPT 2b   GS/Kal   g, e   pp. 120-36   11 min.
                Pet   g   pp. 116-28

Senta and Erik only in the scene from excerpt 2.

EXCERPT 3   GS/Kal   g, e   pp. 135/3/1-75   23 min.
                Pet   g, e   pp. 128/4/1-60

This scene has Senta, dramatic soprano; the Dutchman, dramatic baritone or bass-baritone; and Daland, bass.

Senta has been gazing at the picture of the Flying Dutchman on the wall of her home when she beholds the Dutchman himself in the doorway. Her father Daland has promised him Senta's hand in exchange for gold and treasures and he sings of this in the important aria "Mögst du, mein Kind." Leaving the two alone to plight their troth in an extended duet, he returns to confirm their union.

EXCERPT 3a   GS/Kal   g, e   pp. 147-69;   13 min.
                      175/3/3-175/5/5
                Pet   g, e   pp. 138-55; 160/3/4-160/5/5

The portion of excerpt 3 using the Dutchman and Senta only. The last twelve bars of act 2 may be used as a conclusion.

LA FORZA DEL DESTINO

(The Force of Destiny)

Giuseppe Verdi (1813-1901)

Spain and Italy, Eighteenth Century

EXCERPT 1   GS   i, e   pp. 13-48   16½ min.
                Int/Kal   i, e   pp. 13-48
                Ric   i   pp. 13-48

The heroine Leonora di Vargas, spinto or dramatic soprano (Bb2-Bb4) capable of sustaining a long line; Don Alvaro, dramatic tenor (Bb3); and the Marquis, bass; with Curra, mezzo-soprano, in a supporting role, are in this scene.

Don Alvaro is in love with Leonora but because he is part Inca, he is certain Leonora's family will not accept him. He therefore comes to her palace with plans of elopement. They are discovered by Leonora's father, the Marquis, who denounces her suitor. Alvaro surrenders by throwing his pistol on the floor; it explodes and fatally wounds the Marquis who curses his daughter as he dies.

EXCERPT 1a   GS   i, e   pp. 16-22   4½ min.
                Int/Kal   i, e   pp. 16-22
                Ric   i   pp. 16-22

The conversation between Curra and Leonora, and Leonora's aria from excerpt 1.

EXCERPT 1b   GS   i, e   pp. 24/3/1-40   6 min.
                Int/Kal   i, e   pp. 24/3/1-40
                Ric   i   pp. 24/3/1-40

Leonora and Alvaro only in the duet from excerpt 1.

EXCERPT 1c   GS   i, e   pp. 16-40   11½ min.
                Int/Kal   i, e   pp. 16-40
                Ric   i   pp. 16-40

The portion of excerpt 1 involving Leonora, Curra, and Alvaro, concluding before the entrance of the Marquis.

EXCERPT 2   GS   i, e   pp. 49-105   27 min.
                Int/Kal   i, e   pp. 116-72
                Ric   i   pp. 116-72

Leonora, spinto or dramatic soprano (B2-B4), and Padre Guardiano, deep bass, have a duet in this scene. Fra Melitone, comic bass or baritone, appears briefly. The offstage chorus is TTBB.

Leonora approaches the monastery at Hornachuelos, praying for mercy in the aria "Madre, pietosa Vergine." She is greeted by Padre Guardiano and, in a long duet, begs for protection. Guardiano bids Leonora depart for a mountain retreat where no one can disturb her. Accompanied by an offstage chorus of monks, she sings a simple prayer "La Vergine degli angeli."

EXCERPT 2a   GS   i, e   pp. 65/3/1-87   10 min.
               Int/Kal i, e   pp. 132/3/1-54
               Ric   i   pp. 132/3/1-54

The portion of excerpt 2 using Leonora and Padre Guardiano only.

EXCERPT 3   GS   i, e   pp. 108/3/4-22/1/1   10 min.
               Int/Kal i, e   pp. 175/3/4-89/1/1
               Ric   i   pp. 175/3/4-89/1/1

This excerpt involves Don Alvaro, dramatic tenor, and Don Carlo, high dramatic baritone.

On a battlefield near Velletri, Italy, Alvaro, in the aria "O tu che in seno agli angeli," is expressing the torture of his soul since the death of the Marquis of Calatrava. In answer to a call for help, he goes off and reappears with his old enemy Don Carlo whose life he has saved. They exchange false names and swear eternal friendship.

EXCERPT 4   GS   i, e   pp. 129-47   12 min.
               Int/Kal i, e   pp. 196-214
               Ric   i   pp. 196-214

This excerpt, also on the battlefield near Velletri, involves the same characters as excerpt 3 with the addition of a surgeon, baritone or bass, and two Spanish soldiers.

Don Carlo brings in Don Alvaro, seemingly mortally wounded, and the two bid farewell in the duet "Solenne in quest'ora." Carlo, left alone, has his doubts about the dying man and sings the aria "Urna fatale." Though he keeps his promise not to remove the seal from a letter Alvaro has given him to destroy, he does look through certain other personal effects. There he finds a portrait of his sister Leonora. Realizing that Alvaro is indeed his old enemy—the man he believes seduced his sister and murdered his father—Carlo is overjoyed to hear that Alvaro is recovering; Carlo may yet have a chance to get revenge.

EXCERPT 5   GS   i, e   pp. 265-78   9 min.
               Int/Kal i, e   pp. 332-45
               Ric   i   pp. 332-45

This is another scene between Don Alvaro, dramatic tenor, and Don Carlo, powerful dramatic baritone.

At the monastery at Hornachuelos, Don Alvaro has taken refuge from the world. Don Carlo comes, once more seeking revenge in the form of a duel. Alvaro tries in vain to convince his enemy that he is now a man of peace and cannot fight. Alvaro swears that he has never dishonored Leonora; revenge, he says, lies only with God. Don Carlo's cries of "coward" eventually get the better of Alvaro, and the two rush away from the sacred place to end their feud.

EXCERPT 6   GS   i, e   pp. 279-300   13 min.
              Int/Kal   i, e   pp. 346-67
              Ric   i   pp. 346-67

In this final scene Leonora, dramatic soprano, has her aria "Pace, pace, mio Dio" with its *pianissimo* Bb4. Other characters are Alvaro, dramatic tenor, and Padre Guardiano, bass. Don Carlo, baritone, has one line offstage.

Leonora has taken refuge in a grotto near the monastery where she prays for peace from the memories which torment her. In the duel (see excerpt 5) Don Alvaro has mortally wounded Don Carlo and comes upon the grotto while seeking help. For the first time since the opening scene in the opera, the lovers meet. Hearing that her brother is dying, Leonora rushes off to help him only to be stabbed by him before he expires. An effective trio ends the opera as Leonora dies in her lover's arms and is blessed by Padre Guardiano.

DER FREISCHÜTZ

(The Free-Shooter)

Carl Maria von Weber (1786-1826)

Bohemia, Seventeenth Century

EXCERPT 1   GS/Kal   g, e   pp. 39-57   15 min.
              Pet   g   pp. 37/3/1-50

Max is a lyric or dramatic tenor (C2-A3) and Caspar is a bass-baritone with a wide range (F#1-F#3) whose role lies in a high tessitura. Zamiel is a mute role.

Max is desperately trying to win the hand of Agathe by being the victor in a shooting match. After singing his great aria "Durch die Wälder, durch die Auen," he is joined in front of the tavern by his fellow forester, Caspar. Caspar suggests they meet that night in a mysterious spot known as Wolf's Glen where Max may obtain some "free" bullets that will help him win the contest. During this scene, Zamiel, the devil in the figure of the Black Huntsman, appears twice among the trees.

EXCERPT 2   GS/Kal   g, e   pp. 58-93   22 min.
               Pet   g   pp. 51-82

Agathe is a lyric or young dramatic soprano (B2-B4) who must sing some florid passages and who needs a good low register. Ännchen sings below Agathe in the duet and trio but is a lyric soprano or soubrette. Max, lyric or dramatic tenor, is also in the scene.

In a room in Kuno's home, Ännchen tries to cheer her cousin Agathe, Kuno's daughter. Unsuccessful, she leaves Agathe alone to sing her great scene "Leise, leise, fromme Weise." Max arrives to court Agathe but says he must leave soon, giving a false reason for wanting to go to the haunted Wolf's Glen. In the trio that follows, the two girls try in vain to dissuade him.

EXCERPT 2a   GS/Kal   g, e   pp. 58-79   16 min.
               Pet   g   pp. 51-70

The portion of excerpt 2 for Agathe and Ännchen only.

EXCERPT 3   GS/Kal   g, e   pp. 115-31   15 min.
               Pet   g   pp. 104-16

In addition to Agathe and Ännchen (see vocal descriptions, excerpt 2), there is an SA chorus of bridesmaids with four solo verses to be sung by a member or members of the women's chorus.

Agathe, alone in her room is already in her bridal dress and singing the beautiful cavatina "Und ob die Wolke." She is still fearful

about the coming events and Ännchen sings her a story about her
aunt who had been frightened in a bad dream. The bridesmaids
enter and sing the Bridal Wreath Chorus.

LA GIOCONDA

Amilcare Ponchielli (1834-1886)

Venice, Seventeenth Century

EXCERPT 1   GS/Ric   i   pp. 20-27   5 min.
                Int   i, e   pp. 22-29
                Kal   i, e   pp. 19-28

Gioconda, a ballad singer, is a dramatic soprano (D3-A#4); La
Cieca, her blind mother, a mezzo-soprano or contralto who needs
warmth and expression; Barnaba is a dramatic baritone (C#2-E3).

Barnaba, hiding in the grand courtyard of the Ducal palace, has
designs on La Gioconda who presently appears leading her blind
mother La Cieca. When Gioconda spurns Barnaba's advances and
runs away, he plans a cruel revenge.

EXCERPT 2   GS/Ric   i   pp. 86-106/2/2   12 min.
                Int   i, e   pp. 88-108/2/2
                Kal   i, e   pp. 92-112/2/2

Enzo, tenor (F2-A3) needs dramatic strength for this duet. Barnaba, dramatic baritone (C#2-G3) requires strength throughout
the range. Gioconda and her mother (silent) appear briefly in this
scene as does Isepo, tenor.

After the crowd has gone into the Basilica di San Marco, Enzo
remains, overcome by the sight of his former fiancée Laura with
her husband Alvise Badoero. Barnaba, a spy, addresses Enzo and
proposes a tryst for him and Laura that night aboard Enzo's ship.
Barnaba sees this as a way to further his own designs on Gioconda,
who is in love with Enzo. Barnaba then employs the service of the
public scribe Isepo in writing an anonymous letter to Alvise informing him of his wife's meeting with a lover. Gioconda overhears
this; despaired of Enzo's faithlessness, she enters the church with

her mother. Barnaba addresses the Doge's palace in a monologue, "O monumento!"

EXCERPT 2a   GS/Ric   i   pp. 101/3/5-6/2/2   11 min.
               Int   i, e   pp. 88-101; 103/3/5-8/2/2
               Kal   i, e   pp. 92-105; 107/3/5-12/3/2

Excerpt 2 eliminating all of the lesser characters by cuts.

EXCERPT 2b   GS/Ric   i   pp. 86-98   6 min.
               Int   i, e   pp. 88-100
               Kal   i, e   pp. 92-104

This is the duet section for Enzo and Barnaba from excerpt 2.

EXCERPT 3   GS/Ric   i   pp. 147-70   13½ min.
               Int   i, e   pp. 149-72
               Kal   i, e   pp. 152/2/7-77

Laura, mezzo-soprano (Bb2-Bb4), needs a strong upper register, Enzo, tenor (D2-Bb3), needs strength and a feeling for lyric line. The offstage lines of Barnaba, baritone, may be omitted.

Enzo, waiting for Laura on his ship, sings the aria "Cielo e mar." Barnaba then brings Laura to Enzo. The lovers, reunited, resolve to sail away together. As Enzo goes below to arouse his crew, Laura falls on her knees in prayer.

EXCERPT 4   GS/Ric   i   pp. 166/2/2-77   6 min.
               Int   i, e   pp. 168/2/2-79
               Kal   i, e   pp. 173/2/2-86

A confrontation scene between Gioconda, dramatic soprano (B2-Bb4), and Laura, mezzo-soprano (Bb2-Bb4).

Laura, aboard Enzo's ship, prays to the Virgin for protection (see excerpt 3). Gioconda, aware of Enzo's meeting with the other woman, steals aboard the ship to confront her rival. Each defies the other in a duet which is perhaps the most dramatic number in the score.

EXCERPT 5   GS/Ric   i   pp. 197-231   15 min.
                   Int   i, e   pp. 199-233
                   Kal   i, e   pp. 207-42

This is a scene for Gioconda, dramatic soprano; Alvise, bass (G1-F3); and Laura, his wife, high mezzo-soprano. There is an offstage chorus in this excerpt.

Alvise, punishing his wife Laura for her infidelity, tells her she must take poison as soon as the serenade in the ballroom ends. When Alvise leaves, Gioconda, anticipating the fate of the woman who once saved Gioconda's mother's life, rushes in and substitutes for the poison a drug which will produce a deathlike sleep.

EXCERPT 5a   GS/Ric   i   pp. 197-218/1/2   10 min.
                   Int   i, e   pp. 119-220/1/2
                   Kal   i, e   pp. 207-37/1/2

This is the scene from excerpt 5 using only Laura and Alvise.

EXCERPT 6   GS/Ric   i   pp. 303-53   30 min.
                   Int   i, e   pp. 305-55
                   Kal   i, e   pp. 313-65

Act 4 complete takes place at a ruined palace on the island of Giudecca, and requires the following cast: Gioconda, dramatic soprano, who sings the aria "Suicidio!" in this scene; Laura, high mezzo-soprano; Enzo, lyric-dramatic tenor; Barnaba, baritone; and two ballad singers, tenor and bass; and an offstage chorus.

Gioconda has brought the unconscious Laura, whose husband thinks she is dead, to the island. Enzo, Laura's lover, arrives after being released from prison with Gioconda's aid. Gioconda's purpose is to restore Laura to Enzo and when she wakes from a presumed death, he is estatic. After helping the lovers escape, Gioconda wishes only to die; she has promised her love to the spy Barnaba in exchange for Enzo's freedom. Barnaba arrives to claim his love. She stabs herself and does not hear when he tells her that he has killed her mother.

EXCERPT 6a   GS/Ric i   pp. 303-42   23 min.
               Int   i, e pp. 305-44
               Kal   i, e pp. 313-54

The portion of excerpt 6 without Barnaba.

EXCERPT 6b   GS/Ric i   pp. 343-53   7 min.
               Int   i, e pp. 345-55
               Kal   i, e pp. 355-65

Gioconda and Barnaba only in the concluding portion of excerpt 6.

GIULIO CESARE

(Julius Caesar)

George Frideric Handel (1685-1759)

Alexandria, Egypt, 48 B.C.

EXCERPT 1   Int   i, e   pp. 27-36   10½ min.

The role of Cornelia calls for a low mezzo-soprano or contralto going no higher than a D4 but with a mature sound. Her son Sextus is usually played by a tenor; sometimes the part is taken by a high mezzo-soprano in a trouser role. Curio, bass, has a small part in this scene.

Cornelia, widow of Pompey, recovering from a fainting spell, attempts suicide. Curio intervenes, proposing marriage. Sextus swears vengeance for the murder of his father in a *bravura* aria.

EXCERPT 2   Int   i, e   pp. 70-86   11 min.

In addition to Cornelia and Sextus, described in excerpt 1, Cleopatra, a dramatic-coloratura or lyric soprano with great agility, is necessary to this scene. Nirenus, bass, sings a supporting role.

Cornelia and Sextus pay their last respects to the dead Pompey and dedicate themselves to vengeance. Cleopatra comes forward sympathetically and assures them that her minister Nirenus can bring them within reach of the murderer Ptolemy. (It is suggested that the B section and *da capo* of Cleopatra's aria be omitted to keep the scene approximately 11 minutes.)

EXCERPT 3   Int   i, e   pp. 96-107   12 min.

Another scene for Cornelia, mature mezzo-soprano or contralto, and Sextus, tenor or mezzo-soprano trouser role, with Achilla, baritone (A1-F3), and at least two silent guards.

Sextus, as a result of having drawn his sword on Ptolemy, has been ordered to prison, and his mother to the seraglio. Achilla makes overtures of freedom for both if Cornelia will wed him. She indignantly refuses; brokenhearted, she sings a parting duet with her son.

EXCERPT 3a   Int   i, e   pp. 102/4/1-7   7 min.

This is the portion of excerpt 3 that includes only Cornelia and Sextus.

EXCERPT 4.   Int   i, e   pp. 108-23   15½ min.

Cleopatra, dramatic-coloratura or lyric soprano with agility; Nirenus, bass, with a very small part; and Caesar, bass-baritone (originally a male alto) appear in this scene.

Cleopatra, disguised as her maid Lydia, has succeeded in capturing the personal interest of Caesar. In this scene she provides a musical entertainment for her guest. Caesar then sings her praises in a very florid aria.

EXCERPT 4a   Int   i, e   pp. 108-17/1/3; 267/3/1-73 14 min.

The same scene as excerpt 4 with the omission of Caesar's aria, replacing it with the duet "Più amabile beltà."

EXCERPT 5   Int   i, e   pp. 124-50 (can be   22 min.
                              shortened by omitting *da capo* repeats)

Cornelia, Sextus, and Achillas (see excerpt 1 for vocal requirements) are heard in this scene with Ptolemy (Tolomeo), bass. Nirenus, bass, again plays a short role.

In the seraglio garden, Cornelia has been set to work. Achillas again proposes marriage and is rejected as is Ptolemy who has similar ideas. Cornelia is prevented from committing suicide by Sextus who has been smuggled in by Nirenus. The latter plots to bring them again within striking distance of the tyrant, and Sextus sings another "vengeance" aria.

HÄNSEL UND GRETEL

(Hansel and Gretel)

Engelbert Humperdinck (1854-1921)

Once upon a Time—Germany

EXCERPT 1   B&H/GS/Kal   e   pp. 12-66   23 min.
              Sch   g   pp. 12-66

The children Hansel and Gretel are sung by young women. Gretel, a lyric soprano (C3-Bb4), should have a trill; Hansel, mezzo-soprano (C3-Ab4), should have a boyish appearance. Their parents, Gertrude and Peter, are sung by a dramatic soprano or mezzo-soprano (B2-B4) and a baritone (Bb1-F3) respectively.

The children are introduced in a lively, frolicsome scene in their cottage. This includes a simple folk dance. They are interrupted by their mother who, scolding them, sends them into the woods to pick berries. Peter, the father, comes home from a successful day, bringing provisions. When he learns that Hansel and Gretel are in the woods, he sings the ballad of the witch. The frightened parents rush out in search of the children.

EXCERPT 1a   B&H/GS/Kal   e   pp. 12-33   8½ min.
               Sch   g   pp. 12-33

This is the opening portion of the scene with Hansel and Gretel only.

EXCERPT 1b   B&H/GS/Kal   e   pp. 12-41   12 min.
                Sch   g   pp. 12-41

The scene from excerpt 1 that includes Hansel, Gretel, and Gertrude only.

EXCERPT 2   B&H/GS/Kal   e   pp. 72/4/2-95/1/1   15 min.
                Sch   g   pp. 72/4/2-95/1/1

In addition to Hansel, mezzo-soprano, and Gretel, lyric soprano, one important solo is sung by the Sandman, lyric soprano. A few girls' voices should be heard offstage; women or children may be used on stage as the fourteen angels during the well-known prayer at the end of the scene.

Hansel and Gretel have picked berries in the woods but before returning home they proceed to eat them all. It gets dark and the children lose their way. Soon the Sandman arrives, sprinkling sleep into their eyes; Hansel and Gretel sing a simple prayer before falling asleep.

EXCERPT 3   B&H/GS/Kal   e   pp. 103-62/2/2   30 min.
                Sch   g   pp. 103-62/2/2

Hansel and Gretel as described in excerpt 1 (here Gretel has an optional D5) are joined by the Dew Fairy, a light lyric soprano with several A4's, and the Witch. The Witch may be sung by almost any voice category except coloratura soprano and *basso profondo*. Written in a range from Bb2 to B4, it is indicated in the score for mezzo-soprano. Transposed an octave lower, it is frequently performed by a *tenore buffo* and even occasionally by a comic baritone.

The Dew Fairy wakes the children from their night's sleep in the woods. They sight a gingerbread house to which they are lured by hunger. From the house the Witch appears whose habit it is to feed children generously and bake them in an oven until they become gingerbread. Seeing through this, Hansel devises a way to get out of the dilemma—they push the old Witch into the oven.

HELP! HELP! THE GLOBOLINKS!

Gian-Carlo Menotti (1911-)

America, 1968

EXCERPT 1   GS   e, g   pp. 30-51   9½ min.

Dr. Stone is a high baritone (C#2-G3 or A3); Mme Euterpova is a dramatic soprano (E3-B4) and caricature of an overbearing music teacher; Timothy, a comic character role, is a tenor (E2-Gb3).

Dr. Stone, the dean of St. Paul's School, and Timothy, the janitor, are worried about the absence of the children. Mme Euterpova, the music teacher, storms into the office, first complaining about the children not taking their instruments home to practice, then confessing her love for Dr. Stone who coldly rejects her.

EXCERPT 2   GS   e, g   pp. 70-79   3½ min.

In this short ensemble, Dr. Stone sings only one pitch (A2). Mme Euterpova, dramatic soprano (Db3-A4), and Timothy, tenor (Eb3-Ab3), appear along with Miss Newkirk, mezzo-soprano (C3-Eb4); Mr. Lavender-Gas, baritone (A1-Eb3) and Dr. Turtlespit, bass (F1-Bb2). Each character should be clearly defined.

Dr. Stone, nearly metamorphosed by a Globolink, has been taught by Mme Euterpova to make one sound to ward off any other Globolinks. Timothy, when threatened by a Globolink kills the creature with a blast of a tuba. Rejoicing, Mme Euterpova assigns instruments to each of the other teachers and they all march off to conquer the threatening Globolinks. (The march could be repeated to lengthen the scene.)

L'INCORONAZIONE DI POPPEA

(The Coronation of Poppea)

Claudio Monteverdi (1567-1643)

Rome, 62 A.D.

EXCERPT 1   Fab   i, e   pp. 17-42   15 min.
               UE   i, g   pp. 17-64

Poppea, lyric soprano with florid singing in the middle range;
Nerone, tenor, an authoritative character with most of his singing
in the middle range; Ottone, lyric baritone with some florid passages in the upper register; and two soldiers, both tenors, make up
this scene. (Music often lies low for the voice category indicated
in this opera.)

Outside Poppea's house, the warrior Ottone returns to Rome
only to find that his mistress Poppea has become the mistress of
Emperor Nerone. Poppea extracts a promise from Nerone that his
wife Ottavia will be dethroned in her favor.

EXCERPT 1a   Fab   i, e   pp. 31/1/4-42   7 min.
               UE   i, g   pp. 47-64

This is the portion of excerpt 1 using only Poppea and Nerone.

EXCERPT 2   Fab   i, e   pp. 43-52   5 min.
               UE   i, g   pp. 65-81

Poppea, lyric soprano described in excerpt 1, and her nurse
Arnalta, a slightly comic character sung by a very low mezzo-
soprano or contralto, are the characters in this scene.

In Poppea's bedroom, Arnalta, an old nurse, warns Poppea that
her design on Nerone and the throne may be dangerous; Poppea
laughs, believing that love is on her side.

EXCERPT 3   Fab   i, e   pp. 53-82   19 min.
               UE   i, g   pp. 82-136

Nerone, tenor (D2-G3), with Ottavia, dramatic mezzo-soprano
(C3-G4); Seneca, mature bass with agility at the extremes of the

range; Drusilla and Pallade, sopranos; and Valletto, tenor, all with easy vocal parts in the middle range.

In the Imperial Palace, the Empress Ottavia, aware of Nerone's love affair with Poppea, is oblivious to the consoling words of Drusilla. Seneca, a philosopher, advises the Empress to maintain her dignity. A vision of the goddess Pallas warns Seneca of impending death. Nerone informs Seneca that he intends to dispose of Ottavia and marry Poppea, and becomes enraged when Seneca disapproves.

EXCERPT 4   Fab   i, e   pp. 83-95   7 min.
               UE   i, g   pp. 137-56

Poppea, lyric soprano, and Nerone, tenor, with silent servants in this scene.

Nerone is alone with Poppea in her bedroom. Bestowing her charms on him, she suggests that Seneca, the one major obstacle between her and the throne, be removed. Nerone at once dispatches a guard to the old philosopher with an execution notice.

EXCERPT 5   Fab   i, e   pp. 96-108   6½ min.
               UE   i, g   pp. 157-85

Poppea, lyric soprano; Drusilla, soprano; and Ottone, lyric baritone, make up the cast for this scene.

Outside Poppea's house, Ottone laments that he can no longer visit Poppea. When she comes out, she reveals her ambitions and spurns her former lover. Drusilla tries to convince Ottone that fidelity to Poppea is hopeless and finally he agrees to love Drusilla instead.

EXCERPT 5a   Fab   i, e   pp. 100/3/2-108   4 min.
               UE   i, g   pp. 173-85

This scene is taken from excerpt 5 and uses only Drusilla and Ottone.

EXCERPT 6   Fab   i, e   pp. 109-17   5 min.
               UE   i, g   pp. 215-24

Damigella, soprano, and Valletto, tenor, may be light voices. There are no special vocal demands.

In the palace garden, Damigella and Valletto sing a charming love duet.

EXCERPT 7   Fab   i, e   pp. 137-46   4½ min.
                UE   i, g   pp. 225-35/1/6; 236-39

This is a drinking song for two tenors, Nerone and Lucano. Lucano usually sings below Nerone in the duet.

EXCERPT 8   Fab   i, e   pp. 147-61   8½ min.
                UE   i, g   pp. 240-78

The characters in this scene are Drusilla, soprano (D3-G4); Ottavia, dramatic mezzo-soprano (F3-G4); and Ottone, lyric baritone (A1-B2).

In her chamber in the palace, Ottavia no longer able to bear her disgrace, tells Ottone to murder Poppea. He agrees, though still feeling love for his former mistress. He borrows Drusilla's cloak to disguise himself as a woman in order to gain access to Poppea's house.

EXCERPT 8a   Fab   i, e   pp. 153-61   4½ min.
                 UE   i, g   pp. 262-78

From excerpt 8, only the scene between Drusilla and Ottone is included here.

EXCERPT 9   Fab   i, e   pp. 162-78   11 min.
                UE   i, g   pp. 279-309

Amor, with the highest soprano part in the opera (G3-Bb4), appears in this scene with Poppea, lyric soprano; Arnalta, low mezzo-soprano or contralto; and Ottone, lyric baritone.

Arnalta sings Poppea to sleep with a gentle lullaby. When Ottone steals into the room disguised in a woman's cloak, Amor, the god of love, prevents him from striking the sleeping Poppea.

EXCERPT 9a   Fab   i, e   pp. 162-68/3/2   5 min.
                 UE   i, g   pp. 279-90

The portion of excerpt 9 with Poppea and Arnalta only.

L'INFEDELTÀ DELUSA
(Deceit Outwitted)

Franz Josef Haydn (1732-1809)

Italy, Early Eighteenth Century

EXCERPT 1   UE   i, g, e   pp. 17-84/1/1; 85/2/2-86   16 min.

The five characters in the opera, all appearing in this excerpt, are Vespina and Sandrina, lyric-coloratura sopranos (C3-C5); Filippo and Nencio, high tenors (C2-C4); and Nanni, bass-baritone (F1-F3) requiring strength in the extremes of his range.

Nencio, a wealthy countryman, and the elderly Filippo plan for Filippo's daughter Sandrina to marry Nencio. Sandrina enters and is told of the plan; she is distressed because she has loved Nanni for three years. Her father insists she obey his wishes.

EXCERPT 2   UE   i, g, e   pp. 87-108/1/1;   11½ min.
                            109/1/1-23/1/1; 124/2/3-29

Sandrina, lyric-coloratura soprano; and Nanni, bass-baritone, with sustained F1's and F3's, are in this scene.

Sandrina wonders how she will obey her father's will and marry Nencio when she is in love with Nanni. Nanni appears and is puzzled because Sandrina seems to reject him. She sings a long aria, "Che imbroglio è questo," telling him she must leave him. Left alone, Nanni swears vengeance in an aria, "Non v'è rimedio."

EXCERPT 3   UE   i, g, e,   pp. 130-70   10½ min.

Vespina, lyric-coloratura soprano; and Nanni, bass-baritone, have a brilliant dramatic duet in this scene.

Vespina sings an aria while preparing the evening meal in her home. Her brother Nanni comes home, furious because a marriage is being arranged between his beloved Sandrina and the wealthy Nencio. Vespina is also infuriated because she loves Nencio; brother and sister join in a duet of vengeance.

EXCERPT 4   UE   i, g, e   pp. 171-227   13½ min.

Finale of act 1 using the same characters as excerpt 1.

Outside Filippo's house, Nencio sings an aria mocking the artificiality of city women. Sandrina approaches him and advises him to marry Vespina who loves him dearly. Nencio retorts that he is now in love with Sandrina. Vespina and Nanni who have been hiding, at this moment come forward and confront the deceitful Nencio. A quarrel develops which Filippo tries in vain to calm.

EXCERPT 5   UE   i, g, e   pp. 238-71/1/1;   18 min.
                         275/2/1-96; 301/2/4-305

An amusing scene with Vespina, soprano, dressed as an old lady, singing the comic aria "Ho un tumore in un ginocchio." Filippo, tenor, has an aria, "Tu, tu sposarti." Nanni (bass), Sandrina (soprano), and Nencio (tenor), sing only in recitatives.

Vespina, disguised as an old lady, approaches Filippo's house, she makes up the story that her daughter was once married to Nencio but that he tired of her and left her with three starving children. Filippo is convinced, and no longer wishes his daughter to marry Nencio. When Nencio enters upon the scene, he gets a strict upbraiding from Filippo.

EXCERPT 5a   UE   i, g, e   pp. 243-75   10 min.

From excerpt 5, this is Vespina's aria, with Filippo and Sandrina in recitatives.

EXCERPT 6   UE   i, g, e   pp. 306-57   10 min.

A scene for Vespina, soprano, appearing in two different male disguises, and Nencio, tenor.

Vespina, now dressed as a German serving man, approaches Nencio, whom she loves. The servant urges Nencio to drink wine with him because it is his master's wedding day; the bride is none other than Sandrina. Nencio thus believes that Filippo has found a richer son-in-law, and though he does not mind losing Sandrina, he refuses to be made a fool of. As he approaches Filippo's house, Vespina appears again, this time dressed as the Marquis of Ripafratta whose servant she appeared as earlier. The Marquis tells Nencio that he is not really going to marry Sandrina but rather intends to marry her off to one of his servants, thereby making Sandrina a kitchen maid. Nencio is only too glad to be a witness at the wedding ceremony and expresses his delight in the aria "Oh, che gusto!"

EXCERPT 7   UE   i, g, e   pp. 358-72/2/3;   17 min.
                               375/3/1-423

Sandrina and Vespina each have soprano arias; all five characters described in excerpt 1 sing an ensemble.

Vespina explains that there is just one more masquerade necessary to make their plot work; Filippo and Sandrina meanwhile make preparations for Sandrina's wedding. The notary and servant who arrive presently are really Vespina and Nanni in disguise. The contract is cleverly signed before the arrival of the "Marquis" and the servant's name is substituted. The servant reveals himself as Nanni, now married to Sandrina. Filippo and Nencio are furious but there is nothing they can do to change it. Vespina then reveals her series of disguises and all agree to a double wedding.

L'ITALIANA IN ALGERI

(The Italian Girl in Algiers)

Gioacchino Rossini (1792-1868)

Algiers, Late Eighteenth Century

EXCERPT 1   GS   i, e   pp. 38-55; 60/1/2-61   11 min.
                    Ric   i   pp. 31-46/3/3; 49/3/1-50

Lindoro, a high lyric tenor, here sings a technically difficult aria extending to C4 (B3 if aria is transposed down as it often is). Mustafà is sung by a *basso buffo* or *basso cantante* (B1-E3) with comic acting ability.

In the palace of the Bey of Algiers, Mustafà, the Bey, asks Lindoro, an Italian now captive in his service, if he would like to get married. It is the Bey's design to get rid of his own wife. In the duet that follows they speak of the kind of woman each prefers for a marriage partner.

EXCERPT 2   GS   i, e   pp. 65-71; 74-92 (opt.   11½ min.
                               cuts 90/1/4-90/4/2; 92/1/1-92/2/2)
                 Ric   i   pp. 54-59; 62-77 (opt. cuts 75/3/5-
                               76/2/2; 77/1/4-77/2/3

Isabella, a mezzo-soprano (A2-A4) with particular flexibility in the lower range, has a coloratura aria in this scene. Taddeo is a *basso buffo* but the role is often sung by a baritone (B1-E3).

The shipwrecked Isabella arrives at the seashore and sings an aria in which she laments her lost love, Lindoro, but comments that she knows how to look after herself. She and her traveling companion, Taddeo, sing an enchantingly silly duet lamenting their fate, argue about the situation, then make up and decide that the relationship of uncle and niece will have its advantages.

EXCERPT 3   GS   i, e   pp. 111-99   15 min.
                 Ric   i   pp. 94/4/1-155

In addition to Mustafà, Isabella, Lindoro, and Taddeo (voice descriptions in excerpts 1 and 2); Elvira, soprano with two sustained C5's; Zulma, mezzo-soprano whose part in the ensemble lies between Elvira and Isabella; Ali, Captain of the Guard, baritone, is included in this scene.

In his palace, Mustafà meets the latest arrival to his harem, the Italian beauty, Isabella. Isabella, seeing Mustafà for the first time, is amused at the sight of the grotesque Bey, and she has humorous music as she makes up to him. Taddeo in his role of "uncle" prevents the relationship from going too far. Lindoro, Elvira, and her companion Zulma enter to bid a last farewell. Mustafà is disposing of his wife Elvira in favor of Isabella. Lindoro recognizes Isabella as the sweetheart from whom he has been parted, and Isabella, overjoyed at seeing Lindoro, takes matters into her own hands. Things do not go according to Mustafà's plan; confusion is the result and the seven sing one of the most clever patter ensembles of all time.

EXCERPT 4   GS   i, e   pp. 226/2/1-78   17 min.
                Ric   i   pp. 179/2/1-220

Elvira, soprano; Zulma, mezzo-soprano; Isabella, mezzo-soprano (Bb2-Gb4); Lindoro, lyric tenor; Taddeo, comic bass or baritone; and Mustafà, *basso buffo*, are heard in this scene. Zulma has only recitatives in the excerpt in which a few slaves (silent) may be used.

Isabella has engratiated Elvira and Zulma; they assist her in adorning herself for a rendezvous with Mustafà. But Isabella has a plan: Elvira must join them, and of course, "Uncle" Taddeo and the servant Lindoro must also be present. Enraged by this arrangement, Mustafà leads off a quintet of pandemonium.

EXCERPT 4a   GS   i, e   pp. 226/2/1-31/2/5;   6½ min.
                              235-39
                Ric   i   pp. 179/2/1-84/3/5; 188-92/1/5

This is only Isabella's aria with Elvira and Zulma in recitatives from excerpt 4. The men need not sing the accompanying comments.

EXCERPT 4b   GS   i, e   pp. 240-78   10 min.
                Ric   i   pp. 192/2/1-220

The quintet of Elvira, Isabella, Lindoro, Taddeo, and Mustafà make up this scene from excerpt 4.

EXCERPT 5   GS   i, e   pp. 284-99 (suggested   6½ min.
                             cuts in score)
                Ric   i   pp. 226-39 (suggested cuts: 226/2/2-
                             227/5/3; 239/2/2-39/3/3)

Lindoro, Taddeo, and Mustafà, as described in excerpts 1-4.

A plan is put into action that will enable Lindoro, Taddeo, Isabella, and other Italians to escape the captivity of Mustafà. The two men inform Mustafà that he is to be initiated into that ancient and noble Italian order of the "Pappataci" (literally, "eat and be silent"). Mustafà reacts with delight and the rollicking "Pappataci" trio follows.

LAKMÉ

Leo Delibes (1836-1891)

India, Mid-Nineteenth Century

EXCERPT 1   Int   f, e   pp. 24-40   7½ min.

Lakmé is a lyric soprano who needs the flexibility of a coloratura with a strong B4; Mallika, mezzo-soprano (B2-G#4), is a companion to Lakmé. Nilakantha, a Brahmin priest, bass (A1-D3); and Hadji, his servant, a tenor, appear briefly in a recitative in this scene.

The scene takes place in the garden of a Hindu temple. Nilakantha bears hatred for a British invader who has forbidden the priest to practice his religion. Nilakantha leaves his daughter Lakmé alone with her slave Mallika, and they sing a charming duet.

EXCERPT 1a   Int   f, e   pp. 30-40   5 min.

The portion of excerpt 1 using only Lakmé and Mallika.

EXCERPT 2   Int   f, e   pp. 41-67   9½ min.

This is the quintet for the five English characters in the opera, combined with Gerald's lyric aria "Fantaisie aux divins mensonges." Ellen and Rose are both sopranos with no particular technical demands, and Mrs. Benson, a comic governess, is a mezzo-soprano. Gerald should have A3's and Bb3's for his lyric tenor role; Frédéric is a lyric baritone (Bb1-F3).

Fascinated by what they see inside the garden, each of the English people expresses his or her own feelings about the adventure. Frédéric warns of poisonous flowers and also tells of the beauty of the priest's daughter Lakmé. The girls want a sketch of Lakmé's jewels; Gerald, an artist, agrees to stay behind and draw the sketch.

EXCERPT 3   Int   f, e   pp. 68-75   6 min.

Lakmé and Mallika (see descriptions in excerpt 1) are in this scene; Mallika appears only briefly.

Lakmé and Mallika return to the garden. Lakmé dismisses Mallika after a short conversation, then sings an aria expressing her mixed feelings of sadness and happiness.

EXCERPT 4   Int   f, e   pp. 78-93/1/5   6½ min.

A scene between Lakmé, lyric-coloratura soprano, and Gerald, lyric tenor.

Gerald comes out of hiding and Lakmé becomes alarmed; one word to her father could bring about Gerald's death. He is obviously infatuated with her and they join in a passionate duet.

EXCERPT 5   Int   f, e   pp. 146-66   13½ min.

This excerpt is included for its "Bell Song," Lakmé's coloratura aria extending upward to an E5. Nilakantha, bass, has an F3 in this scene. The chorus can be omitted, Lakmé thus addressing the "Bell Song" to the audience.

The Brahmin priest Nilakantha disguises himself as a beggar and believes that the person who has dared to break into the sacred temple gardens will reveal himself upon hearing Lakmé's song. Lakmé obliges as the crowd gathers around her.

EXCERPT 6   Int   f, e   pp. 184-98   8 min.

Lakmé and Gerald (voice descriptions in excerpts 1-2) sing another duet when Gerald returns. Lakmé proposes that they elope to a part of the forest known only to her.

EXCERPT 7   Int   f, e   pp. 222-82 (trad. cut in   24 min.
                                     score)

A scene for Lakmé, soprano to C5; Gerald, tenor to B3; Frédéric, baritone; and Nilakantha, bass, who sings only briefly in a high range. A chorus is offstage.

Lakmé has brought the wounded Gerald into the forest. He is more enamored than ever of the Hindu beauty who nurses him back to health. She gives him a draught of sacred spring water said to cause all who drink it to remain forever in love. Frédéric arrives and reminds Gerald of his duty to his country, urging him to leave with his regiment. Lakmé, unhappy at this prospect, takes a leaf of a deadly blossom and bites it. Just then Nilakantha enters, furious at the sight of Gerald near his daughter. Lakmé stops her father from having her lover killed by telling him she is dying for Gerald's sake. The poison from the flower takes effect and she collapses.

EXCERPT 7a   Int   f, e   pp. 222-45   11½ min.

This scene from excerpt 7 uses Lakmé, Gerald, and the chorus.

EXCERPT 7b   Int   f, e   pp. 222-34   7 min.

The same scene as excerpt 7a without the chorus.

EXCERPT 7c   Int   f, e   pp. 256-82   12½ min.

This portion of excerpt 7 involves Lakmé, Gerald, Nilakantha, and the men's chorus offstage.

EXCERPT 7d   Int   f, e   pp. 256-77   10½ min.

The scene from excerpt 7 with Lakmé and Gerald only, and the chorus of soldiers offstage.

LIZZIE BORDEN

Jack Beeson (1921-)

Fall River, Massachusetts, About 1880

EXCERPT 1   B&H   e   pp. 28/1/3-45/1/6   7½ min.

A confrontation scene between Andrew Borden, bass-baritone or dramatic baritone (Bb1-F#3), and his daughter Elizabeth, mezzo-soprano (Bb2-Ab4), with some dramatic singing.

Andrew is seated at his desk going over his financial ledgers; Lizzie is making a housedress. She tells her father that the dress will not do for the church meeting; she must have a gown made by a dressmaker. He strictly forbids it and tells Lizzie to go find a dress of her late mother. Left alone, Andrew sings boastfully of his wealth, cursing all idlers.

EXCERPT 2   B&H   e   pp. 51-74   12 min.

A scene for Lizzie, mezzo-soprano, and her younger sister Margret, lyric soprano (C3-B4). The voice of their stepmother Abigail, soprano, is heard offstage.

Lizzie urges her sister Margret to accept the marriage proposal of Capt. Jason MacFarlane and, if necessary, elope with him.

EXCERPT 3   B&H   e   pp. 75-178   39 min.

The six leading characters all appear in act 2 complete. Abigail, soprano (C#3-C#5), is indicated in the score as "spinto with coloratura." Jason is a lyric baritone (Bb1-F3); the Reverend Mr. Harrington, a tenor (E2-Ab3). Andrew, bass-baritone; Margret, lyric soprano; and Lizzie, mezzo-soprano, complete the scene.

Abigail is seated at the harmonium, accompanying herself in a song. When a key does not work, she complains about the harmonium and convinces her husband to buy a new piano she has seen. She also convinces him to do over the house and remove all traces of his first wife Evangeline. This irritates Lizzie, and a family quarrel develops, to be interrupted by the arrival of Capt. Jason MacFarlane and the Reverend Mr. Harrington. Andrew tells Harrington to look elsewhere for church funds and refuses Jason when he asks for Margret's hand in marriage. Andrew offers him his older daughter Lizzie instead, and the act closes with a long dramatic aria for Lizzie.

EXCERPT 3a   B&H   e   pp. 75-105 or 107   13 min.

The opening of act 2 with Andrew, Abigail, and Lizzie; includes Abigail's song.

EXCERPT 3b   B&H   e   pp. 142-78   16 min.

The end of act 2 including Lizzie's aria; Andrew, Jason, and Lizzie only, with Abigail's voice offstage.

EXCERPT 4   B&H   e   pp. 184-215   12½ min.

A scene for Lizzie, Margret, and Jason, whose voice categories are described in excerpts 1-3.

Left alone in the house, Lizzie and Margret await the arrival of Jason. When he comes, he convinces Margret to elope. After they leave, Lizzie tries on her mother's wedding dress and fantasizes in front of the mirror.

EXCERPT 5   B&H   e   pp. 206/2/2-47/2/5   14 min.

Lizzie, mezzo-soprano, and Abigail, spinto soprano, are in this scene.

The scene begins with Lizzie in her mother's wedding dress (excerpt 4). Her stepmother Abigail chides her for her silly behavior and they quarrel. The scene ends as Abigail tears the frills from Lizzie's dress and Lizzie smashes the mirror with her fists.

LOHENGRIN

Richard Wagner (1813-1883)

Antwerp, Early Tenth Century

EXCERPT 1   GS   g, e   pp. 115-35   13 min.
                Kal   g, e   pp. 105-27
                Pet   g   pp. 84-101

Ortrud, mezzo-soprano or dramatic soprano, needs sustained power to A4. Frederick of Telramund is a dramatic baritone (C2-G3) and must be capable of sustaining a high tessitura.

In the courtyard of King Henry's fortress, Telramund blames his wife for having deceived him. Ortrud replies that the strange knight who defeated her husband in combat (but spared his life) did so by magic; if the knight were to divulge his name and state, he would lose his powers so that Telramund could overcome him.

EXCERPT 2   GS   g, e   pp. 136-55/4/4   16 min.
                Kal   g, e   pp. 128-46/5/2
                Pet   g   pp. 102-18/5/2

In this scene Elsa, spinto or dramatic soprano (D3-G4) requiring a fine lyric line, sings with Ortrud, mezzo-soprano or soprano

(Bb2-Bb4) of contrasting quality with a strong upper register.

Elsa, about to be married to a knight, appears on the balcony of the fortress, breathing the night air and singing of her happiness. The girl is startled at hearing her name through the darkness. Ortrud appears, and in a long dialogue with Elsa, plants the seeds of doubt in the girl's mind in order to accomplish the demise of the unknown knight.

EXCERPT 3   GS   g, e   pp. 270-93/5/6   21 min.
              Kal   g, e   pp. 267/2/6-93/5/2
              Pet   g   pp. 201/3/2-22/5/5

The title role of the opera is sung by a dramatic tenor (E2-A3) capable of sustaining long, difficult phrases. In this scene he appears with Elsa, spinto or dramatic soprano (C3-B4). Frederick of Telramund, four pages, and two ladies are present but silent in this scene.

In the bridal chamber, Lohengrin is alone with his bride for the first time. As he tenderly calls her by name, she regrets that she cannot respond by uttering his. She grows more and more insistent that he reveal his identity to her. Telramund and his pages steal into the chamber; Lohengrin picks up his sword and strikes Telramund dead. He then promises Elsa that in the presence of the King he will disclose his name and title.

LOUISE

Gustave Charpentier (1860-1956)

Paris, About 1900

EXCERPT 1   GS   f, e   pp. 1-73   37½ min.

The complete first act of *Louise* involves the four main characters of the opera. Louise is a lyric or lyric-spinto soprano (Db3-Bb4), youthful in manner, with stamina and a wide dynamic range. Julien, her beau, is sung by a lyric tenor (E2-Bb3) with strong, solid high notes as well as subtlety. Louise's parents are sung by a mezzo-soprano (B2-G4) and a bass-baritone (A1-E3) with a strong

but lyric upper range. Both should display mature vocal and dramatic qualities.

The scene represents the kitchen of Louise's tenement with its
balcony and on the other side of the stage, Julien's balcony.
Julien is serenading Louise from his balcony; Louise comes out
onto hers and begins a conversation with him. Louise's mother enters the apartment and, after a time, drags Louise into the kitchen
and shuts the door to the balcony. She disapprovingly mocks
Louise's love for Julien. The Father opens a letter Julien has written requesting Louise's hand in marriage. The Father wishes to
consider the request but the Mother will not hear of it. Avoiding
an argument, the Father asks Louise to read the newspaper to him.
She does so, breaking down in tears at the mention of Paris in the
spring.

EXCERPT 2   GS   f, e   pp. 147/5/3-205   14 min.

This excerpt provides an excellent ensemble for any number of
women's voices; eleven of them sing solo lines. Louise, soprano,
has very little singing. Principal soloists are Irma, soprano (E3-A4);
Camille, soprano (E3-A4); and Gertrude, mezzo-soprano (C3-E4).
Other soloists are Blanche, Elise, Marguerite, and an Errand Girl,
all sopranos; Suzanne, Madeleine, and a Forewoman, mezzo-
sopranos. The scene lends itself well to individual characterizations.
Julien, strong lyric tenor (E2-A3), sings serenades in the street,
accompanied by guitar. (Can be played by a guitarist in costume
onstage.)

In the dressmaker's shop, the girls are all sitting around the
tables, sewing and chattering. They see Louise lost in thought, and
begin gossiping about her being in love. After some of the girls
voice their own fantasies on the subject of love, they are serenaded
from the street by Julien. This at first pleases the girls, then begins
to bore them. Louise, unable to cope with the situation, feigns illness and runs out. Later she is seen going off arm in arm with
Julien, much to the girls' amusement.

EXCERPT 2a   GS   f, e   pp. 147/5/3-75   8 min.

The portion of excerpt 2 using the girls only.

EXCERPT 3   GS   f, e   pp. 210-17/1/1; 233/2/1-   17 min.
                              62 (*D* in 217/1/2 is changed to *B#*
                              in 233/2/1)

This scene contains Louise's aria "Depuis le jour," a favorite of sopranos, with its B4 *pianissimo* swelling to *forte*. The roles of Louise and Julien, tenor, require great stamina in the duet that follows. An offstage chorus is heard enhancing the mood of the love duet.

As the sun sets on Paris, Louise and Julien, in their Montmartre garden, sing of the happiness they share in their love. Their cry of freedom is heard against a background of the lights of Paris coming up one by one.

EXCERPT 4   GS   f, e   pp. 340-51/2/6;   33½ min.
                              357/1/2-404

The characters in this scene are Father, bass-baritone; Mother, mezzo-soprano; and Louise, lyric-spinto soprano. The Father has an optional G3 in this scene. Once again an offstage chorus is heard.

Louise's parents' home looks much the same as in excerpt 1, but the balcony of Julien's home has been torn down. Louise's father is ill and in his frustration curses children who would defy their parents. The Mother cannot think of allowing Louise to go back to Julien. The Father sings a lullaby to Louise, treating her as a child. But voices from Paris call to the young woman and Louise runs off, leaving her father cursing the city which has stolen his daughter from him.

LUCIA DI LAMMERMOOR

Gaetano Donizetti (1798-1848)

Scotland, About 1700

EXCERPT 1   GS/Kal   i, e   pp. 29-42/2/5   12 min.
                                 (opt. cut 40/4/3-42/1/1)

Ric   i   pp. 34-49 (opt. cut 47/3/3-49/2/2)

A scene for lyric-coloratura soprano (C3-D5), containing the aria "Regnava nel silenzio." The supporting role of Alisa is a mezzo-soprano.

Lucia, waiting in a park near a fountain, relates to her confidante Alisa the legend of the fountain, affirming her love for Edgardo di Ravenswood, an enemy of her family.

EXCERPT 2   GS/Kal   i, e   pp. 42/4/1-59 (opt.   12½ min.
                               cut 58/2/2-58/4/3)
               Ric   i   pp. 50/2/1-72 (opt. cut 70/3/4-71/2/2)

Edgardo should be a strong lyric tenor capable of maintaining the high tessitura of his music (F2-Bb3 with opt. Eb4). He joins Lucia, lyric-coloratura soprano, for this scene.

Edgardo comes to meet Lucia and tells her that he has been ordered to France and must bid her farewell. He wishes to end the feud between him and her brother, but she advises Edgardo to keep their love a secret.

EXCERPT 3   GS/Kal   i, e   pp. 62/4/1-81 (opt.   12½ min.
                               cuts 65/1/2-65/4/1; 67/2/2-67/4/3;
                               77/5/5-79/4/5; 80/2/2-81/1/2)
               Ric   i   pp. 77-99 (opt. cuts 79/4/1-80/2/1;
                               82/1/3-82/4/1; 94/4/4-97/1/1;
                               97/3/4-98/2/3)

Lucia, lyric-coloratura soprano, sings with her brother Enrico, baritone with strong high notes (B1-G3).

Enrico shows Lucia a forged letter indicating that Edgardo has been unfaithful and advising her to accept an arranged match with Arturo Bucklaw. The action unfolds in the music of an extended duet in three sections.

EXCERPT 4   GS/Kal   i, e   pp. 92/3/1-155 (trad.   15 min.
                               cut 138/1/5-53/1/5)
               Ric   i   pp. 113-82 (trad. cut end of 163-
                               180/1/2)

This scene is built around the well-known sextet and includes a not-too-difficult chorus. The six principals are Lucia, soprano (to D5); Alisa, mezzo-soprano (F3-A4); Edgardo and Arturo, both tenors with strong A3 (Edgardo is usually the heavier voice of the two); Enrico, baritone; and Raimondo, bass.

The marriage contract between Arturo and Lucia is signed. Edgardo appears and, after the singing of the sextet "Che mi frena in tal momento," rushes at his eternal enemy Enrico, who shows Lucia's former suitor the signed contract. In furious rage, Edgardo curses the faithless Lucia and her hated family.

EXCERPT 5   GS/Kal   i, e   pp. 173-216   21 min.
             Ric   i   pp. 206-52

Another chorus scene is included in order to provide the setting for the "Mad Scene" of Lucia, a brilliant display of vocal fireworks (up to Eb5) and intense acting. The other main character is Raimondo who sings a haunting lyric bass aria. Enrico, baritone, and Normanno, tenor, sing supporting parts.

While the wedding guests are still feasting and celebrating, the chaplain Raimondo appears with the shocking news that Lucia has murdered her bridegroom Arturo in the bridal chamber. Soon the disheveled Lucia herself appears in a lengthy display of mental derangement. At the end of the scene, Lucia falls dead.

EXCERPT 6   GS/Kal   i, e   pp. 219-40   16½ min.
             Ric   i   pp. 255-80

This aria for Edgardo, tenor, is very demanding because of its high tessitura; supported by Raimondo, bass, and a men's chorus.

Edgardo visits the tombs of his ancestors to console his grief at Lucia's apparent treachery. When he sees a funeral procession and finds out that his beloved is dead, he stabs himself.

DIE LUSTIGEN WEIBER VON WINDSOR

(The Merry Wives of Windsor)

Otto Nicolai (1810-1849)

Windsor, Early Fifteenth Century

EXCERPT 1   GS e   pp. 17-32 (trad. cut in score)   8 min.
             Kal g, e pp. 13-29 (trad. cut 27/3/4-29/2/3)
             Pet g   pp. 17-32 (trad. cut in score)

A duet scene between Mistress Ford (Frau Fluth), a lyric or spinto soprano (A2-B4) with agility, and Mistress Page (Frau Reich), low mezzo-soprano also with great agility (A2-G4).

In a garden between the Ford and Page homes, the two ladies greet each other with the news that both have received the same love letter from Sir John Falstaff. Repulsed by his amorous pretensions, they begin to plot their revenge on the fat knight.

EXCERPT 2   GS e   pp. 34/3/2-45 (trad. cut in   5 min.
                      score)
             Kal g, e pp. 32/1/2-43 (trad. cut 40/1/6-
                      43/1/3)
             Pet g   pp. 34/3/2-45 (trad. cut in score)

A scene between Fenton, lyric tenor (D2-A3) not difficult, and Mr. Page (Herr Reich), bass (G1-E3) requiring rapid articulation.

Fenton appears in Page's garden to ask the hand of Page's daughter Anne in marriage; in the duet that follows, Page stubbornly refuses Fenton's request.

EXCERPT 3   GS e   pp. 46-102   22½ min.
             Kal g, e pp. 44-109 (trad. cut 97/1/4-
                      105/1/6)
             Pet g   pp. 46-108 (trad. cut in score)

Mistress Ford, soprano, opens the scene with a recitative and aria demanding a trill and agility from C3 to an optional C5. Others in the excerpt are Mistress Page, low mezzo-soprano with agility; Mr. Page, bass; Sir John Falstaff, the fat knight, bass

(G1-D3), capable of comic, mock-romantic acting; Ford, baritone (C2-F3) dramatic role; Slender (Spärlich), tenor (E2-A3), and Dr. Caius, baritone or bass (C2-F3 or G3), comic roles. Two serving men can be part of a mixed ensemble completing the scene.

Mistress Ford awaits Falstaff in her home. She and Mistress Page have sent an anonymous note to Mr. Ford informing him of the rendezvous. A large laundry basket is brought in; when Mistress Page interrupts the couple to tell Mistress Ford her husband is coming home, the women hide Falstaff in the basket and laugh as he gets dumped in the Thames River. The plan works out perfectly—the jealous Ford is embarrassed in front of his neighbors.

EXCERPT 4   GS   e   pp. 103-24   12 min.
              Kal g, e pp. 111-32
              Pet g   pp. 111-32

A scene containing an aria for Falstaff with a sustained E1, assisted by a men's ensemble and a duet for Falstaff and Ford. (See vocal descriptions for excerpt 3.)

Falstaff is drinking with his cronies in the Garter Inn; Ford enters, announcing himself as Mr. Brook seeking the aid of the fat knight in winning favor of a certain Mistress Ford. He is astonished to learn that Falstaff has been hidden in a basket and dumped in the river but still plans to return to visit the lady again that very day. The two anticipate the upcoming rendezvous with glee.

EXCERPT 4a   GS   e   pp. 109-24   9 min.
              Kal g, e pp. 116-32
              Pet g   pp. 117-32

The duet between Falstaff and Ford only, without the men's ensemble.

EXCERPT 5   GS   e   pp. 125-43   16 min.
              Kal g, e pp. 133-52
              Pet g   pp. 133-51

A duet for Anne Page, lyric soprano (D3-Bb4), and Fenton, tenor (E2-Ab3), and their quartet with Slender and Dr. Caius, characters described in excerpt 3.

Anne's two unwanted suitors Slender and Dr. Caius, unknown to each other, plan to meet her during her daily walk in the garden. They are forced into hiding upon the arrival of Fenton with whom she is in love. A romantic duet soon gives way to an amusing quartet.

EXCERPT 5a   GS   e   pp. 129/3/1-44   6½ min.
               Kal g, e pp. 137/3/1-44
               Pet g   pp. 136/3/1-44

Fenton's aria and the duet between Anne and Fenton.

EXCERPT 6   GS   e   pp. 144-74   12 min.
               Kal g, e pp. 153-91 (trad. cut 181/2/1-
                         189/1/2)
               Pet g   pp. 152-89 (trad. cut 179/2/1-
                         187/1/2)

The same characters as excerpt 3, with two serving men (silent) and no chorus. This includes a lengthy duet for Ford and Mistress Ford; Falstaff has only speaking and *falsetto* singing in this scene.

Falstaff has just arrived at Mistress Ford's house when Mistress Page announces the unexpected arrival of Mr. Ford. The women cleverly disguise Falstaff as an old woman whom Ford hates and whom he promptly drives out of the house. Another vain search for Falstaff ensues and again the jealous Ford is ridiculed.

EXCERPT 6a   GS   e   pp. 145-58   7 min.
               Kal g, e pp. 155-68
               Pet g   pp. 153-66

The duet between Ford and Mistress Ford, with the silent serving men.

MACBETH

Giuseppe Verdi (1813-1901)

Medieval Scotland

EXCERPT 1   GS   i, e   pp. 4-37   12 min.
                Ric   i   pp. 4-34

A scene for Macbeth, baritone (C2-F3), and Banquo, bass (F1-
Eb3), both voices requiring dramatic strength as well as ability to
sustain a lyric line. Dominating the scene, the three witches of
Shakespeare's drama are indicated in Verdi's score as a three-part
chorus (soprano, mezzo, alto). The brief roles of Ross and Angus
are condensed into a chorus of messengers, unison basses (A1-D3).

A group of witches dance upon the heath. Returning from battle, Macbeth and Banquo are greeted as Thane of Cawdor and pro-
genitor of future kings, respectively. The two generals are amazed
when messengers of King Duncan arrive with the news that the
Thane of Cawdor has been executed for treason and the title assigned to Macbeth.

EXCERPT 2   GS   i, e   pp. 38-49/3/3; 52/4/1-76   19½ min.
                Ric   i   35-45/1/3; 48-71

Lady Macbeth should be sung by a dramatic soprano (Bb2-C5)
with dark timbre and considerable flexibility. The role often taken
by a dramatic-coloratura mezzo-soprano, includes in this scene the
brilliant aria "Vieni, t'affretta." Macbeth, baritone, joins her in a
dialogue and duet; a servant, bass, appears briefly.

In the great hall of Macbeth's castle, Lady Macbeth is reading a
letter from her husband describing the meeting with the witches.
Her contemplations are of murdering the King. When Macbeth returns she convinces him to commit the murder that very night.
She then completes the crime by smearing with blood the King's
sleeping servants so it will appear that they were the murderers.

EXCERPT 2a   GS   i, e   pp. 54-76   12½ min.
                Ric   i   pp. 49-71

The duet portion of the scene only; the servant does not sing in
this excerpt.

EXCERPT 3   GS   i, e   pp. 112-20   6 min.
                   Ric i   pp. 107-15

   Lady Macbeth, dramatic soprano, sings the extremely dramatic
aria "La luce langue." Macbeth, dramatic baritone, has only a few
lines of recitative.
   Macbeth is now King but he is uneasy not only with his own
conscience but also with the memory of the witches' prophecy
that Banquo, not Macbeth, will be the sire of future kings. Lady
Macbeth urges her husband to murder Banquo and, left alone,
sings her aria of fierce determination.

EXCERPT 4   GS   i, e   pp. 278-90   10½ min.
                   Ric i   pp. 262-74

   This is the famous "Sleepwalking Scene" in which Lady Macbeth, described in excerpt 2, after singing most of the opera in the
middle range, must sing a sustained lyric aria ending with a *pianissimo* Db5. Supporting roles are a Lady-in-Waiting, soprano or
mezzo-soprano; and a Physician, bass.
   In a room of the castle, the Lady-in-Waiting and a Physician
comment on their mistress's apparent loss of mind through a guilty
conscience. Lady Macbeth herself wanders in, walking and talking
in her sleep, recalling the murders of Duncan and Banquo, and trying to rub the spot of imaginary blood from her hand.

          MADAMA BUTTERFLY

          (Madame Butterfly)

          Giacomo Puccini (1858-1924)

          Nagasaki, Japan, 1904-1907

EXCERPT 1   GS   i, e   pp. 1-57   15 min.
                   Kal i, e   pp. 1-43/1/2
                   Ric i, e   pp. 1-43/1/2
                   Ric i   pp. 1-59

   Butterfly is a lyric spinto soprano (Db3-Bb4) who in this scene

has an optional Db5. The role requires a secure vocal technique
and the impression of an Oriental. Others in the scene are Lt. B. F.
Pinkerton, tenor (G2-Bb3), who sings two short but important
arias; Sharpless, baritone, who must have a G3; and Goro, tenor
(F#2-G3), a character role. Lesser roles in this scene are Suzuki,
mezzo-soprano, and two servants, silent. There is a three-part
women's chorus.

Pinkerton eagerly awaits his bride Cio-Cio-San, known as
Madame Butterfly. The marriage broker Goro points out the vir-
tues of the house where Pinkerton and his Japanese bride will live
and introduces Pinkerton to Suzuki and the other servants. The
American consul Sharpless arrives and the two Americans drink a
toast to their homeland. Soon the anticipated moment comes.
Butterfly and her friends appear, singing of love.

EXCERPT 1a   GS   i, e   pp. 46-57   3 min.
                Kal i, e   pp. 35/1/2-43/1/2
                Ric i, e   pp. 35/1/2-43/1/2
                Ric i   pp. 47/1/2-59

The portion of excerpt 1 with Butterfly and the girls only, eliminating Sharpless's one line.

EXCERPT 2   GS   i, e   pp. 122-56   8 min.
                Kal i, e   pp. 106/2/1-33
                Ric i, e   pp. 95/2/1-120
                Ric i   pp. 124-64

The love duet for Butterfly, who needs a strong C5, and Pinkerton (see vocal descriptions in excerpt 1). Suzuki, mezzo-soprano,
sings very little in this scene.

Butterfly, disowned by her relatives for giving up her religion to
marry an American, is being comforted by her husband. Soon she
overcomes her sorrow and shyness and sings ecstatically of her
love. The scene climaxes in the passionate love duet.

EXCERPT 3   GS   i, e   pp. 157-74   6 min.
                Kal i, e   pp. 134-50
                Ric i, e   pp. 121-37
                Ric i   pp. 167-91/2/3

Butterfly sings the famous aria "Un bel dì vedremo"; her role demands subtlety as well as strength. Suzuki, lyric mezzo-soprano (C3-F#4), requires warmth and consistency of tone.

Three years after her marriage to Lieutenant Pinkerton, Butterfly is waiting in her house for him to return. Her servant Suzuki has her doubts, but Butterfly's faith is constant as she describes the scene she imagines will take place when her husband comes home.

EXCERPT 4	GS	i, e	pp. 203/4/1-26/2/2	11 min.
	Kal	i, e	pp. 177/4/1-99/2/2 (Italian words different from other scores)	
	Ric	i, e	pp. 164/4/1-86/2/2	
	Ric	i	pp. 224/4/2-51/2/1	

The main characters are Butterfly and Sharpless, both previously described. Suzuki is silent in this scene as is the small child.

Sharpless calls on Butterfly and attempts to read her a letter telling that Pinkerton is now married to an American wife. Overcome by the sight of the letter, Butterfly interrupts, insisting that the letter means Pinkerton will return to her. When Sharpless suggests that Butterfly find another husband, she shows him her child, obviously Pinkerton's son, and sings in a pathetically moving aria, "Che tua madre," that she would rather die than return to the Geisha trade. Sharpless leaves, unable to finish reading the letter.

EXCERPT 5	GS	i, e	pp. 233-49/2/2	6½ min.
	Kal	i, e	pp. 206-20/2/2	
	Ric	i, e	pp. 193-208/2/2	
	Ric	i	pp. 261-82/1/4	

Butterfly sings the "Flower Duet" with Suzuki. It is important that the voices blend well.

A salute of a cannon from the harbor announces the arrival of a man-of-war. Through her telescope Butterfly recognizes Pinkerton's ship and, delirious with joy, orders Suzuki to help her decorate the room with flowers.

EXCERPT 6   GS   i, e   pp. 271/3/1-324   7½ min.
                Kal   i, e   pp. 241-79 (trad. cut 271/2/5-
                                    272/4/3)
                Ric   i, e   pp. 229-66
                Ric   i   pp. 309/3/1-63

In this scene, the four main characters already described—Butterfly, Suzuki, Pinkerton, and Sharpless—appear. Kate Pinkerton, mezzo-soprano, has a lesser role and again the child is there but silent.

Butterfly has been watching all night for Pinkerton's arrival. At daybreak when Sharpless, Pinkerton, and his American wife, Kate, arrive, Suzuki is shocked to learn of the second marriage. Pinkerton, overcome with remorse, hurries from the scene after singing the aria "Addio, fiorito asil." Soon Butterfly learns the truth and tearfully agrees to give up her child to be reared in America if his father will come to take him. She then commands Suzuki to leave her alone and bids farewell to her son in an intensely powerful aria. By the time Pinkerton returns to claim the child, Butterfly has stabbed herself.

EXCERPT 6a   GS   i, e   pp. 275-97/1/2   7½ min.
                Kal   i, e   pp. 243/1/2-57/2/2
                Ric   i, e   pp. 231/1/2-45/2/2
                Ric   i   pp. 313-35/2/2

The portion of excerpt 6 with Suzuki, Pinkerton, and Sharpless. Kate Pinkerton is silent.

EXCERPT 6b   GS   i, e   pp. 311/3/1-24   6 min.
                Kal   i, e   pp. 268/3/1-79 (trad. cut 271/2/5-
                                    272/4/3)
                Ric   i, e   pp. 256/3/1-66
                Ric   i   pp. 350/3/1-63

This is the final scene from excerpt 6 with Butterfly, Suzuki, and the child only. It requires Pinkerton's final entrance calling Butterfly's name.

MANON

Jules Massenet (1842-1912)

France, 1721

EXCERPT 1   GS   f, e   pp. 75/3/2-102/2/3   11½ min.
              Kal   f, e   pp. 83/3/2-110/3/1

The role of Manon is scored for lyric soprano (C3-A4) who should have considerable flexibility and a trill. The leading tenor role, Des Grieux, requires a strong-voiced, lyric tenor (F2-A3). A trio of women may be seen at the opening of the scene, if desired, or may sing offstage where Manon can have imagined to have seen them. Lescaut, Manon's cousin, speaks offstage and a Postboy (silent) is needed.

Manon is waiting at an inn at Amiens to be taken to a convent. She attracts the attention of the Chevalier des Grieux; they fall in love almost immediately and decide to run off to Paris together.

EXCERPT 2   GS   f, e   pp. 115-68   25 min.
              Kal   f, e   pp. 123-77

Act 2 features Manon, soprano (D3-B4), and Des Grieux, tenor (E2-A3), both in very subtle arias: "Adieu, notre petite table" and "En fermant les yeux," respectively. The characters of Lescaut and De Bretigny, both baritones, are introduced. Both sing in the same range (Bb1-E3) but Lescaut should be the higher of the two. A maid appears in a speaking role.

In the apartment of Manon and Des Grieux in Paris, Des Grieux is writing a letter to his father asking permission to marry Manon. Manon's cousin Lescaut and a wealthy nobleman, De Bretigny, arrive. Lescaut asks to read the letter Des Grieux has written; De Bretigny suggests that he could provide for Manon since her lover is about to be taken away at the instigation of his father. After the visitors leave, Des Grieux goes to post his letter while Manon bids a sad farewell to the surroundings they have shared. When Des Grieux returns he describes a dream he has had. There is a knock at the door; Des Grieux answers and is captured.

EXCERPT 2a   GS   f, e   pp. 155-58   10½ min.
              Kal   f, e   pp. 163/1/2-77

The latter part of excerpt 2 with only Manon and Des Grieux.

EXCERPT 3   GS   f, e   pp. 197/4/1-214   7 min.
              Kal   f, e   pp. 207/3/1-25

This scene is built around Manon's elegant "Gavotte," an aria
requiring some coloratura technique and in which a D5 is usually
interpolated. De Bretigny, a baritone, sings a supporting role
backed by a chorus of vendors, townspeople and nobility.
De Bretigny brings Manon to the fête at the Cours-la-Reine,
Paris, where she sings of her life of luxury and is applauded by the
crowd.

EXCERPT 4   GS   f, e   pp. 246-82   22 min.
              Kal   f, e   pp. 257-94

The demanding tenor aria (F2-Bb3) for Des Grieux, "Ah, fuyez,
douce image," is found in this scene, as well as an aria for his
father, the Count, bass with an F3. Manon, lyric soprano (D3-B4)
with flexibility, has some dramatic moments, too. A chorus of
men and women sing offstage, the women appearing and singing
briefly onstage. The porter of the seminary is a speaking part.
Des Grieux has entered the religious profession and at the opening of this scene a chorus of devout women are praising the young
abbe's first sermon. His father tries to dissuade him from taking
the holy orders. Left alone, Des Grieux cannot banish Manon from
his thoughts. Manon herself enters; gradually Des Grieux is once
more lured into her clutches, ending the scene in a rapturous love
duet.

EXCERPT 4a   GS   f, e   pp. 246-63/2/2   12 min.
              Kal   f, e   pp. 257-74/1/4

This uses Des Grieux's aria, the Count, and the women's chorus.

EXCERPT 4b   GS   f, e   pp. 252/3/3-63/2/2   9 min.
              Kal   f, e   pp. 263/3/3-74/1/4

The portion of excerpt 4 using only Des Grieux and the Count.

EXCERPT 4c   GS   f, e   pp. 258-82   14 min.
                Kal   f, e   pp. 268/3/4-94

This scene centers around Des Grieux, Manon, and the chorus, with the porter appearing briefly.

EXCERPT 4d   GS   f, e   pp. 269-82   6½ min.
                Kal   f, e   pp. 281-94

This is the portion of excerpt 4 using Des Grieux and Manon only.

EXCERPT 5   GS   f, e   pp. 349-80   17 min.
                Kal   f, e   pp. 361-96

The final scene between Manon and Des Grieux (see earlier vocal descriptions) again requiring a great deal of subtle singing. Lescaut, baritone, has no difficult singing in this scene. A chorus of guards is needed.

Lescaut and Des Grieux resolve to rescue Manon from being deported to Louisiana. Lescaut bribes the guards to leave Manon a while with Des Grieux. Happily reunited with her, Des Grieux suggests they go off and start a new life together. Too weak to do so, she dies in her lover's arms.

EXCERPT 5a   GS   f, e   pp. 363/4/3-80   9 min.
                Kal   f, e   pp. 378/3/1-96

This is the end of the opera with Manon and Des Grieux only.

MANON LESCAUT

Giacomo Puccini (1858-1924)

Amiens, Paris, Le Havre, and Louisiana, About 1721

EXCERPT 1   Int   i, e   pp. 40-50/4/1; 73/1/6-   13 min.
                              89/2/1
                Ric   i   pp. 40-50/4/1; 73/1/6-89/2/1
                Kal   i, e   pp. 47/2/1-61; 86/2/2-105/2/1

As in Massennet's *Manon*, Manon and Des Grieux are soprano
(D3-Bb4) and tenor (E2-Bb3), the lyric voices being of a somewhat
heavier texture in the tradition of Italian opera. Edmondo is a
lighter tenor (E2-Gb3), and Lescaut, baritone, is heard from offstage in this scene.

The first act takes place outside an inn at Amiens. Manon on her
way to a convent is approached by Des Grieux. Her brother Lescaut calls; she must go, but will return later. Left alone, Des
Grieux sings the aria "Donna non vidi mai." Edmondo is instru-
mental in helping Manon and Des Grieux elope to Paris.

EXCERPT 2   Int   i, e   pp. 103-22/1/4   10 min.
               Ric   i   pp. 103-22/1/4
               Kal   i, e   pp. 120-43/2/1

Manon, lyric soprano, appears singing the dramatic aria "In
quelle trine morbide." The role of her brother Lescaut, baritone
(Bb1-F#3), has no excessive vocal demands in this excerpt. Some
silent servants complete the scene.

Manon, tired of humble life with Des Grieux, has become the
mistress of Geronte, a wealthy old libertine. She does, however,
ask her brother about Des Grieux; she is informed that her former
lover has become a gambler. As soon as he accumulates enough
money, he intends to win her back.

EXCERPT 3   Int   i, e   pp. 149-87   16 min.
               Ric   i   pp. 149-87
               Kal   i, e   pp. 174-220

This excerpt includes, in addition to Manon and Des Grieux
who sing an extended duet, Lescaut (see vocal requirements in excerpts 1-2), and Geronte, bass (B1-F3). A Sergeant, bass, and some
silent guards are required.

In the luxurious apartment of Geronte, Manon receives a surprise visit from Des Grieux. At first he reproaches her for her frivolity, but soon he is won over by her beauty. Geronte discovers
them and goes to get the police. Manon, having developed a love
of luxury, takes time to gather up her jewels before leaving with
Des Grieux. The police arrive before they have a chance to escape;
Manon is arrested for immoral conduct.

EXCERPT 3a   Int   i, e   pp. 149-63   7 min.
               Ric   i   pp. 149-63
               Kal   i, e   pp. 174-91/1/4

The portion of excerpt 3 ending with the love duet of Manon
and Des Grieux before Geronte's entrance.

EXCERPT 3b   Int   i, e   pp. 149-73   13 min.
               Ric   i   pp. 149-73
               Kal   i, e   pp. 174-201

Manon, Des Grieux, and Geronte only in the first scene from
excerpt 3.

EXCERPT 4   Int   i, e   pp. 193-203   7 min.
               Ric   i   pp. 193-203
               Kal   i, e   pp. 226-39

Another scene involving Manon, Des Grieux, and Lescaut (see
vocal descriptions in excerpts 1-2). A lamplighter, tenor, has a
short, simple solo.
   Near the harbor of Le Havre, Manon is waiting to be deported
to Louisiana with other undesirables. Des Grieux and Lescaut try
in vain to free her.

EXCERPT 5   Int   i, e   pp. 236-63   17 min.
               Ric   i   pp. 236-63
               Kal* i, e   pp. 274-304

The entire act involves only Manon and Des Grieux, and is demanding for both, especially Manon's aria "Sola, perduta, abban-
donata." Mature voices are required.

EXCERPT 5a   Int   i, e   pp. 236-54/4/1   13½ min.
               Ric   i   pp. 236-54/4/1
               Kal* i, e   pp. 274-94

This is the scene from excerpt 5 with Manon and Des Grieux
only to the end of Manon's aria.

---

*In the Kalmus score, the aria is slightly different from the other
  scores.

EXCERPT 5b   Int   i, e   pp. 248/4/1-63   10 min.
                   Ric   i   pp. 248/4/1-63
                   Kal*   i, e   pp. 288/3/1-304

This begins with Manon's aria from excerpt 5 and goes through the end of the act.

MARTHA

Friedrich von Flotow (1812-1883)

England, About 1710

EXCERPT 1   GS/Kal   e, g   pp. 9-44   12½ min.

This excerpt features the two women of the cast, Lady Harriet Durham, lyric-coloratura soprano (D3-D5) and Nancy, her maid, low mezzo-soprano (G2-G4). Sir Tristram, bass, sings a character part which is not difficult. They are supported by a women's chorus and three servants (tenor, baritone, and bass).

Lady Harriet, Maid of honor to Queen Anne, is seen in her boudoir, bored with courtly life. Her maid Nancy reminds her that love is missing in her life. With that, Harriet's ridiculous cousin Sir Tristram is announced. His proposed elegant diversions merely induce laughter. The song of the servant maids (offstage) on the way to the Richmond Fair inspires Lady Harriet and Nancy to don peasant costumes and join the merrymakers.

EXCERPT 1a   GS/Kal   e, g   pp. 9-24   8½ min.

This scene from excerpt 1 uses Harriet, Nancy, and the women's chorus (Ladies of the Court) in the opening of the opera.

EXCERPT 2   GS/Kal   e, g   pp. 104-46   23 min.

In addition to the two women described in excerpt 1, there appear in this scene two gentlemen farmers, Lionel and Plunkett.

---

*In the Kalmus score, the aria is slightly different from the other scores.

Lionel is a robust lyric tenor who sings in a high tessitura; Plunkett is a bass-baritone requiring rapid articulation.

At the fair of Richmond, Lionel and Plunkett have hired two servant girls, "Martha" and "Julia" who are really Lady Harriet and Nancy in disguise. After arriving at the farmhouse, the girls balk at working for the men. As "Julia" breaks a spinning wheel and storms out of the room pursued by Plunkett, Lionel begins a courtship with "Martha." Plunkett returns, scolding "Julia" for having created more chaos. The clock strikes twelve, and the four sing a lovely "Good Night Quartet."

EXCERPT 2a   GS/Kal   e, g   pp. 129-41   9 min.

This is the courtship scene between Lady Harriet (Martha) and Lionel.

EXCERPT 3   GS/Kal   e, g   pp. 205-31   17½ min.

This scene includes the same characters as excerpt 2—Lady Harriet, Nancy, Plunkett, and Lionel.

Lionel, having been arrested for paying court to Lady Harriet and later pardoned, is alone at the farmhouse. When Lady Harriet comes to confess her love for him, he reviles her and leaves her in tears. Plunkett and Nancy, however, have cultivated a real romance and their aim is to find a way to reunite Lady Harriet and Lionel.

EXCERPT 3a   GS/Kal   e, g   pp. 213-21   6½ min.

This includes the portion of excerpt 3 with Lady Harriet and Lionel. Lady Harriet's aria (pp. 205-10) may be included lengthening the scene to 11½ minutes.

EXCERPT 3b   GS/Kal   e, g   pp. 223-31   4½ min.

The duet between Nancy and Plunkett only.

IL MATRIMONIO SEGRETO

(The Secret Marriage)

Domenico Cimarosa (1749-1801)

Geronimo's House in Bologna, Eighteenth Century

EXCERPT 1   Ric   i   pp. 10-27   10 min.

The opening scene introduces Carolina and Paolino who are secretly married. Carolina, the younger and more attractive of the two sisters, is a light coloratura soprano (F3-C5); Paolino, a junior business partner of his father-in-law, is a light high tenor (E2-C4).

Carolina and Paolino, in a series of duets, sing of their love and their desire to reveal their marriage. Then they bid each other a lighthearted farewell.

EXCERPT 2   Ric   i   pp. 41-53   6 min.

In addition to Carolina, light coloratura soprano, the older and less amenable sister, Elisetta, appears in this scene. Indicated for mezzo-soprano in the score, the part is only slightly lower (D3-B4) than Carolina; the role is really more feasible for a lyric soprano. Fidalma is a mature mezzo-soprano (B2-G4) with flexibility.

Geronimo has arranged a match for Elisetta with Count Robinson, an English lord. This causes Carolina to provoke her ill-tempered sister, much to the dismay of Fidalma, their aunt. The trio brings the quarrel to a musical climax.

EXCERPT 3   Ric   i   pp. 75/3/1-93/2/4   9 min.

The three ladies in excerpt 2 are joined by Count Robinson, bass or baritone, (A1-Eb3) requiring agility.

Count Robinson, having arrived at the house, mistakes first Carolina, then Fidalma, for Elisetta, the bride he has been promised. The Count reacts with surprise when he meets Elisetta and a quartet develops.

EXCERPT 4   Ric   i   pp. 102-14   8 min.

A duet for Paolino, light high tenor, and Count Robinson, bass or baritone.

The Count confides to Paolino his misgivings about the match with Elisetta, declaring his preference for the younger and prettier Carolina. Paolino, secretly married to Carolina, is more than a little upset by this.

EXCERPT 5   Ric   i   pp. 127/1/3-62   16 min.

The finale of act 1, involving the six characters of the opera. In addition to those already described, this includes Geronimo, bass (G1-E3) who should have more of a *buffo* quality than the romantic Count.

Preparations are being made for a banquet to honor Count Robinson when the Count himself enters, wooing Carolina. Elisetta reacts violently to this and Fidalma manages to silence the quarrel. Geronimo tries his best to discover the cause of all the fuss but his deafness, Paolino's unwillingness to let him find out that the Count wishes to marry Carolina, Fidalma's preoccupation with avoiding a family quarrel, and the fact that everybody talks at once causes the first act to end in chaos.

EXCERPT 6   Ric   i   pp. 163-78   9½ min.

A duet for Count Robinson, bass or baritone, and Geronimo, comic bass.

Alone with the Count, Geronimo still is puzzled but after some length of time realizes that his prospective son-in-law is not pleased with his bride-to-be. An agreement is made: the Count will resign half the dowry he has been promised if he is allowed to marry Carolina instead of Elisetta.

EXCERPT 7   Ric   i   pp. 179/6/1-94   7½ min.

A trio for Carolina, soprano; Paolino, lyric tenor; and Fidalma, mezzo-soprano.

Paolino having heard the new arrangement (excerpt 6) desperately confides in Fidalma. Fidalma, herself secretly in love with Paolino, mistakes this for a proposal of marriage and immediately accepts. Carolina arrives in the middle of all this but Paolino to whom she is secretly married has no chance to explain.

EXCERPT 8   Ric   i   pp. 207/2/3-20/3/5   8 min.

A scene between the Count, baritone or bass, and Elisetta, soprano or high mezzo-soprano.

The result is amusing as the Count tries, by depicting himself as an ogre and a monster of iniquity, to break off his engagement to Elisetta.

EXCERPT 9   Ric   i   pp. 220/4/1-32/2/6   5½ min.

Trio for Elisetta, Fidalma, and Geronimo (see previous excerpts for voice categories).

Fidalma betrays Carolina and Paolino by telling Geronimo that the young couple are in love; Elisetta is upset because the Count evades her. They decide there is only one way to get rid of their rival Carolina—that is by sending her off to a convent, a proposition to which her father readily agrees.

EXCERPT 10   Ric   i   pp. 232/3/1-58   12 min.

Quintet for all the characters previously described except Paolino.

Geronimo tells Carolina that she must go to a convent. The Count offers to help her in her distress. She is just about to tell him the whole truth about her secret marriage to Paolino when Elisetta, Fidalma, and Geronimo enter and unmercifully taunt the poor girl.

EXCERPT 11   Ric   i   pp. 266-304/2/7   19 min.

Finale of act 2; the same six characters as excerpt 5. Because of the action of this scene, it is important that the set have five practical doors, or hallways which one might imagine lead to bedroom doors.

It is night. Geronimo gives Paolino a letter to deliver to the Mother Superior of the convent Carolina is to enter; however, Paolino retires to Carolina's room. The Count comes out of his room hoping to help Carolina; he is surprised instead by Elisetta. They politely bid each other goodnight but Elisetta's suspicions are aroused. Paolino and Carolina appear next, planning their elopement. Disturbed by a noise they hide in Carolina's room. Elisetta then rouses Geronimo and Fidalma from their rooms to come and catch the Count in Carolina's room. The Count appears, but out of his own room, awakened by the noise. Finally Carolina and

Paolino come forth and admit they were married two months before. All is forgiven and the Count agrees to marry Elisetta.

MEDEA

Luigi Cherubini (1760-1842)

Ancient Greece

EXCERPT 1   Ric   i   pp. 10-27/5/6 (suggested   12 min.
                              cut 27/3/2-27/5/3)

In this excerpt, Glauce, lyric soprano (F3-C5) with flexibility, sings an exacting aria with flute obbligato. Two handmaidens, sopranos (or soprano and mezzo-soprano) and a women's ensemble complete the scene.

In the courtyard of Creon's palace in Corinth, Glauce is attended by her handmaidens on the eve of her wedding to Jason. She is apprehensive about the possibility of revenge on the part of Medea, Jason's abandoned first wife. Glauce's attendants attempt to reassure her.

EXCERPT 2   Ric   i   pp. 64-85   13 min.

The characters in this excerpt are Medea, high dramatic soprano (Bb2-B4), and Jason, dramatic tenor (D2-G3). Both should be mature voices.

Medea pleads in vain with Jason to return to her once more, reminding him of the sacrifices she has made for his sake.

EXCERPT 3   Ric   i   pp. 86-110/1/4; 114/2/1-   10½ min.
                              124/2/2

The characters are Medea, high dramatic soprano; Neris, mezzo-soprano (D3-G4) who sings a lyric aria; and Creon, a powerful bass (Bb1-Eb3). A chorus of men completes the scene.

Outside King Creon's palace, Medea laments having to give up her children to Jason and his new wife. King Creon appears and orders Medea banished from his kingdom; she pleads with him for asylum for one more day; reluctantly he gives in to her request. Left alone with Medea, her attendant Neris declares that she will faithfully follow her mistress into exile.

EXCERPT 4   Ric   i   pp. 119/2/1-39/1/6   13½ min.

The scene begins with Neris's aria, described in excerpt 3, and continues with a duet for Medea and Jason (see vocal requirements, excerpt 2).

In spite of Neris's attempts to calm her mistress's wrath, Medea swears vengeance upon Jason and Glauce, but recoils at the thought of killing her own children. Jason appears; Medea threatens him and feigns maternal grief until he is persuaded to place the children in her care. Seemingly grateful, she bids him a final farewell.

EXCERPT 4a   Ric   i   pp. 125/3/3-39/1/6   7 min.

The duet portion of excerpt 4 with Medea and Jason only.

EXCERPT 5   Ric   i   pp. 162-79   15 min.

An aria for Medea, high dramatic soprano, with the supporting role of Neris, mezzo-soprano to Ab4, in the recitative. Two children, silent, are necessary in this scene. A long introduction could provide a dramatic pantomime for Medea.

In front of the temple of Hera, Medea invokes the infernal gods in the realization of her revenge. Still unable to strike the fatal blow to her children, she tearfully embraces them and sings a contemplative aria.

THE MEDIUM

Gian-Carlo Menotti (1911-)

Baba's House in a Large City, 1945

EXCERPT 1   GS   e, f   pp. 43/1/2-60   8 min.

Madame Flora (Baba), a medium, is sung by a mature mezzo-

soprano with a range from A2-A4. Her daughter Monica is a youthful light lyric soprano. Toby, a gypsy boy, is a silent role usually
performed by a dancer, actor, or mime artist.

Baba has been frightened during her last seance; she has felt a
hand touch her in the dark. After her clients have left she tries to
blame the phenomenon on Toby. Monica calms her and sings to
her the lullaby "The Black Swan."

EXCERPT 2   GS   e, f   pp. 61-84/3/3   13½ min.

This scene uses the same persons described in excerpt 1.

While Baba is out of the house, Monica and Toby indulge in a
bit of play. Toby puts on a puppet show which Monica applauds.
Then she sings a waltz tune to which they dance around the room.
The waltz turns into a sort of love duet, Monica singing what she
imagines to be the thoughts Toby cannot express. Baba returns
and questions Toby about a hand she felt touching her in the dark.
When he does not react, she whips him.

MEFISTOFELE

Arrigo Boito (1842-1918)

Medieval Germany

EXCERPT 1   Kal   i, e   pp. 77/2/1-96   11 min.
               Ric   i, e   pp. 89-110

The roles of Faust and Mefistofele are, as in Gounod's *Faust*,
scored for tenor (F2-Bb3) and bass (Gb1-E3). Faust requires a
somewhat weightier timbre than his French counterpart. The role
of Mefistofele is in exactly the same range as that of the Gounod
work (Gb1-E3), and with similar dramatic requirements.

Faust is meditating alone in his study. A gray friar whom he
has seen earlier enters the room throwing off his disguise to reveal
himself as Mefistofele, the spirit that denies all good. He offers to
Faust the privilege of traveling all over the world with him in
search of knowledge; Faust agrees, the contract is signed and they
both leave.

EXCERPT 2   Kal   i, e   pp. 97-116   10 min.
              Ric   i   pp. 111-33

Margherita is a lyric-spinto soprano (D3-A#4) needing a trill;
Marta, a mezzo-soprano (C3-E4). The other two characters are
described in excerpt 1, Faust requiring a strong B3 for this scene.

Faust, now a young man under the assumed name of Enrico,
arrives with Mefistofele in Margherita's garden. While Faust woos
Margherita, Mefistofele flirts with her mother, Marta. An effective
quartet develops as the two couples wander in the garden. Faust
gives Margherita a sleeping potion for her mother, and the girl
surrenders to his embrace.

EXCERPT 3   Kal   i, e   pp. 178-99   16½ min.
              Ric   i   pp. 205-30

Margherita, lyric-spinto soprano; Faust, lyric or dramatic tenor;
and Mefistofele, bass, appear in this scene. An offstage chorus is
heard in one crucial line. Margherita should have a trill and lyric
subtlety to meet the requirements of the aria "L'altra notte in
fondo al mare."

Margherita has been imprisoned for poisoning her mother and
drowning her own child. Faust arrives urging her to fly away with
him as they recall their lovemaking in a beautiful duet. Mefistofele,
who has made plans for their escape, returns; Margherita is terri-
fied at the sight of him. Refusing to leave the prison, she dies in
Faust's arms. Mefistofele condemns her, but a chorus of heavenly
voices announces salvation.

DIE MEISTERSINGER VON NÜRNBERG

(The Mastersingers of Nuremberg)

Richard Wagner (1813-1883)

Nuremberg, Mid-Sixteenth Century

EXCERPT 1   GS/Kal   g, e   pp. 19-40   9 min.
              Pet   g   pp. 23/2/5-44

The role of Eva is written for a high, strong lyric or spinto soprano (F#3-Ab4); Magdalena, for a mezzo-soprano (E3-F4). Walther is a lyric or young dramatic tenor (F2-A3) with ability to sustain long phrases; David is a lyric tenor with a less difficult role (F#2-G3).

Walther arrives at the church to catch a glimpse of his beloved Eva. Eva, in order to have a few words with Walther, sends her companion Magdalena back to look for her kerchief. Learning that Eva's father has offered the hand of his daughter to the man who wins the singing contest of the Mastersingers' guild, Walther is determined to win the contest. Magdalena's suitor David arrives; Magdalena demands that he instruct Walther in the rules of the Mastersingers.

EXCERPT 2   GS/Kal   g, e   pp. 212/3/5-36/3/2   13 min.
               Pet   g   pp. 198/4/5-220/4/3

Hans Sachs should be sung by a bass-baritone (A1-E3) with a great deal of warmth and dramatic sense. Eva is a lyric or lyric-spinto soprano with a strong voice. Magdalena's lines need not be sung.

In his cobbler's workshop, Sachs, recalling the beauty of Walther's freestyle song, sings the monologue "Was duftet doch der Flieder." Eva appears, despairing of her chances to have Walther for a husband because his song does not meet the rules of the Mastersingers. Sachs, a middle-aged widower hoping to win Eva for himself, offers some fatherly advice to the girl and accepts with manly resignation her love for Walther.

EXCERPT 3   GS/Kal   g, e   pp. 352/5/2-93/4/2;   26½ min.
                        397/4/1-402/3/4
               Pet   g   pp. 323/5/1-61/1/2; 364/3/1-67

A scene for David, Sachs, and Walther (see vocal descriptions in excerpts 1-2). Walther must have the stamina for at least one verse of his "Preislied."

It is early morning on the day of the singing contest. Sachs, reading by the window, fails to notice David entering with a basket of cakes and a bouquet of flowers. David, apologizing for his mischief the night before, is asked to sing the St. John's Day song he has prepared for the day's celebration. Suddenly realizing that it is Hans Sachs's name day, too, he offers Sachs the flowers and cakes. Left alone, Sachs meditates on the madness of the world. Walther enters describing a dream he has had during the night and singing the song inspired by that dream. Sachs then writes down the poem and instructs Walther in the technical devices needed to make the song acceptable to the judges of the contest.

EXCERPT 3a   GS/Kal   g, e   pp. 352/5/2-74/1/6   13½ min.
               Pet   g   pp. 323/5/1-42/3/6

This is the portion of excerpt 3 using only Sachs and David.

EXCERPT 3b   GS/Kal   g, e   pp. 366/2/5-93/4/2;   20 min.
                           397/4/1-402/3/4
               Pet   g   pp. 335/5/5-61/1/2; 364/3/1-67

Excerpt 3b uses only Sachs and Walther from excerpt 3.

EXCERPT 4   GS/Kal   g, e   pp. 403-19; 422-   11 min.
                           426/3/2; 428/1/2-30/1/2
               Pet   g   pp. 368/6/2-85/3/3; 387/3/2-91/3/1;
                           392/4/2-94/3/2

Beckmesser, the town clerk, is sung by a comic baritone or a *basso buffo*. The role lies in a high tessitura and contains an A3 in *falsetto*. Sachs should be sung by a weighty bass-baritone.

Sachs's workshop is now empty. Walther's poem has been written down and left on the table. Beckmesser snoops around and pockets the poem for himself. When Sachs returns, Beckmesser scolds him for entering the contest and produces the manuscript he has found. Knowing that Beckmesser cannot possibly do justice to the poem. Sachs allows the clerk to keep the manuscript but not to divulge its authorship.

EXCERPT 5   GS/Kal   g, e   pp. 431-63   17½ min.
               Pet   g   pp. 395-422

Sachs, Walther, Eva, Magdalena, and David (see vocal descriptions for excerpts 1-2) appear in this scene. Magdalena and David sing only briefly in the quintet.

Eva, clad in festival costume, pays a visit to Sachs' workshop. Knowing what is really on her mind, Sachs pretends to busy himself adjusting her shoes. Walther enters and at the sight of his beloved, sings a verse of the "Preislied" which he sang for Sachs earlier. Eva, overjoyed, expresses her gratitude to Sachs. All join voices in the sublime quintet "Selig wie die Sonne," each expressing his or her own true feelings of happiness.

A MIDSUMMER NIGHT'S DREAM

Benjamin Britten (1913-1976)

Ancient Athens, Sometimes Set in England in Elizabethan Times

EXCERPT 1   B&H   e, g   pp. 45/1/2-65   7½ min.

The group of rustics in this scene are Flute, tenor, singing the top line in the ensemble—must have falsetto for passages where he plays a female role; Snout, tenor (D2-Ab3); Starveling, high lyric baritone; Bottom, bass-baritone with a flair for comic acting; Quince and Snug, basses.

A group of six rustics are rehearsing for the play-within-the-play to be presented at the nuptial festivities of Theseus, Duke of Athens.

EXCERPT 2   B&H   e, g   pp. 216/2/1-28/2/6   6½ min.

A quartet for Helena, soprano (C3-A4); Hermia, mezzo-soprano (B2-F4); Lysander, tenor (C2-A3); Demetrius, baritone (B1-D3). All should be good musicians with strong voices though none of the parts presents any unusual difficulties.

Through a series of mistakes, the two pairs of lovers have quarreled and have fallen asleep in a wood. During the night Puck has used a magic herb to cure them of their troubles and in the morning they are reconciled, deciding that their misunderstandings were a dream.

EXCERPT 3   B&H   e, g   pp. 228/3/1-49/1/6   7 min.

Another rehearsal scene for the six characters described in excerpt 1. Bottom thinks a ballad telling of his adventures should be composed to be sung at Theseus's wedding.

EXCERPT 4   B&H   e, g   pp. 263-300/2/3   15½ min.

This is the actual play-within-the-play with the six rustics described in excerpt 1. It is extremely amusing as is the original play-within-the-play in the Shakespeare drama, and requires good singing actors. Cuts may be made to eliminate the members of the Court who are watching the play.

MIGNON

Ambroise Thomas (1811-1896)

Germany and Italy, Late Eighteenth Century

EXCERPT 1   GS/Kal   f, e   pp. 60-127   27 min.
              (trad. cuts 66-73; 79/5/2-82/1/2)

The title role of Mignon calls for a mezzo-soprano or dark-timbred lyric soprano (C3-A4 with optional B4 or D5); Philine should be sung by a coloratura soprano; Wilhelm is a lyric tenor (D2-B3) singing mostly in the middle range; Lothario is a bass-baritone role requiring *cantabile* singing; Laertes is a second tenor. Other roles are Frederic, trouser role for a mezzo-soprano, and Giarno, bass.

In the courtyard of a German inn, Lothario, an old wandering minstrel who has been searching for his lost daughter, meets Mignon. She has been adopted by a band of gypsies and mistreated by their leader Giarno. She is rescued by Lothario and Wilhelm Meister, a young student. Laertes and Philine, members of an acting company, observe the scene. Mignon becomes attached to Wilhelm who questions her about her childhood. Moved by her nostalgic romance "Connais-tu le pays," Wilhelm arranges to buy her freedom from the gypsies. The aged Lothario who has befriended the girl, comes back to bid her good-bye; together they sing the duet "Légères hirondelles." Wilhelm is persuaded to join the theatrical company as a poet and he has little choice but to allow Lothario and Mignon to accompany him.

EXCERPT 1a   GS/Kal   f, e   pp. 60-87   7 min.
                         (trad. cuts 66-73; 79/5/2-82/1/2)

A trio from excerpt 1 for Wilhelm, Laertes, and Philine only.

EXCERPT 1b   GS/Kal   f, e   pp. 89/2/1-108; 119-27   16 min.

The portion of excerpt 1 using Mignon, Wilhelm, Lothario, with Giarno.

EXCERPT 1c   GS/Kal   f, e   pp. 89/2/1-98   7 min.

Mignon's aria with some singing for Wilhelm.

EXCERPT 1d   GS/Kal   f, e   100/4/3-108   4 min.

Duet for Mignon and Lothario only.

EXCERPT 2   GS/Kal   f, e   pp. 165-69/3/1;   30 min.
                         171/4/2-201/4/4; 350-54; 202/2/2-21

The characters are Mignon, Philine, Wilhelm, Laertes, and Frederic, all described in excerpt 1.

Philine is seated at her dressing table when Wilhelm enters accompanied by Mignon dressed as a page. Philine mocks her and goes off with Wilhelm with whom she is infatuated. Mignon, jealous of the sophisticated actress, proceeds to apply makeup to herself as she sings the "Styrienne." As she dresses in one of Philine's costumes, Frederic breaks in, rejoicing to be near Philine in the gavotte "Me voici dans son boudoir." When Wilhelm returns he and Frederic exchange words over Philine and finally draw swords, but their duel is interrupted by Mignon wearing Philine's dress. Wilhelm, in the tender aria "Adieu, Mignon" tells the girl that they must part. Philine returns and her remarks irritate Mignon further until she violently wishes that Philine would be burned alive.

EXCERPT 2a   GS/Kal   f, e   pp. 165-69/3/1;   19 min.
                                   171/4/2-201/4/4

The portion of excerpt 2 with Philine, Mignon, Wilhelm, and
Laertes only.

EXCERPT 2b   GS/Kal   f, e   pp. 191-201/4/4;   17 min.
                                   350-54; 202/2/2-17/2/3

Mignon, Wilhelm, and Frederic only from excerpt 2.

EXCERPT 2c   GS/Kal   f, e   pp. 191-201; 206/2/5-   14 min.
                                   217/2/3

Mignon and Wilhelm only with arias for both.

EXCERPT 3   GS/Kal   f, e   pp. 223-38   8 min.

A dramatic scene for Mignon, mezzo-soprano or lyric soprano
(Bb2-Bb4 with opt C5) and her duet with Lothario, bass-baritone.
Alone in the gardens of the castle of Baron Rosenberg, Mignon
is about to drown herself, despairing of her unrequited love for
Wilhelm. She is halted by the sounds of Lothario's lute and confides to him her tale of sorrow and desire for vengeance. The half-
crazed old man reacts curiously when she expresses the hope that
heaven's lightning will strike and burn the castle where Philine and
the actors are playing.

EXCERPT 4   GS/Kal   f, e   pp. 277-339   28 min.

Act 3 complete calls for Mignon, Lothario, and Wilhelm, all described in excerpt 1. Philine, coloratura soprano, sings parts of her
polonaise "Je suis Titania" offstage. The supporting character of
Antonio, bass, and an offstage chorus complete the scene.
Wilhelm has brought the ailing Mignon and the distraught
Lothario to an old castle in Italy, which he decides to purchase.
Lothario sings a lullaby to the sleeping girl and, left alone, Wilhelm
also sings a tender romance, "Elle ne croyait pas." When Mignon
awakens, Wilhelm assures her of his love despite echoes of Philine's
voice in the distance. Lothario, once more in familiar surroundings,
has recovered his reason and memory. He is in his very own castle

and Mignon turns out to be his lost daughter. The three rejoice in their newly found happiness.

EXCERPT 4a   GS/Kal   f, e   pp. 301/2/3-39   18½ min.

Same as above but omitting Lothario's and Wilhelm's arias, the chorus and the role of Antonio.

EXCERPT 4b   GS/Kal   f, e   pp. 301/2/3-18/2/1   9 min.

A portion of excerpt 4 for Mignon, Wilhelm, and Philine only.

EXCERPT 4c   GS/Kal   f, e   pp. 321-39   8½ min.

The final trio with Mignon, Wilhelm, and Lothario only.

THE MOTHER OF US ALL

Virgil Thomson (1896-)

In and around Susan B. Anthony's House and at Political Gatherings, United States, Mid-Nineteenth Century

EXCERPT 1   GS   e   pp. 19-30   5 min.

The opera focuses on the character of Susan B. Anthony, scored for a dramatic soprano (C3-B4) who must project authority on stage at all times. Anne, her confidante, is a low mezzo-soprano or contralto (A2-D3). The two narrators, Gertrude S. and Virgil T., call for soprano (could be mezzo-soprano) and baritone, respectively.

This scene is narrated in the form of a series of quotes from the two women. Susan B. is seated beside a table in her home, pasting press clippings in a scrapbook. Anne is knitting.

EXCERPT 2   GS   e   pp. 66-78   8 min.

This excerpt calls for Susan B., dramatic soprano; Daniel Webster, bass (A1-C#3); Chris the Citizen, baritone (D2-F3); and three tenors: Jo the Loiterer, Andrew Johnson, and Thaddeus Stevens,

none of whom sings above an F3. Donald Gallup, a negro man, and
a negro woman are short speaking roles.

Susan B. Anthony is on her front porch, daydreaming. She sees
in her dream a negro man and woman, and upon questioning them
realizes they cannot help her in her fight for woman suffrage.
Donald Gallup, a college professor, comes next into the vision. He
cannot help her in her fight either, nor can the Very Important
Persons of politics, whom she next sees. She is asked by two Civil
War veterans, Jo and Chris, to explain the difference between rich
and poor.

EXCERPT 3   GS   e   pp. 79-98   12 min.

The characters of this scene are as follows: Susan B. Anthony,
dramatic soprano; Angel More, light lyric soprano; Anne, low
mezzo-soprano or contralto; Jenny Reefer, Indiana Elliot, and
Constance Fletcher, lyric mezzos; John Quincy Adams, lyric tenor;
Jo the Loiterer, second tenor; Indiana Elliot's brother, baritone to
G3; Daniel Webster and Ulysses S. Grant, basses. A chorus, singing
only a few responses, can either be part of the action, or separated
from it, as a Greek chorus.

It is the wedding day of Indiana Elliot and Jo the Loiterer.
Susan B. ponders on the difficult lot of women. The wedding party arrives and before the wedding ceremony gets under way there
are many digressions. When Daniel Webster blesses the couple and
they kiss, Susan B. prophesies that all their children, women as
well as men, will have the right to vote.

EXCERPT 4   GS   e   pp. 99-114   9 min.

Susan B. Anthony, dramatic soprano, is again the central figure.
Others are Indiana Elliot, mezzo-soprano; Jo the Loiterer, Andrew
Johnson, and Thaddeus Stevens, all tenors with nothing above an
F#3. Anne and Jenny, mezzos, have very little to sing in this
scene. The chorus performs the same function as it does in excerpt
3.

Susan B is at home doing her housework. Anne comes in followed by Jenny Reefer, to tell her that she will be asked to speak
at a political meeting. Jo arrives followed by Indiana who though
married to him, refuses to take his name. Eventually all characters

urge Susan B. to speak at the meeting; at first she firmly refuses
but eventually consents to do it.

EXCERPT 5   GS   e   pp. 115-33   10½ min.

This scene again calls for a large cast, most of whom have been
described in earlier excerpts. The new character is Lillian Russell,
lyric or dramatic soprano. Others are Susan B., Anne, Jenny, Constance Fletcher, Indiana Elliot, Jo the Loiterer, John Adams, and
Daniel Webster. The chorus plays an important part at the end of
the scene.

Anne and Susan return from a political meeting at which the
politicians, afraid of woman suffrage, have written the word
"male" into an amendment to the Constitution. Jenny Reefer
rushes in to announce that she has converted Lillian Russell to the
cause of woman suffrage. Daniel Webster reproaches Susan for her
impatience. Jo and Indiana resolve their quarrel over the change
of name (see excerpt 4) and everybody crowds around Susan B.
Anthony to thank her for her successful leadership.

EXCERPT 5a   GS   e   pp. 115-21/3/5   4½ min.

Susan B. and Anne only appear in this portion of excerpt 5.

NORMA

Vincenzo Bellini (1801-1835)

Gaul, About 50 B.C.

EXCERPT 1   B&H/Kal   i, e   pp. 30-51   16 min.
              GS/Ric   i   pp. 49-85

The soprano role of Norma (Db3-Bb4) is one of the most difficult of all operatic roles, requiring a combination of strength for
the sustained line and extreme agility for the florid dramatic coloratura passages. This excerpt features her aria "Casta diva" in
which she is supported by her father, Oroveso, a mature bass (C2-
Eb3), and by a chorus.

Norma, the high priestess of the Druids, is secretly in love with Pollione, the proconsul of the Roman enemy. Not wishing danger upon her lover, she addresses her people saying that the time is not yet ripe to rise against their oppressors. She prays to the moon goddess for peace.

EXCERPT 2   B&H/Kal   i, e   pp. 52-68   9½ min.
             GS/Ric   i   pp. 86-109

A duet for Adalgisa, mezzo-soprano or soprano (Bb2-C5), and Pollione, tenor (C2-Bb3), both roles requiring vocal strength and flexibility.

The Roman proconsul Pollione has forsaken the priestess Norma for Adalgisa who has also taken vows of chastity. The lovers meet in the forest of the Druids and together plan to seek safety and happiness in Rome.

EXCERPT 3   B&H/Kal   i, e   pp. 69-106   22 min.
             GS/Ric   i   pp. 110-58

A scene for Norma, Adalgisa, Pollione (described in excerpts 1-2), with Clotilda, mezzo-soprano supporting role; a brief chorus part; and two children, silent.

Norma is in her dwelling with the two children she has borne Pollione, and with her companion Clotilda. Norma laments her unhappy fate when Adalgisa enters confessing, for the first time to the priestess, her own love for Pollione. Pollione comes upon the scene and a fiery trio ensues.

EXCERPT 3a   B&H/Kal   i, e   pp. 72/3/4-84   12 min.
             GS/Ric   i   pp. 115/3/1-30

The duet from excerpt 3 with Norma and Adalgisa only.

EXCERPT 4   B&H/Kal   i, e   pp. 107-26   15 min.
                       (trad. cut 126/1/5-126/3/3
             GS/Ric   i   pp. 159-87 (trad. cut 187/1/2-/3/1)

This is the better known of the two duets between Norma and Adalgisa. (See excerpts 1-2 for vocal description.) Clotilda appears in a supporting role; the two children are asleep.

Nearly crazed with anger, Norma thinks of killing Pollione and their children, and then letting herself be burned on the funeral pyre. Unable to bring herself to stab the sleeping children, she summons Adalgisa and begs her to take the children and go with Pollione. Adalgisa entreats Norma not to abandon her children as the two women join in the duet "Mira, O Norma."

EXCERPT 4a   B&H/Kal   i, e   pp. 113-26   12 min.
                (trad. cut 126/1/5-126/3/3)
              GS/Ric   i   pp. 167-87 (trad. cut 187/1/2-/3/1)

Excerpt 4 without Clotilda.

LE NOZZE DI FIGARO

(The Marriage of Figaro)

Wolfgang Amadeus Mozart (1756-1791)

The Castle of Count Almaviva Near Seville, Spain, About 1775

EXCERPT 1   B&H   i, e   pp. 8-30   11 min.
             GS   i, e   pp. 14-44
             Kal   i, e   pp. 8-29

Susanna is a lyric soprano who should sound youthful and light in timbre but whose part lies in the middle register. Figaro is sung by both baritones and basses, spanning a range from G1 to F3, and requiring flexibility.

The scene opens on a room in the castle where Figaro, the Count's valet, and his bride Susanna, the Countess's chambermaid, will live. In the course of the two duets bridged by a recitative, Figaro finds out that his master intends to restore a custom granting the master the right to spend the wedding night with his servant's bride. As Susanna goes off to answer her mistress's call, Figaro, in the aria "Se vuol ballare," vows to outwit his master.

EXCERPT 2   B&H   i, e   pp. 31-38/1/6   4 min.
              GS   i, e   pp. 45-53
              Kal   i, e   pp. 30-36

Dr. Bartolo is a comic bass requiring rapid articulation in his aria "La Vendetta." Marcellina, mezzo-soprano, sings only recitatives in this scene.

Dr. Bartolo still bears a grudge against Figaro for having helped the Count win Rosina, the girl Dr. Bartolo himself wanted to marry. When Bartolo discovers that in a weak moment Figaro has promised to marry the aged Marcellina, Bartolo is all too eager to help the old lady get her man.

EXCERPT 3   B&H   i, e   pp. 38/2/1-45   3 min.
              GS   i, e   pp. 54-63
              Kal   i, e   pp. 37-43/3/4

An amusing duet between Susanna, lyric soprano, and Marcellina, mezzo-soprano.

Susanna has overheard Marcellina's plan to marry Figaro if she can; thinking the match ridiculous and being unhappy about the prospect of losing her own bridegroom, she greets the older woman with exaggerated politeness; soon their compliments to each other give way to sarcastic insults.

EXCERPT 4   B&H   i, e   pp. 46-91   21 min.
              GS   i, e   pp. 64-124
              Kal   i, e   pp. 43/4/1-89

In addition to Susanna, lyric soprano; and Figaro, baritone or bass with nothing lower than C2. This scene includes Cherubino, a trouser role for a lyric mezzo-soprano (Eb3-C4) or soprano; Basilio, a comic light-lyric tenor role; and the Count, a strong baritone (A-D3). A small chorus of servants appears briefly.

The Count's page Cherubino takes refuge in Susanna's room, confessing to her his susceptibility to women ("Non so più cosa son"). Hearing the Count's voice the page quickly hides behind a chair. As the Count makes advances to Susanna, he himself is forced to hide because Basilio, the music master, is coming his way. The Count chooses to hide behind the same chair; Cherubino darts around and crouches in the seat of the chair where Susanna covers him with a cloth. The busybody Basilio first taunts Susanna about the Count's philanderings, then about Cherubino. When Basilio mentions Cherubino's infatuation with the Countess, the Count can stand it no longer. He reveals his presence and demands that his page be banished from the castle. Demonstrating how the boy was caught once before, the Count lifts the cloth from the chair, revealing Cherubino once again.

Just then Figaro enters leading a group of peasants in praise of the Count. But the Count finds a way to delay Figaro's wedding and orders Cherubino into military service. Figaro stays behind to give Cherubino a spirited description of his future in the military. The mock-military aria is the famous "Non più andrai."

EXCERPT 4a   B&H i, e   pp. 46-73/1/6   12 min.
              GS   i, e   pp. 64-99
              Kal i, e   pp. 43/4/1-71

The opening section of excerpt 4 with Cherubino, Susanna, the Count, and Basilio. (Can be added to excerpt 3 if desired.)

EXCERPT 5   B&H i, e   pp. 92-158   30 min.
              GS   i, e   pp. 125-216
              Kal i, e   pp. 90-159/1/6
                          (Cuts are frequently made in the reci-
                          tatives to shorten the scene.)

A scene involving Susanna, Cherubino, Figaro, and the Count (described in excerpts 1-4) with the Countess Almaviva. The Countess should have a heavier lyric soprano voice than Susanna's, with a range from C3 to A4 in this scene, and should be capable of sustaining long, legato phrases. Figaro has little to sing in excerpt 5.

The Countess is alone in her boudoir lamenting the lack of attention from her husband in a contemplative aria, "Porgi amor." Her maid Susanna enters and the two women complain of the Count's wayward affections. Figaro proposes a plan to renew the Count's interest in his wife; let him discover a note arranging a tryst between the Countess and a lover. They hope then to send Cherubino, dressed as Susanna, to meet the Count.

Cherubino arrives and sings a serenade, "Voi che sapete," which he has written for the Countess. Then during an aria sung by Susanna, "Venite, inginocchiatevi," Cherubino tries on his feminine disguise in comic bit of business. When they are interrupted by the Count's knock at the chamber door, Susanna and Cherubino hide.

By the time the Count has been allowed to enter the room, he is convinced that his wife is protecting a lover and he insists that she go with him while he gets the tools to unlock the closet door. When the Count and Countess have gone and the door to the chamber has been locked, Susanna assists Cherubino in jumping out the window while she herself goes into the closet.

The Count and Countess return, unlock the chamber door, enter and go to the closet only to find that it is Susanna in the closet, not a lover at all.

EXCERPT 5a	B&H	i, e	pp. 101/3/1-58	24 min.
	GS	i, e	pp. 137/3/1-216	
	Kal	i, e	pp. 101-59/1/6	

This is the scene from excerpt 5 beginning after Figaro's exit. The Countess's aria could precede it, adding 3½ minutes.

EXCERPT 5b	B&H	i, e	pp. 101/3/1-14	7½ min.
	GS	i, e	pp. 137/3/1-54	
	Kal	i, e	pp. 101-13	

This is the portion of excerpt 5 using only the Countess, Susanna, and Cherubino. The Countess's aria could precede this excerpt.

EXCERPT 6	B&H	i, e	pp. 138/1/2-204	20 min.
	GS	i, e	pp. 187-277	
	Kal	i, e	pp. 138-204	

The finale of act 2 actually begins in excerpt 5 with the return of the Count and Countess to the chamber and continues with Figaro's appearance. It also introduces Antonio, a comic baritone or bass; and finally the trio of Marcellina, Bartolo, and Basilio (vocal descriptions in excerpts 2-4) who join the rest to complete the ensemble.

The Count, suspecting his wife's infidelity, is finally coaxed into

forgiveness by the Countess and Susanna. Figaro enters to escort
his bride to the wedding but is detained by the Count. Soon Antonio, the gardener, arrives in an inebriated state, complaining that
someone has jumped onto the flowers (Cherubino in his earlier escape—see excerpt 5). Figaro silences the Count's renewed suspicions by taking the blame himself. Now Figaro must account for
everything the gardener saw, and the ladies prompt him with the
correct answers. By this time the wedding has been delayed long
enough for Marcellina to lodge a formal complaint against Figaro
for breach of promise and the act ends in pandemonium.

EXCERPT 7   B&H   i, e   pp. 205/1/1-/3/2;   9 min.
                             207/3/1-22/3/5
              GS   i, e   pp. 278; 281/1/2-300
              Kal   i, e   pp. 205/1/1-/3/2; 208/1/2-23

A duet between the Count and Susanna (see excerpts 1-4 for
vocal requirements) and a *bravura* aria for the Count. The only offstage line that cannot be eliminated is Figaro's.

The Count has not given up hope of Susanna and when she
comes in to borrow smelling salts for her mistress, he seems within
reach of his prize. She agrees to meet him that evening in the garden. The duet is a masterpiece of encouragement and evasion. But
as Susanna leaves, not really needing the smelling salts, she assures
Figaro offstage that he is certain to win his case. The Count
launches into an aria, resolving to punish Figaro at once.

EXCERPT 8   B&H   i, e   pp. 222/4/1-43/3/3   7 min.
              GS   i, e   pp. 301-28
              Kal   i, e   pp. 224-46

Another brilliant piece of Mozart ensemble, the Sextet, occurs
here. With Susanna, the Count, Marcellina, Bartolo, and Figaro
(all described in earlier excerpts) is Don Curzio, a high *buffo* tenor.

Marcellina arrives with her lawyer Don Curzio to inform Figaro
that he must either marry her or pay damages. Figaro has just
found clues indicating that he is of noble birth and may be able to
afford the cost. Upon closer scrutiny of these clues, it is revealed
that Figaro is none other than the long lost son of Marcellina and
Bartolo who then decide to make the occasion a double wedding.

Susanna and the Count join the sextet and the happiness of the two couples is contrasted with the fury of the Count and Curzio.

EXCERPT 9   B&H   i, e   pp. 252-55   3 min.
                GS   i, e   pp. 341/4/1-47/1/1
                Kal   i, e   pp. 255/4/1-59

A duet between Susanna who sings the higher line, and the Countess.

The Countess dictates the letter to be given to the Count, setting the time and place of meeting in the garden. Susanna writes it down and the two ladies read it together.

THE OLD MAID AND THE THIEF

Gian-Carlo Menotti (1911-)

A Small Town in the United States, About 1940

EXCERPT 1   Ric   e   pp. 13-42   8½ min.

The four characters of the opera are Miss Todd, dramatic mezzo-soprano (G#2-G4); Laetitia, light lyric soprano (C3-D5); Miss Pinkerton, character soprano (D3-A4); and Bob, baritone (A1-F3 or G#3). All four appear in excerpt 1.

Miss Todd receives a visitor, Miss Pinkerton, in her parlor. They gossip and discuss their empty, lonely lives. Laetitia, Miss Todd's maid, announces a male visitor at the back door; Miss Pinkerton, getting up to excuse herself, is promptly escorted out the front door. The stranger turns out to be Bob, a young, handsome vagabond to whom Miss Todd and Laetitia take a great liking.

EXCERPT 1a   Ric   e   pp. 13-26/2/2   4½ min.

Miss Todd and Miss Pinkerton only.

EXCERPT 1b   Ric   e   pp. 13-31/3/1   5½ min.

Miss Todd, Miss Pinkerton, and Laetitia in a scene from excerpt 1.

EXCERPT 2   Ric   e   pp. 43-62   5½ min.

Laetitia, light lyric soprano; Miss Todd, dramatic mezzo-soprano; and Bob, baritone, are in this scene.

Laetitia is assisting Miss Todd in her kitchen and both comment on the handsome stranger whom they had welcomed the night before as their guest. Laetitia takes a breakfast tray to Bob's room and urges him to stay with them another week. Their conversation is interrupted by Miss Todd calling for her maid's assistance.

EXCERPT 2a   Ric   e   pp. 51-62   3 min.

The bedroom scene; Laetitia and Bob only, with Miss Todd's voice calling from offstage.

EXCERPT 3   Ric   e   pp. 63-90   8½ min.

This involves the four characters described in excerpt 1; Bob sings only a few lines.

As the women meet on the street, Miss Pinkerton shows Miss Todd a newspaper article describing an escaped convict who has been seen in town. The description fits Bob, and Miss Todd, panicked, runs home to warn Laetitia. Regardless of the news, Laetitia convinces Miss Todd that their guest must not be ordered to leave.

EXCERPT 3a   Ric   e   pp. 63-71   2½ min.

The portion of excerpt 3 using Miss Todd and Miss Pinkerton only.

EXCERPT 3b   Ric   e   pp. 72-90   6 min.

The latter portion of excerpt 3 for Miss Todd, Laetitia, and Bob.

EXCERPT 4   Ric   e   pp. 91-102   5½ min.

Laetitia, light lyric soprano; Miss Todd, mezzo-soprano; and Miss Pinkerton, character soprano, are in this excerpt.

Alone at her work, Laetitia laments Bob's indifference to women in the aria "Steal me, sweet thief." Miss Pinkerton comes running into the house to tell Miss Todd that the thief is still hiding in town and there have been many robberies in the neighborhood (actually Miss Todd stealing to obtain funds for Bob's support). Before she leaves, Miss Pinkerton suspiciously eyes a pair of trousers Laetitia has just pressed.

EXCERPT 5   Ric   e   pp. 103-19   6½ min.

Laetitia, light lyric soprano; Miss Todd, mezzo-soprano; and Bob, baritone, are involved in excerpt 5.

Bob, making ready to leave, sings his aria "When the air sings of summer." Laetitia is surprised to see him packing, and when she asks him if there is anything she can do to convince him to stay, he replies that he wishes he could have some liquor. Miss Todd, a teetotaler, is shocked at the idea, but the clever Laetitia suggests raiding the liquor store as a means of "sinning against a sin" and at the same time keeping their guest happy.

EXCERPT 6   Ric   e   pp. 129-80   16 min.

The four characters described in excerpt 1 are heard in this scene.

The liquor store has been raided by Miss Todd and Laetitia; Bob is quite content. Miss Pinkerton again visits Miss Todd, this time with the news that the liquor store has been robbed and the thief is still at large. Miss Todd and Laetitia confront Bob with the truth and warn him that he had better go along with their plans to escape the consequences of their own crimes. When he refuses, Miss Todd goes off to call the police; Bob's unknown identity cannot possibly stand up against Miss Todd's good name in the community. Left alone with Bob, Laetitia suggests that he run away with her. He agrees; Bob and Laetitia proceed to steal as many of Miss Todd's belongings as they can stuff in her car before driving away. Miss Todd, returning to her ransacked home, collapses in a chair, and the curtain closes on Miss Pinkerton viewing the scene with triumphant indignation.

EXCERPT 6a   Ric   e   pp. 139-80   13 min.

Same as above without Miss Pinkerton; her appearance at the end of the opera is not necessary.

ORFEO ED EURIDICE

(Orpheus and Eurydice)

Christoph Willibald von Gluck (1714-1787)

Legendary Thrace and Hades

EXCERPT 1   GS   f, e   pp. 18-33/2/3   13½ min.
              Kal   i, e   pp. 12/3/1-26/4/3
              Ric   i   pp. 14-30

The role of Orpheus, originally written for a *castrato*, is nowadays assigned to a mezzo-soprano or contralto as a trousers role. (Occasionally, however, the role has been sung by a baritone, and in a French edition by the composer, the part was rewritten for a tenor.) The range is A2-G4 with a rather low tessitura. Amor, appearing in this scene, is a light lyric soprano (E3-A4).

Orpheus is heard singing the aria "Chiamo il mio ben cosi" with its backstage orchestral echoes. He is lamenting his bride Eurydice. Amor, the god of love, takes pity on the bereaved husband, informing him that he may descend to the realm of Pluto to seek his wife. There is one condition, however: in order for her to return to earth with him, he must not look at her or she will perish.

EXCERPT 2   GS   f, e   pp. 83-109; 125-30   21 min.
              Kal   i, e   pp. 78-105/3/7; 120-25
              Ric   i   pp. 96-126; 147-54

Orpheus and Amor are both described in excerpt 1. This scene contains Orpheus's aria "Che farò senza Euridice." Eurydice (G3-A4) is sung by a lyric soprano voice of a richer quality than that of Amor.

Orpheus and the veiled Eurydice begin their journey back to earth from the netherworld. He is not allowed to look upon her; if he does, she will again be dead. Eurydice becomes increasingly despondent because Orpheus seems no longer to love her. Unable to resist, Orpheus turns to look at her and she collapses. Despairing, he sings the aria "Che farò senza Euridice." The god of love again intervenes, restoring Eurydice to life. The trio section of the final scene is inserted here as a conclusion.

EXCERPT 2a   GS   f, e   pp. 83-106   16½ min.
                 Kal   i, e   pp. 78-101
                 Ric   i   pp. 96-123

This is the scene with only Orpheus and Eurydice, ending with the aria.

EXCERPT 2b   GS   f, e   pp. 102/2/3-9; 125-30   9½ min.
                 Kal   i, e   pp. 97/3/3-105/3/7; 120-25
                 Ric   i   pp. 118/2/2-26; 147-54

This portion of excerpt 2 begins with Orpheus's aria and includes Amor's entrance and the final trio.

OTELLO

(Othello)

Giuseppe Verdi (1813-1901)

Cyprus, Late Fifteenth Century

EXCERPT 1   GS/Kal/Ric   i, e   pp. 94-108   9½ min.

Otello is considered one of the greatest dramatic tenor roles in all opera. In addition to being a forceful actor, he should be capable of sustaining a high tessitura, and of executing a few *sotto voce* passages and a *pianissimo* Ab3. Desdemona is a lyric-spinto soprano role (C3-Ab4) requiring subtlety.

In front of Otello's castle the crowd has welcomed the Moor Otello, governor of Cyprus, back from the war. After the crowd departs, Otello is left alone with his wife Desdemona. They sing a duet version of the lines in Shakespeare's play where Otello is describing how Desdemona fell in love with him when he was recollecting the hardships of battle.

EXCERPT 2   GS/Kal/Ric   i, e   pp. 109-120/2/3   18 min.

This short excerpt contains the "Credo" of Iago, baritone (A#1-F#3) capable of subtle dramaticism and high lyric singing. Cassio is a tenor role with only a few lines to sing.

Cassio, a lieutenant, has been deprived of his power by Otello. Iago begs Cassio to ask Desdemona to intercede for him. It is in this way that Iago hopes to arouse Otello's suspicion of his wife's infidelity.

EXCERPT 3   GS/Kal/Ric   i, e   pp. 153/1/2-201   18 min.

Otello, dramatic tenor (C2-Bb3); and Iago, high lyric baritone (Bb1-G3); have a dramatic duet in this scene. Desdemona, soprano (Bb2-Bb4); and Emilia, mezzo-soprano (Bb2-Eb4), complete the quartet at the beginning of the excerpt.

Desdemona pleads Cassio's cause to Otello. Otello tries to avoid the subject, but her insistence arouses his suspicion still further. She attempts to wipe his brow with a handkerchief but he flings it to the ground. It is picked up by Iago's wife, Emilia. A quartet follows in which Desdemona declares her love for Otello and implores his forgiveness while Iago demands that Emilia give him the handkerchief. Left alone, Otello sings the fervent aria "Ora per sempre addio." Iago pretends to console the Moor but at the same time vows that he has seen Desdemona's handkerchief in Cassio's room. Otello becomes enraged; Iago offers to help him in vengeance as they join in the duet "Si, pel ciel."

EXCERPT 3a   GS/Kal/Ric   i, e   pp. 169/2/2-201   12 min.

The last half of excerpt 3 with Otello and Iago only.

EXCERPT 4   GS/Kal/Ric   i, e   pp. 206-25/3/2   14 min.

This is a dramatic scene between Otello and Desdemona, dramatic tenor to C4 and lyric-spinto soprano to Bb4, respectively.

In the great hall of the castle, Otello calls for Desdemona and asks to borrow her handkerchief. She offers one, but he says it is not the one he has given her. She offers to go to her room and fetch the one he wants, but Otello, convinced of his wife's guilt, denounces her and throws her out of the room.

EXCERPT 5   GS/Kal/Ric   i, e   pp. 324-64   29 min.

Act 4 complete involves seven characters. Otello, dramatic tenor, and Desdemona, lyric-spinto soprano, both have major arias.

Emilia, mezzo-soprano (E3-Ab4), has some dramatic singing near the end of the scene. In briefer roles are Cassio, tenor; Iago, baritone; Lodovico and Montano, basses.

Desdemona is in her bedroom preparing to retire for the night, assisted by Emilia. Desdemona sings the "Canzone del Salice" ("Willow Song") that she remembers from her childhood. When Emilia has bid her goodnight and left, Desdemona kneels in prayer, singing "Ave Maria." Otello enters, contemplates Desdemona for a time, then kisses her. After asking her if she has said her prayers, he again accuses her of loving Cassio. Denials are useless; as Otello becomes more enraged, he strangles her. Emilia knocks frantically on the door; when Otello finally admits her, she is stunned by the tragedy and calls for help. Emilia explains the truth about the handkerchief and Montano exposes Iago's villainy. The remorseful Otello sings the narrative "Niun mi tema," then stabs himself. Once more he kisses the lifeless Desdemona as he dies.

EXCERPT 5a   GS/Kal/Ric   i, e   pp. 324-41/3/5   15 min.

Desdemona's "Willow Song" and "Ave Maria"; Desdemona and Emilia only.

I PAGLIACCI

Ruggero Leoncavallo (1858-1919)

Montalto, Calabria, August 15, 1865

EXCERPT 1   GS   i, e   pp. 68-133   20½ min.
              Kal   i, e   pp. 66-131
              SZ   i   pp. 66-131

This section of the opera, beginning with Nedda's "Stridono lassù" and continuing through Canio's "Vesti la giubba," involves the five principals. Nedda is a lyric soprano (C3-Bb4) requiring some dramatic flare; Canio, a dramatic tenor (D2-A3); Tonio, a baritone (Bb1-F3), requires great acting ability; Silvio, lyric baritone (C2-G3), should have a warm, romantic quality. Beppe, supporting role, is a lyric tenor.

Left alone in the village square, Nedda, a member of a group of traveling players, muses on the jealousy of her husband Canio and wonders if he has read her secret desires. When Tonio, the hunchback of the troupe, tries to woo her, she drives him away with a whip.

Soon she is greeted by Silvio, a villager who loves her. They decide to elope that night. During their love duet, Tonio has called Canio to witness the scene and apprehend the lover at the right moment. Silvio, realizing he has been seen, runs away unidentified by the jealous husband. Threatening to kill his wife, Tonio demands to know her lover's name.

Beppe, another of the players, arrives in time to come between the quarreling couple. Tonio whispers to Canio that he will probably be able to spot the lover at the performance that evening. In one of the most famous of tenor arias, Canio, left alone, grieves over his wife's infidelity and the fact that he must go on stage and make people laugh while his heart is breaking.

EXCERPT 1a   GS   i, e   pp. 68-91   10 min.
                Kal i, e   pp. 66-89
                SZ   i   pp. 66-89

This is the opening of Excerpt 1 with Nedda and Tonio only.

EXCERPT 1b   GS   i, e   pp. 92-117/2/4   10½ min.
                Kal i, e   pp. 90-115/2/4
                SZ   i   pp. 90-115/2/4

This portion of excerpt 1 featuring Nedda and Silvio can be combined with Nedda's aria if so desired.

LES PÊCHEURS DE PERLES

(The Pearl Fishers)

Georges Bizet (1838-1875)

Ancient Ceylon

EXCERPT 1   Chou   f   pp. 29-42   7 min.
                        Kal   f, e   pp. 29-42

This is the complete version of the favorite tenor-baritone duet
"Au fond du temple saint" often done in concert. Nadir, lyric
tenor (Eb2-Bb3), should have a strong upper register; Zurga, lyric
baritone, sings no higher than Eb3 in this excerpt.

On a beach, Zurga, chief of the fishermen, welcomes the return
of his boyhood friend Nadir after a long absence. They recall their
rivalry for the hand of a beautiful Brahmin priestess Leïla, but
their oath of friendship dispels such enmity.

EXCERPT 2   Chou   f   pp. 89/2/6-95; 97-118   20 min.
                        Kal   f, e   pp. 89/2/5-95; 97-118

Nourabad, the high priest of Brahma, is sung by a bass (C2-Eb3);
the priestess Leïla, by a lyric soprano (C3-C5). They appear in this
scene with Nadir, tenor (see vocal description in excerpt 1).

In a ruined temple, Nourabad warns Leïla, on threat of death, to
be faithful to her religious vows. Left alone, she sings of her secret
love in the aria "Comme autrefois." Soon she hears the voice of
Nadir singing a serenade, and when they are together they sing a
passionate love duet.

EXCERPT 2a   Chou   f   pp. 97-118   14 min.
                        Kal   f, e   pp. 97-118

This is the portion of excerpt 2 using only Leïla and Nadir.

EXCERPT 3   Chou   f   pp. 153-75   15 min.
                        Kal   f, e   pp. 153-75

Zurga, baritone with a top F#3; and Leïla, lyric soprano (C3-

B4), are joined by Nourabad, bass, who has very little singing in this scene.

Alone in his tent, Zurga reflects on the breaking of his friendship with Nadir who has been discovered with Leïla and condemned to death. Leïla herself appears: she is willing to die but pleads for Nadir's life. But Zurga gives in to jealousy and Leïla curses him.

EXCERPT 3a   Chou   f   pp. 153-73   14½ min.
               Kal   f, e pp. 153-73

This is the scene from excerpt 3 using only Zurga and Leïla.

PELLÉAS ET MÉLISANDE

Claude Debussy (1862-1918)

Fictional Kingdom of Allemonde, Legendary Time

EXCERPT 1   Dur/Int/Kal   f, e   pp. 1-22/3/1   10 min.

The lyric soprano role of Mélisande lies mostly in the middle range, but the singer of the part should have an ethereal quality in both voice and appearance. Golaud, baritone, needs a dark, mature sound.

Golaud has lost his way in the depth of the forest where he finds a beautiful young woman weeping at the edge of a spring. Her answers to his questions are vague and mysterious; after some time she does tell him her name, Mélisande. It is growing dark and they seek shelter.

EXCERPT 2   Dur/Int/Kal   f, e   pp. 38/6/2-54   6 min.

Mélisande, lyric soprano, sings in middle range (D3-F4) in this scene. Geneviève (C3-F#4), mother of Golaud and Pelléas, is a mezzo-soprano. Pelléas can be sung by a tenor or a high lyric baritone (C2-F#3). If cast with a baritone it is important that his voice be extremely lyric in contrast to the darker sound of his older half-brother Golaud. An offstage chorus of sailors (altos and tenors) is heard briefly.

Mélisande is now married to Golaud. She, Geneviève and Pelléas appear on the terrace of King Arkel's castle to watch the ocean at sunset. Night approaches; Geneviève retires. To Pelléas's casual remark that he must leave the next day, Mélisande responds with the childlike cry, "Why must you go?"

EXCERPT 3   Dur/Int/Kal   f, e   pp. 55-74/1/2   7½ min.

A scene between Pelléas and Mélisande (see excerpts 1-2 for voice description).

To escape the noonday heat, Pelléas and Mélisande have come to an ancient and deserted fountain in the woods, reputed to have the power to restore sight to the blind. Mélisande is fascinated by the water. She throws a ring Golaud has given her up in the air to see it sparkle in the sunlight. The ring slips through her fingers to the bottom of the well where it can never be recovered.

EXCERPT 4   Dur/Int/Kal   f, e   pp. 75/5/1-102   12 min.

A scene for Mélisande and Golaud (see excerpt 1 for vocal description).

Golaud is lying on his bed in a room of the castle, Mélisande at his side. He has been wounded, but he tells her his injuries are not serious and she may go to sleep for the night. Suddenly she bursts into tears; she is not happy in the gloomy palace. Tenderly he takes her hands and notices the ring he gave her is missing (see excerpt 3). Evasive, she replies that she dropped the ring in a grotto by the sea. Golaud orders her to go at once to find it; Pelléas will conduct her safely.

EXCERPT 5   Dur/Int/Kal   f, e   pp. 115-40/1/3   11½ min.

The "Tower Scene" with Pelléas (to A3), Mélisande and briefly, Golaud. (See earlier excerpts for vocal requirements.)

Mélisande is at a window in one of the towers of the castle combing her unbound hair. Pelléas, down below, tells her he must leave; she again begs him to stay. He promises to delay his departure. As she extends to him her hand to kiss, her long magnificent hair falls over Pelléas's face arousing passionate feelings in him. Golaud approaches and reprimands them for their childishness.

EXCERPT 5a   Dur/Int/Kal   f, e   pp. 115-38/2/4   10 min.

The "Tower Scene" excerpt 5, with Mélisande and Pelléas only.

EXCERPT 6   Dur/Int/Kal   f, e   pp. 142-57/5/2   8 min.

This scene for Pelléas, tenor or high lyric baritone, and his half brother Golaud, a baritone with a dark, mature sound, begins in the vaults beneath the castle and moves to a terrace at the entrance of the vaults.

Golaud leads Pelléas into the subterranean vault where the breeze of death blows. Seized with shuddering, they go out onto the terrace and Golaud warns Pelléas to avoid intimate conversations with Mélisande.

EXCERPT 7   Dur/Int/Kal   f, e   pp. 158/2/1-88   11 min.

A new character is introduced in this scene—Yniold, Golaud's son by his first marriage. Though sometimes sung by a boy soprano, the role can be taken by a petite young woman with a lyric soprano voice. Golaud, mature baritone, is also in this scene.

In front of the same tower where Mélisande appeared in excerpt 4, Golaud questions Yniold about his stepmother's behavior. The child's answers are so vague that they only tantalize Golaud's suspicions. A light appears in Mélisande's window; Golaud holds Yniold up high so he can look into the room. Pelléas is there with Mélisande but they do not speak or come near each other.

EXCERPT 8   Dur/Int/Kal   f, e   pp. 189-219   15 min.

King Arkel, Golaud's grandfather, bass (F1-D#3), in addition to Mélisande, lyric soprano with no high singing in this scene; Pelléas, tenor or high baritone; and Golaud, mature baritone, are in this excerpt.

Pelléas meets Mélisande along the corridor of the castle and obtains a rendezvous with her—midnight at the Fountain of the Blind. The old, nearly blind King Arkel enters and, taking Mélisande to his heart, tries to dispel the gloomy forebodings she has. The sight of his wife irritates Golaud so much that finally, in a mad rage, he throws her down and drags her by the hair across the room. Only Arkel understands and pities.

EXCERPT 8a   Dur/Int/Kal   f, e   pp. 196/4/3-219   11½ min.

The same as excerpt 8 with Mélisande, Golaud, and Arkel, beginning with King Arkel's entrance.

EXCERPT 9   Dur/Int/Kal   f, e   pp. 232/2/2-67   13½ min.

This is a love scene for Pelléas, tenor or high lyric baritone, and Mélisande; Golaud appears at the end as a silent character.

Mélisande meets Pelléas at the fountain in the park. He confides that the reason he must leave is that he loves her. She confesses her love for him, too. They soon realize that Golaud is nearby; he has his sword but Pelléas is unarmed. The lovers embrace wildly; the stars of the heavens seem to be falling upon them. Golaud rushes out, stabs Pelléas, and pursues the fleeing Mélisande.

EXCERPT 10   Dur/Int/Kal   f, e   pp. 268-310   24 min.

Mélisande, Golaud, Arkel (see earlier excerpts for vocal descriptions), and a Physician, bass (Bb1-D3), are in excerpt 10.

The ailing Mélisande lies in her bed. Golaud and the Physician converse; she may recover. When she wakes as if from a dream, Golaud begs her forgiveness and asks if she loved Pelléas. She replies that she loved him innocently, but Golaud's doubts still leave him troubled. He makes her suffer so that she is near death. The aged Arkel brings her the child she has borne; Mélisande dies, and Golaud bows his head in grief and remorse.

LA PÉRICHOLE

Jacques Offenbach (1819-1890)

Peru, About 1860

EXCERPT 1   B&H   e   pp. 26-31; 42-50 Music only—8 min.
                            (dialogue with appropriate cuts)
              Kal   e   pp. 34-39; 28-33 (sung by Paquillo and
                            Perichole); 42-48

The title role was written originally for mezzo-soprano (Bb2-A4) but at the Metropolitan Opera it has been performed by sopranos taking high options. In either case, the role requires a lyric voice with warmth in the middle range and flexibility in the upper register. Likewise, Paquillo, originally a tenor role, has been assigned to a high baritone in the tradition of operetta. In the Boosey and Hawkes score, most of his A's and Ab's have lower options.

This excerpt features the two leading singers in some of the best-known duets and arias, with a chorus. Four characters who sing in the opera but only speak in this scene are Guadalena, one of the three cousins; Don Andrès, the Viceroy of Peru; Don Pedro, Governor; and Count Panatellas.

La Périchole and Paquillo, street singers unable to afford a marriage license, try their songs out on the clientele of the tavern of "The Three Cousins" but have little luck. After the crowd has been drawn away by a circus troupe, Périchole falls exhausted. Paquillo goes off to try his luck elsewhere leaving her asleep in the square. Struck by her beauty, the Viceroy invites the hungry girl to dinner and later, revealing his identity, offers her a position in his court. Feeling that she can no longer face a life of poverty, she consents and proceeds to write Paquillo a farewell letter (the famous "Letter Song"). Shortly after she leaves Paquillo finds her gone and sadly echoes part of her song as he reads her letter.

EXCERPT 2   B&H   e   pp. 116-18   Music only—2½ min.
                        (with preceding dialogue)
             Kal   e   pp. 122-23

Paquillo, tenor or baritone, sings this trio with Panatellas, tenor (Eb2-Bb3), and Don Pedro, baritone (Db2-F3).

Paquillo has been goaded into a marriage while too intoxicated to know whom he has married or why. The next day the Governor of Peru and the first gentleman-in-waiting remind him that he must present his bride to the Viceroy's court. The three join in a song on the subject of the fairer sex.

EXCERPT 3   B&H   e   pp. 172-83/2/5   Music only—5 min.
                        (with dialogue)
             Kal*   e   pp. 154-60/3/3

*Paquillo's aria is not included in the Kalmus score.

The same cast as excerpt 2, with the addition of the Turnkey who has spoken dialogue only. Paquillo sings an aria with a range C2-F3 if performed in F Major, or D2-E3 if performed in G Major.

Paquillo has been imprisoned for insulting his wife in the Viceroy's court (he discovered that he had married his faithless sweetheart Périchole). Panatellas and Don Pedro visit the prisoner and commend him for speaking out against the fickleness of women. Left alone, Paquillo broods over his misfortunes, calling desperately for his wife.

EXCERPT 4   B&H   e   pp. 179-207   Music only—14 min.
                      (with dialogue)
              Kal*   e   pp. 160/4/1-77

A scene for Périchole, soprano (C#3-Bb4); Paquillo, tenor or high baritone; and Don Andrès, baritone or *buffo* bass (B1-E3), who needs comic acting ability. The Old Prisoner, tenor (Eb2-Ab3), was originally a speaking role. The Turnkey, speaking role, and two guards, silent, complete the scene.

Paquillo opens with his aria (see excerpt 3). La Périchole arrives to visit him in prison, begging his forgiveness for having left him. She assures him she has resisted the Viceroy's advances. The lovers, reconciled, determine to try to escape by bribing the jailer with jewels Périchole has brought along for that purpose. The "jolly jailer" who has bound the pair in chains turns out to be Don Andrès in disguise. An Old Prisoner comes to their aid; he frees them both and the three proceed to bind the Viceroy to a pillar, pilfer his keys, and escape.

EXCERPT 4a   B&H   e   pp. 179-94   Music only—8 min.
                       (with dialogue)
               Kal*   e   pp. 160/4/1-70/2/6

The portion of excerpt 4 using only La Périchole, Paquillo, and the Turnkey.

---

*Paquillo's aria is not included in the Kalmus score.

PETER GRIMES
Benjamin Britten (1913-1976)
The Borough (Aldeburgh), England, About 1830

EXCERPT 1   B&H   e   pp. 87-103   7 min.

The scene is a dialogue between Peter Grimes (C2-B3), tenor
with dramatic intensity, and Captain Balstrode, dramatic baritone
(A1-G3).

As a storm approaches, Grimes, a fisherman, and Balstrode, a re-
tired merchant skipper, are the only beings left on a street near
the sea. Grimes is in disgrace in the Borough because of his treatment of apprentices; the old Captain advises him to leave town and
enlist as a merchantman or privateer. Grimes is obstinate; his ambition is to become rich and marry Ellen Orford. As the storm rises,
the two men shout at each other. Left alone, the half-mad Grimes
sings his aria "What harbour shelters peace?"

EXCERPT 2   B&H   e   116/1/4-71   14 min.

This scene contains the aria "Now the Great Bear and Pleiades"
for Peter Grimes, dramatic tenor with flexibility. Other roles are
the two Nieces, sopranos; Auntie and Mrs. Sedley, mezzo-sopranos;
Bob Boles, tenor (Bb1-Cb4); Ned Keene (G#1-G3) and Captain
Balstrode, baritones. Ellen Orford, soprano (A#2-C5); Hobson,
bass (F#1-F3); and a young boy, silent, appear briefly at the end
of the scene. A mixed chorus of any size has some unison singing.

The Boar, a pub owned by Auntie, is the setting of this scene.
The storm is still raging when Mrs. Sedley comes in seeking Ned
Keene, the apothecary. Bob Boles gets drunk and makes advances
to the Nieces who have come downstairs in their nightgowns. When
Grimes comes in from the storm and sings a strange song about the
constellations and their significance, the crowd thinks him mad.
Captain Balstrode, to prevent violence, intervenes and suggests a
song. All join in the round in 7/4 time, "Old Joe has gone fishing,"
Grimes singing his own mystical version. Ellen bursts in with the
carter Hobson and Grimes's apprentice. In spite of the storm,
Grimes insists on taking the boy to his hut.

EXCERPT 3   B&H   e   pp. 299-313/2/5;   11½ min.
                         319-26/1/2

A tableau for seven singers and a study in characterizations.
Ellen Orford, lyric soprano (B2-Bb4), needs to be able to sing a
long, sustained line and *pianissimo* Bb4 in her "Embroidery Aria."
Two Nieces are both sopranos; Mrs. Sedley, character mezzo-
soprano (G2-E4); Captain Balstrode, dramatic baritone; Ned
Keene, apothecary, lyric baritone; and Swallow, lawyer, bass, complete the cast. (All three men must have an F3.)

Outside the Boar tavern a rather drunk Swallow flirts with the
two Nieces. Mrs. Sedley, a busybody, tries to convince Keene that
Grimes is guilty of murdering his apprentice. Ellen and Balstrode
arrive seriously worried about Grimes's two-day absence. Ellen
shows the apprentice's wet jersey found on the shore; they both
read into it a sinister significance. Balstrode tries to encourage
Ellen by saying that they may yet be able to help their friend Peter
Grimes.

EXCERPT 3a   B&H   e   pp. 320-26/1/2   6 min.

This is the last portion of excerpt 3, with only Ellen and Balstrode.

PIQUE DAME

(The Queen of Spades)

Peter Ilyitch Tchaikovsky (1840-1893)

St. Petersburg, Late Eighteenth Century

EXCERPT 1   GS/Kal   e   pp. 16/2/3-25;   28½ min.
                         33/3/4-55; 59/2/2-63
            Kal   r   pp. 28-41; 54/2/3-81/2/2; 86/2/2-93

The opening scene features the central figure of the story, Gherman, a tenor with a particularly wide range (D2-B3); and Tomsky,
baritone (A1-G3), who sings an important aria. Main characters in

the story but merely completing the quintet here are Lisa, lyric soprano; her grandmother the Countess, mezzo-soprano; Prince Yeletsky, a baritone or bass. The minor characters of Tchekalinsky, tenor, and Sourin, bass, appear briefly.

At the Summer Garden in St. Petersburg, Gherman, a compulsive gambler, confides in his friend Tomsky that he has fallen in love but does not know the name of the young lady. Tomsky encourages Gherman to learn the lady's name and woo her, but Gherman is afraid she is above him in station.

The young lady and her grandmother enter accompanied by Prince Yeletsky who that morning has become engaged to Lisa. The Countess has noticed Gherman and finds out his name from Tomsky; Gherman likewise learns that Lisa is Yeletsky's fiancée. After Lisa and the Prince leave, Tomsky reveals that the Countess was once a great gambler and knew of a secret winning card series, but in a dream she had been warned she would die when anyone tried to win the secret from her. Gherman, entranced by the story, determines to win Lisa away from the Prince.

EXCERPT 1a   GS/Kal   e   pp. 18/3/1-25   6 min.
                Kal   r   pp. 30/4/3-41

This is the opening section of excerpt 1 using only Gherman and Tomsky.

EXCERPT 2   GS/Kal   e   pp. 64-90/2/1   16½ min.
                Kal   r   pp. 94-131/3/1

Lisa, lyric soprano (Eb3-Ab4), plays a more important part in this scene than does her friend Pauline, mezzo-soprano or contralto, whose melancholy aria ranges from A2-Ab4. Other characters are the Governess, mezzo-soprano; and the chambermaid, Masha, soprano or mezzo-soprano. The scene calls for a chorus of girls.

In Lisa's room her girl friends are gathered around while she and Pauline sing a dreamy duet. The latter obliges Lisa's sad mood with an appropriate aria; then the mood changes as the girls take up a dance tune until the governess comes in to remind them it is time for bed. Though Lisa is engaged to Prince Yeletsky, her thoughts are of the young officer Gherman.

EXCERPT 3   GS/Kal   e   pp. 82-107   16 min.
                   Kal   r   pp. 120/3/1-33

A scene primarily for Lisa, lyric soprano, and Gherman, tenor
with a wide range. Also appearing are the Countess, mezzo-soprano,
and her chambermaid Masha, soprano or mezzo-soprano.

Lisa, alone in her room, is thinking of the young officer Gherman whom she saw earlier. Suddenly Gherman himself appears.
She tries to leave but he persuades her to stay and listen to his
protestations of love. Their conversation is interrupted by a knock
at the door; Gherman hides. The Countess enters to scold her
granddaughter for staying up so late. After the Countess departs,
Lisa surrenders to Gherman's embrace.

EXCERPT 4   GS/Kal   e   pp. 223-45   12½ min.
                   Kal   r   pp. 309-37

Another scene for Lisa and Gherman, including Lisa's aria which
requires a strong B4.

On the canal bank near the Winter Palace, Lisa awaits Gherman.
When he arrives, he talks of eloping with her and they join in a
passionate duet. But when he starts mumbling the secret of the
three cards, Lisa is seized with despair at his passion for gambling.
Deaf to her pleading, he pushes her aside and goes his way. Lisa
throws herself into the river.

I PURITANI

Vincenzo Bellini (1801-1835)

Plymouth, England, About 1650

EXCERPT 1   Kal   i, e   pp. 39-50/1/4; 50/5/1-   10½ min.
                             55/1/5; 58/2/5-60
                   Ric   i   pp. 38-50; 51/4/1-55; 60-61

Elvira, soprano (D3-B4 or opt. D5), is a lyric-coloratura of the
bel canto school with an extremely florid line demanding a secure,
flexible technique. Giorgio, bass (C2-D3), sings mostly in the middle and upper range. An offstage chorus is doubled in the orches-
tration.

In this duet, Elvira's uncle comes to her room in Lord Walton's castle to inform her that her father, a Puritan, has consented to her marriage to the Cavalier, Lord Arturo Talbot, the man she loves.

EXCERPT 2   Kal i, e   pp. 67/2/8-85/3/4;   21 min.
                            88/3/2-111/4/6
              Ric   i   pp. 68/2/8-84/6/3; 86/6/5-110

This portion of the act 1 finale features all seven of the opera's soloists and only a few lines of the chorus. Arturo's "A te, o cara" and Elvira's "Son vergin vezzoza" are part of this scene. In addition to Elvira and Giorgio already described in excerpt 1, Arturo, tenor, is featured with some exposed high notes (C#4). The role of Riccardo, baritone (B1-F#3), has a high tessitura. An important role is that of Enrichetta, mezzo-soprano (C3-F#4); other roles are Gualtiero Walton, bass, and Bruno, tenor (bit part).

Arturo arrives to greet his bride Elvira. Enrichetta, widow of the late King Charles I, is a prisoner in the fortress. Arturo, loyal to the crown, allows her to escape wearing Elvira's bridal veil. Riccardo, hoping at one time to marry Elvira himself, almost draws his sword on Arturo, supposing the lady in the veil to be Elvira. But Enrichetta reveals her identity and Riccardo lets Arturo through.

EXCERPT 3   Kal i, e   pp. 178/5/2-211   26½ min.
              Ric   i   pp. 170/5/2-206

A scene for Elvira, Riccardo and Giorgio (see excerpts 1 and 2 for vocal descriptions). Elvira usually cadences her "Mad Scene" with an Eb5. At the end of the duet "Suoni la tromba," Riccardo customarily soars to an Ab3; Giorgio may, though not necessarily, join him on that pitch.

Believing that Arturo has deserted Elvira on her wedding day, the Puritans have denounced the Cavalier bridegroom. In the Puritan camp of the fortress, Elvira, deranged by the event, is wandering aimlessly, singing beautiful romantic melodies about her lover. After she leaves, Riccardo and Giorgio pledge themselves to fight against the Cavaliers and to avenge Elvira's plight.

EXCERPT 3a   Kal i, e   pp. 178/5/2-95   15½ min.
              Ric   i   pp. 170/5/2-90/2/4

Elvira's aria only from excerpt 3, with Riccardo and Giorgio in supporting roles.

EXCERPT 3b   Kal   i, e   pp. 196-211   11 min.
               Ric   i   pp. 190/3/1-206

This is the duet for Riccardo and Giorgio only from excerpt 3.

EXCERPT 4   Kal   i, e   pp. 212-19/3/3;   19 min.
                                225/5/4-40/5/1
               Ric   i   pp. 207-13/5/4; 219/5/4-36/1/1

Arturo, tenor (F2-D4 or C#4), and Elvira, soprano (E3-B4, opt. D5 or C#4). The C3's are indicated as the top pitches if the duet is transposed down a half step (transposition beginning 232/5/1 in Kalmus or 227/4/1 in Ricordi to the end of the duet). This extremely taxing duet should be attempted only by accomplished singers.

Arturo, fleeing from the enemy, slips into a garden of the castle in hopes of seeing Elvira one more time before leaving England forever. They do not meet and she understands his loyalty to the Queen that caused his departure from the wedding celebration. Her joy brings back her sanity and they sing the duet "Vieni fra queste braccia."

THE RAKE'S PROGRESS

Igor Stravinsky (1882-1971)

England, 1750-1760

EXCERPT 1   B&H   e, g   pp. 1-34   18 min.

Anne Trulove, lyric soprano (B2-A4), sings mostly in the middle range and should display a pleasant, warm quality of sound. Tom Rakewell, tenor (D2-A3), has many florid passages and needs to be an effective actor. Nick Shadow, baritone (Bb1-E3), must act the part of a sly, sinister, formidable character. Trulove, Anne's father, is sung by a bass (G1-D3). The precise ensembles and rhythmic difficulties in the score call for expert musicianship.

Tom is visiting his sweetheart Anne in the garden of her country home. Her father, having secured Tom a position in business which he refuses, is apprehensive about Anne's marrying a lazy husband. Tom, in an aria, announces that he intends to rely on good luck and closes with a wish for money. At once Nick Shadow appears informing Tom that a forgotten uncle has died leaving him a large fortune. It is necessary to go to London to settle the estate, and Nick offers himself as a servant to Tom, wages to be settled in a year and a day. After a quartet in which Tom bids Anne and her father farewell, Nick turns to the audience and announces, "The progress of a rake begins!"

EXCERPT 2   B&H   e, g   pp. 71-93   12 min.

A dialogue between Tom Rakewell and Nick Shadow (see vocal descriptions in excerpt 1).

Alone in his quarters in London, Tom broods on his dissatisfaction with the city and dares not even think about the girl he has left. At the end of his monologue, he utters his second wish—that he were happy. Nick appears with a picture of Baba the Turk, a bearded lady from the circus, and eventually convinces Tom he should take this exotic creature for a wife.

EXCERPT 3   B&H   e, g   pp. 94-114   11 min.

Anne, lyric soprano, and Tom, tenor, appear in this scene with Baba the Turk, mezzo-soprano with less singing here than the others. The chorus of townspeople need not be used, but a few servants (silent) are necessary to the scene.

Anne arrives outside Tom's house; she has come to London to persuade Tom to return to the country. A sedan chair is brought in and from it steps Tom. He begs Anne, his former sweetheart, to go back home, for he is not worthy of her. A veiled head emerges from the sedan chair to ask what the delay is; Tom informs Anne that this is his bride, Baba. A duet in which Tom and Anne express their regrets over what might have been, becomes a trio as Baba grows increasingly impatient. Finally Anne leaves and Baba, aided by Tom, emerges from her sedan chair.

EXCERPT 4   B&H   e, g   pp. 115-39   13½ min.

Baba the Turk, mezzo-soprano, sings a dramatic aria with many
florid passages and a range from A2 to A4. Tom Rakewell, tenor
to F#3, and Nick Shadow, baritone, complete the scene.

Tom is bored listening to his wife Baba chatter endlessly about
her possessions. She flies into a rage at his indifference, throwing
pieces of china about the room. In the middle of a line of her
coloratura, Tom stuffs his wig into her mouth and goes to sleep.
Tom dreams that there is a machine which will turn stones into
bread, and he utters his third wish—"I wish it were true!" Nick
then makes Tom believe that he has in fact invented such a
machine and suggests that a fortune is to be made.

EXCERPT 4a   B&H   e, g   pp. 115-24   4 min.

Taken from excerpt 4, this is the portion using Baba the Turk's
aria with very little singing by Tom Rakewell.

EXCERPT 5   B&H   e, g   pp. 185-208   16 min.

A scene for Tom Rakewell and Nick Shadow (see vocal descriptions in excerpt 1), with Anne, soprano, singing one line offstage.

In a graveyard, Nick informs Tom that a year and a day have
passed since their first agreement, and Nick now demands payment
in the form of Tom's soul. Nick does, however, offer Tom one last
chance to redeem himself in a card game. Tom wins, but as Nick
sinks into the grave he had dug for Tom, he declares Tom hence-
forth insane.

THE RAPE OF LUCRETIA

Benjamin Britten (1913-1976)

Rome, 500 B.C.

EXCERPT 1   B&H   e. g   pp. 1-52   22½ min.

The Male Chorus and Female Chorus in this opera are actually
two singers on either side of the stage narrating the action, much

of which is mimed. Female Chorus is a soprano (Bb2-A4) with a strong middle register; Male Chorus, a tenor (B1-Bb3) whose role is lyric but a good deal of which lies in the middle range. The tessitura of Tarquinius, baritone (Bb1-G3), tends to run high; Junius is also a baritone (Bb1-E3); Collatinus, a bass (Bb1-Eb3).

Male Chorus reads how Tarquinius came to rule Rome by force and, adds Female Chorus, to involve the Romans in a war against the Greeks. The curtain opens on a camp outside Rome. Collatinus, Junius, and Tarquinius are drinking and commenting on the chasteness of Collatinus's wife Lucretia and the faithlessness of the other men's wives. Tarquinius taunts the cuckolded Junius as they drink a toast to Lucretia. Tarquinius, left alone, contemplates the possibility of testing Lucretia's chastity.

EXCERPT 2   B&H   e, g   pp. 62-105   16 min.

This excerpt introduces the three principal women: Lucretia, mezzo-soprano (G2-G4) whose lyric music lies primarily in the low register with a few dramatic high notes; Bianca, mezzo-soprano (A2-F4); and Lucia, lyric soprano (B2-B4) requiring a high *pianissimo*. Female Chorus, soprano (Bb2-Ab4), plays an important role. The roles of Male Chorus, tenor, and Tarquinius, baritone, are not difficult in this scene.

Lucretia is at home sewing while her attendants Lucia and Bianca spin. A quartet evolves in which Female Chorus joins the three women in philosophizing on the fate of womankind. The night is growing very late when Prince Tarquinius arrives. He is greeted courteously by the women who are subject to his command.

EXCERPT 2a   B&H   e, g   pp. 62-91/1/3   10 min.

The quartet for the four women, only, from excerpt 2.

EXCERPT 3   B&H   e, g   pp. 117/2/2-56   17 min.

The roles of Male Chorus, Female Chorus, and Tarquinius have been described in excerpt 1; Lucretia, in excerpt 2. Male Chorus has a *sprechstimme* narrative.

Tarquinius approaches the sleeping Lucretia and kisses her as she dreams of her long-absent husband Collatinus. Lucretia awakens, and for a time Tarquinius seeks in vain to win her love.

Finally he pulls the covers from her bed and forces himself upon her; the curtain falls as Male and Female Choruses sing a unison chorale.

EXCERPT 4   B&H   e, g   pp. 157-229   35 min.

   This scene is scored for Lucia, high soprano; Bianca and Lucretia, low mezzo-sopranos; Junius, baritone; and Collatinus, bass. Male and Female Choruses (soprano and tenor soloists) appear near the end of the scene.

   In the early morning, Bianca and Lucia are busy arranging flowers in Lucretia's house. They leave the orchids, Collatinus's favorite flower, for Lucretia. But Lucretia hysterically tells Lucia to send an urgent message for Collatinus to come home. She makes a wreath of the orchids while singing an arioso about the purity of flowers. Collatinus and Junius arrive, the latter revealing knowledge of Tarquinius's visit. Lucretia starkly tells Collatinus what happened the previous night. He forgives her at once but she stabs herself and dies at his feet. The rest of the characters, joined by Male Chorus and Female Chorus in a *chaconne*, lament the death of the virtuous Lucretia.

EXCERPT 4a   B&H   e, g   pp. 157-73/2/4   6 min.

   Duet for Lucia and Bianca only.

EXCERPT 4b   B&H   e, g   pp. 157-86/1/4   12 min.

   Lucia and Bianca with Lucretia.

EXCERPT 4c   B&H   e, g   pp. 157-201/3/1   27 min.

   Lucia, Bianca, Lucretia, Junius, and Collatinus; opening of the scene to the death of Lucretia.

EXCERPT 4d   B&H   e, g   pp. 193-201/3/1   6½ min.

   Lucretia and Collatinus only.

RIGOLETTO

Giuseppe Verdi (1813-1901)

Mantua, Sixteenth Century

EXCERPT 1   GS/Kal   i, e   pp. 51-56/1/4   4½ min.
                 Ric   i, e   pp. 73-80
                 Ric   i   pp. 60-65

The duet between Rigoletto, baritone (C2-E3) with a mature sound and superb acting ability, and Sparafucile, bass (F1-Eb3).

Rigoletto, hunchback court jester, cursed by Count Monterone, is on his way home at night when approached by Sparafucile, an assassin for hire. He offers his services to Rigoletto, thinking Rigoletto might want to dispose of his rivals. Rigoletto does not need Sparafucile at this moment but ascertains where he can be found should the need arise.

EXCERPT 2   GS/Kal   i, e   pp. 56/2/1-99 (trad.   23 min.
                 cuts 72/1/2-73/5/3; 92/1/5-92/4/5;
                 93/1/3-93/3/1)
                 Ric   i, e   pp. 81-143 (trad. cuts 103/1/3-5/4/3;
                 133/2/2-34/2/4; 134/3/2-35/1/4)
                 Ric   i   pp. 66-116 (trad. cuts 84-85; 108/1/1-
                 108/3/4; 109/1/1-109/2/2)

Rigoletto, baritone (B1-G3), has a demanding part in this scene; his voice should be lyric in quality and dramatic in intensity. His daughter, Gilda, is sung by a lyric or lyric-coloratura soprano (B2-C#5) with subtlety and flexibility. The Duke, tenor (F2-Bb3), appears in a role with a rather high tessitura demanding both strength and lyricism. Giovanna, mezzo-soprano, is an important supporting role.

Rigoletto approaches his house musing on the corruption of the court, Monterone's curse, and the stranger who has offered his services as a hired murderer. His monologue "Pari siamo" builds to a climax as his daughter Gilda rushes from the house to greet him. In a tender duet with Gilda, he also warns Giovanna to keep the girl safely guarded.

As Rigoletto leaves, the Duke of Mantua, who in the disguise of a student, Gualtier Maldé, has met Gilda at church, bribes Giovanna to let him in to see the girl. He sings to her of his love and then, after an extended farewell duet, the disguised Duke leaves and Gilda sings the well-known aria "Caro nome" before retiring to her room.

EXCERPT 2a   GS/Kal   i, e   pp. 56/2/1-69   7 min.
                Ric   i, e   pp. 81-99
                Ric   i   pp. 61-81/1/4

The opening of excerpt 2 with only Gilda and Rigoletto.

EXCERPT 2b   GS/Kal   i, e   pp. 56/2/1-79/2/7   10½ min.
                     (trad. cut 72/1/2-73/5/3)
                Ric   i, e   pp. 81-114 (trad. cut 103/1/3-5/4/3)
                Ric   i   pp. 66-91 (trad. cut 84-85)

This is the portion of excerpt 2 including Gilda, Rigoletto, and Giovanna.

EXCERPT 2c   GS/Kal   i, e   pp. 79/3/1-99 (trad.   12 min.
                     cuts 92/1/5-92/4/5; 93/1/3-93/3/1)
                Ric   i, e   pp. 115-43 (trad. cuts 133/2/2-
                     134/2/4; 134/3/2-35/1/4)
                Ric   i   pp. 92-116 (trad. cuts 108/1/1-
                     108/3/4; 109/1/1-109/2/2)

Gilda, Giovanna, and the Duke are included in 2c.

EXCERPT 3   GS/Kal   i, e   pp. 114-29/1/2;   24 min.
                     138-71
                Ric   i, e   pp. 165-87/1/2; 204-50
                Ric   i   pp. 133-47/2/3; 158-94

Again the Duke, Rigoletto, and Gilda are involved (see vocal requirements in excerpts 1-2). The Duke and Rigoletto have demanding arias "Parmi veder le lagrime" and "Cortigiani," respectively. Borsa, tenor; Marullo, baritone; Ceprano, bass, sing solo parts with a men's ensemble of courtiers. Monterone, a powerful bass-baritone, has a short declamation; an Usher (tenor or baritone) and a Page (soprano or mezzo-soprano) complete the scene.

In the salon of the ducal palace, the Duke is disconsolate. He has returned to the house to woo Gilda and has found it empty. The Courtiers arrive with the news that they have abducted the girl believed to be Rigoletto's mistress and have brought her to him. Overjoyed, the Duke quickly goes to make love to her. Rigoletto in his duty as court jester, enters and slyly looks around for Gilda while entertaining the court. Enraged by their remarks about his mistress, he shouts "Give me my daughter!" When he and Gilda are finally reunited, she recounts the story of the stranger she met in church, and her father consoles her anguish. Count Monterone, on his way to execution for denouncing the Duke, repeats his curse. In spite of Gilda's love for the Duke, Rigoletto swears vengeance upon the man who has so cruelly abused her.

EXCERPT 3a   GS/Kal i, e pp. 138-71   17 min.
              Ric i, e pp. 204-50
              Ric i pp. 158-94

The portion of excerpt 3 without the Duke.

EXCERPT 3b   GS/Kal i, e pp. 153-54/2/4;   10½ min.
                 155/4/1-71
              Ric i, e pp. 226-28/4/4; 229/2/4-50
              Ric i pp. 174-76/4/4; 177/2/4-94

From excerpt 3, a portion with Rigoletto, Gilda, Monterone, and Usher.

EXCERPT 3c   GS/Kal i, e pp. 153-54/2/4;   7½ min.
                 155/4/1-64/1/1
              Ric i, e pp. 226-28/4/4; 229/2/4-39
              Ric i pp. 174-76/4/4; 177/2/4-86/3/1

The scene from excerpt 3 involving only Gilda and Rigoletto.

EXCERPT 4   GS/Kal i, e pp. 172-232   28 min.
              Ric i, e pp. 251-333
              Ric i pp. 195-262

The Duke, Rigoletto, and Gilda (see vocal requirements, excerpt 2) are again featured in the complete last act. The Duke must have a strong B3 for his aria "La donna è mobile." Gilda has dramatic singing in the trio, coloratura singing in the quartet, and extremely lyric requirements in the final duet. Rigoletto usually sings an A3 in the final scene. Sparafucile is sung by a low bass (Gb1-D3) and his seductive sister Maddalena by a mezzo-soprano or contralto (B2-F4) with agility. The music of the men's chorus (offstage) may be played in the accompaniment if a chorus is not available.

The action takes place inside and outside an inn on the deserted banks of the Mincio River. Rigoletto brings his daughter Gilda (dressed as a young cavalier) to the inn to observe the Duke's philanderings. Even when she sees him disguised as a soldier, entering the tavern, calling for wine and a room for the night, and singing that "women are fickle," she protests her constant love for him. Rigoletto, sending his daughter off to Verona, makes the necessary arrangements to have the Duke murdered. Maddalena, enamored of the Duke, persuades Monterone to kill any other guest who might arrive and substitute the body in the sack he is to give to Rigoletto. Gilda has returned and has overheard this. She finds it an easy way to spare the life of the man she loves and end her own sorrow. When Rigoletto discovers his own daughter has been murdered in place of the Duke, he remembers Monterone's curse.

EXCERPT 4a   GS   i, e   pp. 177/2/1-94   5 min.
                Ric i, e   260-78
                Ric i   202-17

This is the famous quartet for Gilda, Maddalena, the Duke, and Rigoletto.

EXCERPT 4b   GS   i, e   pp. 201/2/2-18   5 min.
                Ric i, e   pp. 288-313
                Ric i   pp. 224-44

This is the trio for Gilda, Maddalena, and Sparafucile.

EXCERPT 4c   GS   i, e   pp. 219-32   10 min.
                Ric i, e   pp. 314-33
                Ric i   pp. 245-62

From excerpt 4, this is the final duet between Rigoletto and Gilda, with the Duke singing offstage and a lesser part for Sparafucile.

ROMÉO ET JULIETTE
(Romeo and Juliet)
Charles Gounod (1816-1893)
Verona, Fourteenth Century

EXCERPT 1   GS/Kal   f, e   pp. 33-63   13 min.

This excerpt includes Mercutio, lyric baritone (D2-F#3); Juliet, lyric soprano with flexibility and a trill (C3-D5); Romeo, lyric tenor (D2-A3). Gertrude, mezzo-soprano, and Gregorio, baritone, sing supporting roles. A small ensemble of men (Montagues) have little to sing but must react to Mercutio's song.

When Romeo expresses his premonition of ill, Mercutio responds with the "Queen Mab" aria. Romeo and his companions then draw aside as Juliet sings enthusiastically of her girlish joy in the well-known "Waltz Song." The nurse is called away, and the masked Romeo courts Juliet in the charming duo "Ange adorable," paralleling their first meeting in Shakespeare's drama.

EXCERPT 1a   GS/Kal   f, e   pp. 47-63   7 min.

This is the portion of excerpt 1 involving only Juliet, Romeo, Gertrude, and Gregorio.

EXCERPT 2   GS/Kal   f, e   pp. 78-118   25 min.

This excerpt includes the same characters as excerpt 1a with a men's chorus (Capulets).

Romeo appears near Juliet's house to get another glimpse of her, serenading her with the aria "Ah, lève-toi, soleil." She now appears on her balcony. Romeo hides as they are interrupted for a time by the approach of Gregorio and the men (Capulets) in search of a Montague. After Gertrude sends the men away, Juliet and Romeo resume their conversation until Juliet bids Romeo goodnight.

EXCERPT 2a   GS/Kal   f, e   pp. 82-93/3/3;   21 min.
                              102/4/1-18

This is the same as excerpt 2 with cuts made to leave only the music for Romeo and Juliet.

EXCERPT 3   GS/Kal   f, e   pp. 120/4/1-34   8 min.

A quartet for Romeo and Juliet (see excerpt 1 for vocal requirements) both of whom must have a high B; Gertrude, mezzo-
soprano; and Friar Laurence, bass with a range from G1 to E3.

Juliet and Romeo are secretly married in Friar Laurence's cell.
Friar Laurence hopes that the union will end the feud between the
Capulets and the Montagues.

EXCERPT 4   GS/Kal   f, e   pp. 181-99   11½ min.

An extended duet for Romeo and Juliet, tenor and lyric soprano; both have optional high C's.

Having found his way into Juliet's chamber, Romeo, banished
from Verona for having killed Juliet's cousin Tybalt in a street
fight, receives pardon from Juliet and bids her a tender farewell.

EXCERPT 5   GS/Kal   f, e   pp. 200-214   8½ min.
                        (with aria pp. 215-24 opt.)   13 min.

A scene for Juliet, lyric soprano; Gertrude, mezzo-soprano; and
Friar Laurence, bass; with Juliet's father, Capulet, bass-baritone
(C#2-D3).

Capulet and Friar Laurence arrive in Juliet's chamber to tell her
that her marriage to Count Paris is now being arranged. The priest
advises her to take a potion which will produce a deathlike sleep.
Upon waking, she may escape from her tomb and flee with Romeo.
At this point the score has a dramatic aria for Juliet which is seldom performed at the opera house.

EXCERPT 5a   GS/Kal   f, e   pp. 208-24   9 min.

The portion of excerpt 5 featuring Juliet and Friar Laurence
only.

EXCERPT 6   GS/Kal   f, e   pp. 248-65   12½ min.

This is the final scene between Romeo, tenor, and Juliet, lyric
soprano.

Romeo, believing Juliet to be dead, has come to the tombs of
the Capulets. Not having received the message that she is only
sleeping and that she will soon join him, he takes a deadly poison.

Juliet awakens; they embrace with joy, but soon Romeo's poison begins to take effect. Juliet, finding a dagger among her burial garments, stabs herself in order to join her husband in eternal sleep.

LA RONDINE

(The Swallow)

Giacomo Puccini (1858-1924)

Paris and the Riviera, Late Nineteenth Century

EXCERPT 1   UE   i, e   pp. 5-39/3/5   18 min.

The action centers around two arias of Magda, lyric soprano (C3-C5), "Che il bel sogno di Doretta" and "Ore dolci e divine" requiring sustained *pianissimo* high notes. Other important roles are Lisette, soubrette soprano; Prunier, light lyric tenor or character tenor; and Rambaldo, bass-baritone. The ensemble consists of Yvette and Bianca, sopranos; Suzy, mezzo-soprano; Gobin, tenor; Périchaud, baritone; and Crébillon, bass.

In an elegant Parisian salon, Rambaldo and his mistress Magda are entertaining friends. Prunier, a poet, begins a love ballad he has composed; as he is unable to find a fitting ending, Magda improvises one. As the men go off to one side of the room, Magda and her girl friends consider the relative merits of wealth and romantic love. Magda sings an aria reminiscent of her romantic encounter with a young student at the Café Bullier.

EXCERPT 2   UE   i, e   pp. 91/4/4-98/2/6;   15 min.
                         107/2/5-16; 118/2/1-40

A condensation of act 2 using the quartet of principal singers: Magda, Lisette, and Prunier, all described in excerpt 1, and Ruggero, strong lyric tenor with a C4. This excerpt may be performed with or without chorus. A waiter (silent) is necessary to the scene.

Ruggero, upon the advice of Prunier, has gone to the Café Bullier to spend his first evening in Paris. Magda, wishing to relive an experience from the past, has done likewise. They meet, sit at a table, Magda under the assumed name of Paulette. When they get up to dance, Lisette, Magda's chambermaid, arrives, escorted by the poet Prunier. Of course she recognizes her mistress, but Prunier discreetly dissuades her from the truth and the four sing together of their love.

EXCERPT 3   UE   i, e   pp. 156-208   28 min.

Act 3 complete with Magda, Ruggero, Lisette, and Prunier, all described in excerpts 1 and 2, plus a Majordomo, bass.

Ruggero has brought Magda to his summer house on the Riviera and has written to his family for permission to marry her. He is unaware of her past which would disqualify her for marriage into his family. He sings of their future together in the aria "Dimmi che vuoi seguirmi." Lisette and Prunier enter, quarreling over Prunier's attempt to launch Lisette's acting career. She was a total failure in her debut and now returns to her former position as Magda's maid. When Ruggero shows Magda a letter from his mother welcoming the idea of his marriage, Magda breaks down and tells him the truth about herself and, despite his pleadings, bids him a tender farewell.

EXCERPT 3a   UE   i, e   pp. 156-70/2/5   10 min.

The first part of act 3, with Magda and Ruggero only, including Ruggero's aria.

EXCERPT 3b   UE   i, e   pp. 170-93/1/6   9 min.

Lisette, Prunier, Magda, and the Majordomo.

EXCERPT 3c   UE   i, e   pp. 193/2/1-208   9 min.

The final scene between Magda and Ruggero.

DER ROSENKAVALIER

(The Cavalier of the Rose)

Richard Strauss (1868-1949)

Vienna, 1744

EXCERPT 1   B&H   g, e   pp. 125/3/4-56   21 min.

The final portion of act 1 with the Marschallin, a lyric-spinto or dramatic soprano with a mature vocal quality and sensitivity; and Octavian, a young man played by a mezzo-soprano (Bb2-A4). Also appearing in this scene are four footmen (two tenors, baritone, bass) and a little black boy (silent).

The Marschallin is left alone in her boudoir, having been instructed by her cousin Baron Ochs von Lerchenau to give Octavian a silver rose to present to the Baron's fiancée. Musing before the mirror on her waning youth, the Marschallin realizes that she must soon give up her young lover Octavian. Octavian enters and is confused by her change of mood from the happy woman she was when they had been together earlier. He is stunned when she indicates that one day he will tire of her. After he has left, she realizes too late that she has forgotten to give him the silver rose and has not even kissed him good-bye.

EXCERPT 1a   B&H   g, e   pp. 125/3/4-52/1/6   18 min.

Same as above without footmen and little black boy.

EXCERPT 2   B&H   g, e   pp. 157-91/3/2;   29½ min.
                            194/2/1-229/3/3

A difficult scene involving Sophie, lyric soprano capable of sustaining a C#5; Octavian, mezzo-soprano; Baron Ochs, bass requiring strength at the extremes of his range (F#1-F#3) as well as comic acting ability; Faninal, baritone (Bb1-F#3); and Marianne, soprano (D3-A4). A majordomo, tenor; three Lackeys (tenor, baritone, bass) as well as a number of nonsinging servants complete the scene.

Faninal and his daughter Sophie nervously wait in the reception hall of their mansion for the arrival of the cavalier of the rose; Marianne, the girl's duenna, describes the arrival of a coach. Lackeys announce Octavian who rapturously presents Ochs's silver rose to Sophie. Chaperoned by Marianne, the two young people hold a polite conversation. They are rudely interrupted by Baron Ochs whose crude mannerisms repulse Sophie. While Faninal and Ochs retire to another room, Sophie and Octavian embrace each other, realizing their love.

EXCERPT 2a   B&H   g, e   pp. 161/2/3-86/2/5   12½ min.

The Presentation of the Rose with Sophie, Marianne, Octavian, and the Lackeys.

EXCERPT 3   B&H   g, e   pp. 278/4/2-96   11 min.

A monologue for Baron Ochs, bass, described in excerpt 2, capable of sustaining an E1 as well as an F3. Annina, mezzo-soprano (Bb2-F4), is an important character; a few of Baron Ochs's servants (baritones and basses) sing in unison.

The Baron has been wounded by Octavian who has drawn his sword to protect Sophie's honor. Ochs is seen soothing his wounded vanity with a bottle of wine. Annina, an intrigant, has been hired earlier by Ochs to seek out the chambermaid "Mariandel" (really Octavian in disguise) with whom the Baron has flirted. Annina is now, however, in Octavian's service as she presents Ochs with a note from "Mariandel" agreeing to a rendezvous. The Baron's wounds are recovered quickly as he gleefully waltzes about the room.

EXCERPT 4   B&H   g, e   pp. 421/3/1-51   16 min.

A ravishing trio for Sophie, the Marschallin, and Octavian (see vocal descriptions, excerpts 1 and 2), ending in the final duet between Sophie and Octavian. Essential to the scene are the brief roles of Faninal, baritone, and a little black boy, silent.

In an inn, Baron Ochs has been made a fool of and the Marschallin has intervened, forcing the Baron to renounce his marriage plans with Sophie. After the Baron has left, Octavian tries to explain his true feelings to the Marschallin. Full of understanding, she bids him follow his heart and go to Sophie. In the trio that follows, the Marschallin bravely faces the fact that she is losing her young lover; Octavian comments on the graciousness of the lady; and Sophie is overwhelmed by the reality of the situation. The Marschallin exits leaving the two lovers in an embrace, declaring their love. They run off happily; the curtain closes as the little black boy runs back onstage to pick up Sophie's handkerchief.

THE SAINT OF BLEECKER STREET

Gian-Carlo Menotti (1911-)

Lower East Side, New York City, 1950

EXCERPT 1   GS (revised)   e, g   pp. 73-116/1/2   14½ min.

The scene centers around four women: Annina, strong lyric soprano (D3-B4); Carmela, lighter lyric soprano (E3-B4); Maria Corona, soprano with a more mature quality (C3-Ab4); and Assunta, mezzo-soprano (B2-Ab4). The other leading role is Michele, tenor with a strong B3. Also in the cast are Concettina (speaking role), a girl about five; a boy about ten; a woman, soprano; a tenor voice offstage which could be sung by Michele; other women and children.

An empty lot between two tenements on Mulberry Street has been decorated with lights for the San Gennaro Festival. Concettina is being dressed as an angel by the women; Assunta is seen at an open window singing a lullaby to her baby. Some women ask Annina to join the procession; she replies that her brother will not allow her to do so. Annina's friend Carmela confides that she is engaged to be married. Maria Corona comes rushing in, screaming that the Sons of San Gennaro threaten to take Annina by force if her brother will not let her take part in the procession. Annina is regarded by the community as a saint; her healing power is demonstrated as Maria Corona's dumb son utters a distortion of the word "mamma." Annina's brother Michele appears on the scene telling the other women to leave Annina alone. In a powerful duet, Michele swears to always protect his sister despite her vain efforts to make him understand why she wishes to heal sick people and to become a nun.

EXCERPT 1a   GS (revised)   e, g   pp. 81-99   6 min.

The section of the scene involving only the four leading women.

EXCERPT 1b   GS (revised)   e, g   pp. 101/2/2-   6½ min.
                    116/1/2

The section of excerpt 1 with the duet for Michele and Annina only.

EXCERPT 2   GS (revised)   e, g   pp. 156/3/3-212   19½ min.

A lengthy scene involving Desideria, mezzo-soprano (A2-A4); Michele, tenor requiring a C4 for his aria; Annina, strong lyric soprano; and Don Marco, bass. Also in the scene are the lesser roles of Carmela, soprano; Salvatore, baritone; a Bartender, bass; and a chorus of wedding guests.
    A wedding reception for Carmela and Salvatore is being held in the back room of an Italian restaurant. Desideria, a neighborhood outcast in love with Michele, comes in and asks the bartender to find Michele. Rejected because she was not invited to the wedding, she pleads with her lover in a powerful aria to take her with him into the reception. Don Marco, the parish priest, comes out of the room and blocks Desideria's way. As Michele raises his fist at the priest, Annina and the other guests come out of the reception room. Michele defiantly faces the crowd in his aria "I know that you all hate me." When Annina approaches Michele, Desideria comes forward and vents her jealousy of the sister, rousing Michele's anger to the point of stabbing Desideria. The girl dies in the arms of Annina, who prays for her soul.

EXCERPT 2a   GS (revised)   e, g   pp. 157/3/4-   8 min.
                    82/1/1

Michele and Desideria only, with offstage chorus, through the end of Desideria's aria.

EXCERPT 3   GS (revised)   e, g   pp. 213-50/1/1   13½ min.

A scene for Maria Corona, Annina, and Michele all described in excerpt 1. Don Marco, bass, sings only a few lines.

Maria Corona is selling newspapers in a subway station, conversing with Annina who is nervously waiting nearby. Eventually Don Marco brings in Michele who, after the murder of Desideria, has sought the priest's help in the confessional. Annina tells her brother that she is dying and wants to take the veil. Michele protests violently and as he leaves, he curses her and throws her down the stairs.

EXCERPT 4   GS (revised)   e, g   pp. 257/4/1-75   8 min.

A scene for Annina, Assunta, and Carmela, all described in excerpt 1, with a chorus of women and Don Marco, bass, in a short role. According to the score, Salvatore, Maria Corona, and her son are also in the scene but do not sing.

Annina is deathly ill and in her room, being watched over by Assunta and a group of women praying. Carmela offers Annina her wedding dress if she be allowed to take the veil that day. The priest confirms that this will be possible, and Annina expresses her joy in the short aria "Oh, my love, at last the hour is come."

SAMSON ET DALILA

(Samson and Delilah)

Camille Saint-Saëns (1835-1921)

Gaza, 1136 B.C.

EXCERPT 1   GS   f, e   pp. 79-99   13 min.
               Kal   e   pp. 58-77

This excerpt includes the aria "Printemps qui commence" for Delilah, mezzo-soprano with a strong low register, here singing nothing higher than an E4. Samson is a heroic tenor role, in this scene going only as high as F#3. The Old Hebrew is sung by a bass (E1-D3). A group of Philistine women sing and dance.

The gates of the temple of Dagon swing open; the seductress Delilah appears, followed by Philistine women bringing garlands of flowers. The Israelite hero Samson succumbs to Delilah's charms, despite warnings from the Old Hebrew.

EXCERPT 2   GS   f, e   pp. 100-37/1/1   16 min.
              Kal   e   pp. 78-110/1/1

Delilah, mezzo-soprano (F2 or Ab2-G4 or Bb4), sings the aria "Amour, viens aider" and a powerful duet with the High Priest of Dagon, dramatic baritone (C2-F3).

Delilah waits outside her dwelling for Samson, calling upon the god of love to aid her in gaining power over the leader of the enemy. The High Priest offers Delilah all the wealth of the temple if she will succeed in discovering the secret of Samson's great strength.

EXCERPT 3   GS   f, e   pp. 137-79   20 min.
              Kal   e   pp. 110-48

The great scene between Samson, dramatic tenor (E2-Bb3), and Delilah, mezzo-soprano (A2-Bb4), with a group of Philistine soldiers (silent).

Samson arrives at the dwelling of Delilah. The powerful Israelite is still hesitant, but gradually his sense of duty is overcome by temptation. As she sings a sensuous love song, "Mon coeur s'ouvre à ta voix," a storm gathers, forcing Samson to remain in her dwelling for the night. Delilah, triumphantly discovering the secret of Samson's strength, summons the soldiers to take Samson captive.

EXCERPT 3a   GS   f, e   pp. 137-62/2/1   14 min.
              Kal   e   pp. 110-31/4/1

Same as above without soldiers, concluding at the end of Delilah's aria; therefore considerably less demanding vocally.

THE SEAGULL

Thomas Pasatieri (1945-)

Russia, 1890s

EXCERPT 1   Bel   e   pp. 81-90/1/3   2½ min.

This short excerpt is a trio for three women's voices: Irina Arkadina (Eb3-Bb4), spinto soprano with some agility; Masha (Db3-Ab4), lyric soprano; and Nina (Bb2-G4), lyric mezzo-soprano. Dr. Dorn, tenor, sings one solo line.

In the garden of Sorin's estate, Mme Arkadina, a famous actress, and the two young girls Masha and Nina are being photographed by Dr. Dorn. The mature actress buoyantly boasts of the secrets of her eternal youth.

EXCERPT 2   Bel   e   pp. 97/3/1-104   4 min.

A scene between Nina, lyric mezzo-soprano (F3-G4), and Constantine, baritone (C#2-G3), who sings an aria with a high tessitura and requiring agility.

Constantine, a young writer in love with Nina, appears with a seagull he has shot, confessing that someday he intends to die in the same way as the seagull. He grows bitter about the failure of his play and Nina's coolness toward him.

EXCERPT 3   Bel   e   pp. 124-35/3/1   5½ min.

This excerpt has a long aria for Masha, powerful lyric soprano (Bb2-C5). Trigorin, baritone, a leading character in the opera, sings only a few lines. (The entrance of Nina, indicated in the score, may be omitted.)

In Sorin's dining room, Masha drunkenly confesses that even though she plans to marry Medvedenko, a schoolteacher, she is in love with the young writer Constantine.

EXCERPT 4   Bel   e   pp. 141/2/2-54/2/1   5½ min.

A highly emotional scene between Mme Arkadina (Bb2-B4) and Constantine (Bb1-G#3) described in excerpts 1 and 2.

Constantine has attempted suicide and his mother, Mme Arkadina, is bandaging his head wound. They recall their happiness when Constantine was a child. Abruptly Constantine harangues Arkadina for her involvement with Trigorin who is too cowardly to accept Constantine's challenge to a duel and who is philandering with Constantine's sweetheart Nina. A violent quarrel ends in reconciliation.

EXCERPT 5   Bel   e   pp. 187-212/3/1   11½ min.

An extended duet for Nina, high mezzo-soprano (B2-C5) and Constantine, high baritone (C2-G3). Trigorin, baritone, sings one offstage line.

Constantine remains writing at this desk while other guests are dining. Nina bursts into the study and Constantine, spurred by Nina's fear of being discovered, locks the doors. He tells Nina he still loves her in spite of her past affair with Trigorin. Nina confesses she will always love Trigorin even though he abandoned her. Left alone, the dejected Constantine throws his manuscripts into the stove.

LA SONNAMBULA

(The Sleepwalker)

Vincenzo Bellini (1801-1835)

A Swiss Village, Early Nineteenth Century

EXCERPT 1   GS/Kal   i, e   pp. 78-85/3/6   9½ min.

A duet for Amina, coloratura soprano (D3-C5) capable of sustaining a florid *bel canto* line, and Elvino, extremely high lyric tenor (F2-C4).

Amina, betrothed to Elvino, has captured the attentions of Count Rodolfo, a stranger in the village. For this, Elvino reproaches her severely. Her tears stop him and he begs her forgiveness. The lovers then unite in a duet of reconciliation.

SUMMER AND SMOKE

Lee Hoiby (1926-)

Glorious Hill, Mississippi, Early Twentieth Century

EXCERPT 1   Bel   e   pp. 11-39   15 min.

A scene for eighteen-year-old Alma Winemiller, soprano (D3-Ab4), and John Buchanan, Jr., baritone (B1-F3), supported by the Reverend Mr. Winemiller, bass baritone (C2-B2), and Mrs. Winemiller, speaking role; Roger Doremus, tenor, and Rosa Gonzales (mute in this scene) are on stage briefly. Other mute characters may be used at the director's discretion.

Alma, waiting on a park bench near the fountain for the youthful Roger Doremus who is playing in the Fourth of July band concert, is approached by John, now a medical student home from college. Their interest in one another, kindled in childhood, is renewed and he invites her to go riding with him some afternoon. He is distracted, however, by the appearance of the more accessible Rosa Gonzales and follows after her, leaving Alma.

EXCERPT 2   Bel   e   pp. 40-66   12 min.

Nellie Elwell, soprano (C#3-Bb4), Alma, soprano (C3-Ab4), and the eccentric Mrs. Winemiller (speaking role with some pitches indicated) are in this scene. The Reverend Mr. Winemiller (B1-F3) makes a brief appearance.

While Alma Winemiller is giving Nellie a singing lesson, Mrs. Winemiller sneaks into the room, interrupts the lesson, and reveals Alma's longing for John. The scene turns into an argument between Alma and her mother.

EXCERPT 3   Bel   e   pp. 205-30/2/2   12 min.

Rev. Winemiller has offstage speaking lines and one singing line in this excerpt featuring John (C#2-F3) and Alma (D3-Ab4). In place of the procession of mourners indicated on p. 231 of the piano-vocal score, the death of Dr. Buchanan could be conveyed by the Reverend Mr. Winemiller's return to the room just as John begins his exit.

Alma has called Dr. Buchanan, John's father, asking him to break up a noisy, drunken party next door, a party celebrating the forthcoming marriage of John Buchanan to Rosa Gonzales. In the ensuing argument with Papa Gonzales, Dr. Buchanan has been shot and seriously wounded. Excerpt 3 begins as John and Alma confront one another and exchange recriminations. When Alma is requested by the dying Dr. Buchanan to sing for him, she leaves John remorsefully waiting alone and joins her father at Dr. Buchanan's bedside (offstage).

EXCERPT 4   Bel   e   pp. 257-81/3/1   9 min.

Scenes 10 and 11 of act 2 of the opera may be combined for an interesting excerpt. Nellie (C#3-A4) and John (B1-F3) are featured in the first three minutes, while Nellie and Alma (C#3-Bb4) supported briefly by Mrs. Bassett (C3-E4) and Rosemary (D3-Gb4) are featured in the second portion (scene 11).

Nellie, now a mature young lady, surprises John with a visit to his office. She is on a Thanksgiving vacation from school. John is attracted to her and kisses her. Then, with ambivalence and self-restraint, he sends her away. After a short interlude, the scene changes to the park during the Christmas season. Nellie gives Alma a present inscribed: "To Alma from Nellie and John." Shocked by the implication of the inscription, Alma quickly leaves before Nellie can tell her the news of her engagement to John.

SUOR ANGELICA

(Sister Angelica)

Giacomo Puccini (1858-1924)

A Convent in Italy, Late Seventeenth Century

EXCERPT 1   Ric   i, e   pp. 56/3/2-82/3/2   17 min.

Sister Angelica should be sung by a lyric-spinto soprano (A2-C4) capable of sustaining a high *pianissimo*. The Princess is a dramatic mezzo-soprano or contralto (G#2-F#4).

Sister Angelica, forced by her family to enter a convent, receives a visit from her aunt the Princess. The purpose of the visit is for Angelica to sign over her half of the family's inheritance, for her younger sister is to be married. The Princess remains unforgiving of Angelica's mortal sin, and when Angelica inquires about her illegitimate son, her aunt replies that the child has been dead for two years. Angelica faints with horror, recovering in time to sign the document. Left alone, she sings an aria, "Senza mamma," to her child up in heaven.

SUSANNAH

Carlisle Floyd (1926-)

New Hope Valley, Tennessee, Early Twentieth Century

EXCERPT 1   B&H   e   pp. 21-34   11 min.

The role of Susannah calls for a lyric-spinto soprano (Bb2-Bb4) with strength at the extremes of her range and a youthful appearance. Sam is a dramatic tenor (D2-A3) and Little Bat, a character tenor.

Susannah Polk is accompanied home from a square dance by Little Bat, a shifty-eyed youth. While they are sitting on the front porch, Susannah looks at the stars and sings the aria "Ain't it a pretty night." At the arrival of Susannah's brother Sam, Little Bat dashes off and Sam joins his sister in a folk song and some horseplay.

EXCERPT 1a   B&H   e   pp. 21-29/2/3   8 min.

The portion of excerpt 1 with Susannah and Little Bat only, up to the end of Susannah's aria.

EXCERPT 2   B&H   e   pp. 51-62   7½ min.

Same characters as excerpt 1.

Susannah, who has been seen bathing naked in the creek, is sitting on the front steps of her house when Little Bat comes to call.

His father and the other elders have condemned her for exposing herself, and Little Bat has even been forced into confessing that Susannah has let him make love to her. Susannah, angered at the lie, drives Little Bat away from the house. Sam, who has overheard, comes from the house and tries to comfort Susannah in the aria "It's about the way people is made."

EXCERPT 3   B&H   e   pp. 63-73   8½ min.

Another scene for Susannah, lyric-spinto soprano, and Sam, dramatic tenor.

Susannah and her brother Sam are standing in front of their house discussing the change in Susannah's life since the day she was seen bathing. He urges her to go to the revival meeting; she protests that she has done nothing wrong. She also begs Sam not to go off on a hunting trip and leave her alone, and above all, not to get drunk. He leaves, promising to return the next day, while Susannah promises him that she will attend the revival.

EXCERPT 4   B&H   e   pp. 93-104   12 min.

Susannah, lyric-spinto soprano, sings the folklike ballad "The Trees on the Mountains" with many sustained Bb4's. Blitch, bass-baritone (Bb1-F3), is also in this excerpt.

Susannah is in front of her home singing a sad folk song. The Reverend Olin Blitch comes to visit her and urges her to pray God for forgiveness. She continues to protest that she has done nothing wrong, and tells the preacher how miserable she has been. Seeing that the poor girl will not give in to his spiritual pleading, Blitch then tells her about his lonely life and how he needs a woman just as any other man does. Knowing that her brother is away for the night, he accompanies her into the house.

EXCERPT 5   B&H   e   pp. 112-30   10 min.

Susannah, Sam, and Little Bat, described in excerpt 1, are in this scene. The four elders (tenor, tenor, baritone, bass) could be members of the chorus needed for this excerpt.

Sam returns home, slightly drunk, from a hunting trip. When his sister Susannah tells him she was seduced by the Reverend Mr. Blitch, Sam takes his shotgun and heads for the place where Blitch

is baptizing folks. A shot is heard in the distance; Little Bat runs
to tell Susannah that Sam has killed the preacher. When the people come to drive Susannah out of the valley she confronts them
with a gun and stubbornly refuses to move from her house. Only
Susannah and Little Bat remain; she gently draws him to her, then
slaps his face. He runs off, leaving Susannah to spend the rest of
her life a lonely and embittered woman.

IL TABARRO

(The Cloak)

Giacomo Puccini (1858-1924)

Paris, Early Twentieth Century

EXCERPT 1   Ric   i, e   pp. 31/1/2-63 (sug-   12 min.
                        gested intro. pp. 30/1/1-30/2/4)

The principal characters in this excerpt are Giorgetta, lyric-
spinto soprano (C3-C5) with dramatic qualities; Frugola, mezzo-
soprano (Bb2-A4); and Luigi, strong lyric or dramatic tenor (F2-
Bb3). Other important characters are Tinca, tenor; Talpa, bass;
and Michele, baritone, who sings only one line in this scene.

Frugola, a junk collector, comes to Michele's barge looking for
her husband Talpa and strikes up a conversation with Giorgetta,
Michele's wife. Frugola chats at length about her domestic life and
her cat. Soon the longshoremen are ready to quit work for the day;
Tinca will head for the nearest tavern, but Luigi says that everything, even love, is forbidden to the poor. As Talpa and Frugola
prepare to go home, they tell of their dream of a little cottage of
their own. Giorgetta's dream is to go back to her native village of
Belleville. Luigi, born in the same village, joins her in a nostalgic
duet.

EXCERPT 2   Ric   i, e   pp. 65-120   21 min.

This is the portion of the opera involving the three leading characters: Giorgetta, lyric-spinto soprano; Luigi, strong lyric or

dramatic tenor; and Michele, dramatic baritone (G1 or Bb1-G3). Two lovers, soprano and tenor, appear briefly, but a cut from 98/3/2 to 101/2/2 could eliminate that section of music.

Luigi who loves Giorgetta, explains to her husband Michele that he has remained upon the barge after work to thank Michele for hiring him for the next journey. When Michele goes to light the lanterns, Giorgetta tells Luigi she will light a match when it is safe for him to return. Michele then begs Giorgetta to love him as she once did, and they reminisce of happier days when their child was still alive. Michele's aria "Nulla! Silenzio!" reveals his anguish and growing jealousy. He lights his pipe; naturally, Luigi thinks it is Giorgetta's signal and jumps onto the barge. Michele catches him and forces a confession from him before strangling him to death. Giorgetta nervously comes out of the cabin, telling Michele she only wanted to be near him. He then beckons her to come under his cloak which he opens to reveal the corpse of Luigi.

THE TAMING OF THE SHREW

Vittorio Giannini (1903-1966)

Padua, Sixteenth Century

EXCERPT 1   Ric e pp. 19/3/1-43/2/2   6 min.

A trio for Lucentio, tenor (E2-B3); Tranio, baritone (B1-E3); and Biondello, bass (G1-D3).

Lucentio has fallen in love with Bianca, daughter of Baptista. Yet unknown in Padua, Lucentio and his servant Tranio agree to exchange clothing so that Lucentio may gain entrance to Baptista's house posing as a tutor to Bianca. This arrangement baffles the other servant Biondello, and a lively trio develops.

EXCERPT 2   Ric e pp. 44-104   20½ min.

Required for this scene are Katharina, soprano with dramatic ability; Lucentio and Gremio, leading tenors and Grumio, second tenor; Petruchio, high dramatic baritone; Hortensio and Tranio, baritones; Baptista, leading bass, and Biondello, lesser bass.

Petruchio and his servant Grumio arrive in Padua and knock at
Hortensio's house. Petruchio wishes to take a wife; Hortensio suggests Katharina, daughter of Baptista Minola. Petruchio is determined to have her despite her reputation for being ill-tempered.
He also agrees to introduce Hortensio as a music teacher. Lucentio
appears, disguised as a tutor for Katharina's young sister Bianca,
hoping to woo her. In addition, Bianca has two other suitors:
Gremio, who has been responsible for finding a tutor for Bianca,
and Tranio, disguised as and speaking for his master Lucentio. The
men knock on Baptista's door; they are admitted in their respec-
tive capacities. Katharina responds to the music lesson of Hortensio by breaking the lute over his head. She reacts equally unfavor-
ably to the courtship of Petruchio; the curtain falls as she defiantly hurls objects about the room.

EXCERPT 2a   Ric e   pp. 84/3/4-104   7 min.

The final portion of excerpt 2 with Petruchio, Katharina, and
Baptista. The lines of Gremio and Tranio on p. 102 need not be
sung.

EXCERPT 3   Ric e   pp. 105-43/3/1   12½ min.

The characters in this excerpt are Lucentio and Grumio, tenors;
Petruchio and Hortensio, baritones; Katharina and Bianca, sopranos. It is important that Bianca have a pleasant lyric timbre in
contrast to the rougher dramatic quality of Katharina.
Hortensio and Lucentio have come to Baptista's garden in the
roles of musician and scholar, respectively. They attempt to woo
Bianca while giving her lessons. Katharina's suitor Petruchio and
his servant Grumio arrive, both dressed in garish rags purposely
to taunt the shrewish Kate whom they mock as they exit.

EXCERPT 4   Ric e   pp. 143/3/2-54/4/2   3 min.

A scene for the contrasting soprano voices of Katharina and
Bianca, and Baptista, bass.
A dramatic argument between the two sisters. Katharina is
fiercely jealous of the younger Bianca who has many suitors but
cannot marry until Katharina has found a husband. Their father

Baptista desperately tries to quell the fight and comfort the weeping Bianca.

EXCERPT 5   Ric   e   pp. 154/4/3-72   9 min.

A love duet for Bianca, lyric soprano (Eb3-B4), and Lucentio, tenor (Eb2-B3).

As the evening grows dark, Lucentio stealthily enters Baptista's garden to woo Bianca, this time revealing his true identity. She soon yields to his pleadings, and the two sing rapturously of their love.

EXCERPT 6   Ric   e   pp. 310/4/2-23   7 min.

The final duet between Katharina, soprano (F3-A4), and Petruchio, baritone (C#2-G3).

Petruchio has married the shrew Katharina, and, as exemplified in this duet, has succeeded in taming her. Their love is now complete and harmonious.

THE TENDER LAND

Aaron Copland (1900-)

A Farm in the Midwest, June, About 1930

EXCERPT 1   B&H   e   pp. 26-86   24 min.

Laurie, a lyric soprano (C3-A4, opt. C5), sings mostly in the middle range; she is a seventeen-year-old girl and should have a youthful quality. Ma Moss, her mother, is a low mezzo-soprano (G2-F4); Grandpa, a bass (F1-D3); Martin, tenor, has a range from C2-Bb3; Top, baritone, from A1-F#3.

Laurie, Ma Moss's elder daughter, is graduating from high school. As two strangers, Top and Martin, enter her sheltered and isolated world, she begins to get a feeling for a larger life than she has known. The strangers are accepted into the community as harvesters.

EXCERPT 1a   B&H   e   pp. 26-40/2/4   9 min.

The opening of excerpt 1 uses only Laurie and Ma Moss.

EXCERPT 1b   B&H   e   pp. 40/3/1-67/2/2   6½ min.

This portion of excerpt 1 uses Laurie, Martin, Top, and Grandpa.

EXCERPT 2   B&H   e   pp. 131/4/4-44   9½ min.

Laurie and Martin, lyric soprano and tenor, have this scene together. Martin has some dramatic passages and a B3.

At Laurie's graduation party Martin is dancing with Laurie. They stop for a while and in the conversation, Martin confesses that he is tired of wandering about the land and would like to settle down. The pair fall in love and sing a simple but heartfelt duet.

EXCERPT 3   B&H   e   pp. 157-71/4/3   8 min.

Another scene for Laurie and Martin.

Martin has fallen in love with Laurie but Grandpa disapproves. Martin and his friend Top have been ordered to leave the farm the next morning. Martin, unable to sleep, comes out of the shed into the night; Laurie, also unable to sleep, appears at her window. She comes rushing out of the house knowing that Martin cannot stay close to her as he had wanted to. She begs to run away with him and they make plans to elope at daybreak.

EXCERPT 4   B&H   e   pp. 171/4/4-84/4/2   7 min.

Martin, tenor, and Top, baritone, sing mostly in the middle range in this scene.

Martin, having planned to elope with Laurie, muses about his future. His friend and co-worker Top comes along and convinces Martin that nomadic life is not right for a girl like Laurie. Martin is heard singing "Laurie, forgive me" as the two men wander off.

EXCERPT 5   B&H   e   pp. 184/4/3-203   12 min.

In addition to Laurie, lyric soprano, and Ma Moss, mezzo-soprano, there is in this scene a speaking character, Laurie's younger sister, Beth, who should either be a child or a young girl capable of giving the impression of a twelve-year-old.

Laurie, anticipating elopement with Martin, comes out to the shed at daybreak only to find him gone. Her mother and sister console her but she has changed. She feels she must break away from the protection of her family and start a new life. As she goes down the road, her mother turns her protectiveness to the younger daughter, beginning the cycle anew.

TOSCA

Giacomo Puccini (1858-1924)

Rome, 1800

EXCERPT 1   GS   i, e   pp. 1-72/2/3   26½ min.
              Ric   i   pp. 1-72/2/3
              Kal/Ric   i, e   pp. 1-81/1/3

A scene featuring Mario Cavaradossi, strong lyric tenor (Eb2-Bb3) capable of sustaining high notes, and Floria Tosca, lyric-spinto soprano (Eb3-Bb4), with Angelotti, bass, and Sacristan, *basso buffo*.

Cesare Angelotti, a political prisoner, seeks asylum at the Church of Sant'Andrea della Valle, where his sister has left women's clothes for his disguise. He barely has time to conceal himself before the Sacristan appears, going about his duties. A moment later the painter Cavaradossi returns to work and compares, in the aria "Recondita armonia," the blue-eyed Mary Magdalen he has been painting to the beauty of his beloved Floria Tosca, the opera singer. Making sure that the Sacristan has left, Angelotti reappears, relieved to find his old friend Cavaradossi who promises him aid in escaping. Once more Angelotti hides as Tosca arrives to meet her lover. Mario calms the jealous Tosca in a passionate love duet and arranges to meet her that evening. Tosca leaves; Mario and Angelotti hurriedly complete their escape plans.

EXCERPT 1a   GS   i, e   pp. 30/3/1-57 (suggested   13 min.
                                   intro. from 29/4/4)
               Ric   i   pp. 30/3/1-57 (suggested intro. from
                                   29/4/4)
               Kal/Ric   i, e   pp. 36-68/2/4 (suggested intro.
                                   from 35/1/3)

The duet between Tosca and Cavaradossi only.

EXCERPT 2   GS   i, e   pp. 72-126   14½ min.
              Ric   i   pp. 72-126
              Kal/Ric   i, e   pp. 82/3/1-144

Continued from excerpt 1, this is the second half of act 1. Tosca
and the Sacristan have been described in excerpt 1; Scarpia is a
dramatic baritone (B1-F3) capable of subtle lyricism and powerful
acting; Spoletta, a tenor. A choir of men and boys sings in the beginning of the scene, and a full chorus appears in the procession at
the end, reciting in unison parts of the Roman Catholic mass.

The members of a choir appear in the Church of Sant'Andrea
della Valle to prepare for a festival to celebrate Napoleon's defeat.
Their excitement is hushed by the entrance of Baron Scarpia, chief
of police. An escaped prisoner, Cesare Angelotti, has been traced
to the church. A fan is discovered; it belongs to the Marchesa Attavanti, Angelotti's sister, left as part of a disguise for her brother
who dropped it in his haste. Another clue is a lunch basket refused
by Cavaradossi but which has now been found completely empty,
its contents devoured by the hungry prisoner. Tosca returns to discover that Mario has disappeared; Scarpia takes this as an opportu-
nity to play on her jealousy. She has already noticed Mario's painting of Mary Magdalen resembling the Marchesa Attavanti; when
Scarpia shows her the fan, she is convinced of Mario's infidelity.
As the weeping Tosca leaves the church, Scarpia orders her followed. During a religious procession, Scarpia gloats over the anticipation of destroying his rival and having Tosca for himself, his
voice blending with the chorus in a majestic and powerful "Te
Deum."

EXCERPT 3   GS   i, e   pp. 127-250   39 min.
              Ric   i   pp. 127-250
              Kal/Ric   i, e   pp. 145-272

The complete act 2, because of its through-composed music, becomes awkward when divided into shorter segments, as in excerpts
3a, 3b, and 3c. Only five characters are involved, in addition to an
offstage chorus. Tosca, soprano (C3-C5) has many sustained high
notes and a great deal of dramatic singing and acting, as well as
the extremely lyric "Vissi d'arte." Mario Cavaradossi, tenor (Eb2-
Bb3), though a short role in this scene, has many dramatic out-
bursts. Scarpia, baritone (B1-Gb3), requires strength and subtlety
in an extensive role. Supporting roles are Spoletta, tenor, and
Sciarrone, baritone.

In his apartment in the Palazzo Farnese, Scarpia awaits news of
his prey—Angelotti and Cavaradossi. He sends a note to Tosca who
is singing a victory cantata nearby, informing her that he has word
of her lover. Scarpia's henchmen bring in the captured Cavaradossi
who refuses to admit Angelotti's hiding place. Tosca arrives in time
to see her lover consigned to the torture chamber. Scarpia begins
working on Tosca to get the answers he wants; hearing Mario's cries
of agony, she relents. Just then Sciarrone arrives with the news that
Napoleon has not been defeated after all; Mario's shout of victory
enrages Scarpia to the point of pronouncing a death sentence on
the captured painter. Then Scarpia names his price for Mario's freedom: Tosca's love. After resisting his advances, she finally consents.
He informs her that a mock execution will be necessary, and gives
Spoletta some secret instructions. While Scarpia writes out a pass-
port for the lady to leave Rome, Tosca takes a knife from the table.
As Scarpia turns to embrace her, she drives the knife into his heart.

EXCERPT 3a   GS   i, e   pp. 165/3/3-250   30 min.
               Ric   i   pp. 165/3/3-250
               Kal/Ric   i, e   pp. 184-272

Same as excerpt 3 without the offstage chorus.

EXCERPT 3b   GS   i, e   pp. 203/2/1-50   18½ min.
                Ric   i   pp. 203/2/1-50
                Kal/Ric   i, e   pp. 223/2/1-72

Tosca, Scarpia, and Spoletta only from excerpt 3.

EXCERPT 3c   GS   i, e   pp. 203/2/1-27   8½ min.
                Ric   i   pp. 203/2/1-27
                Kal/Ric   i, e   pp. 223/2/1-47

Tosca and Scarpia only from excerpt 3, concluding with "Vissi d'arte."

EXCERPT 4   GS   i, e   pp. 264/3/2-97/2/3   11½ min.
                Ric   i   pp. 264/3/2-97/2/3
                Kal/Ric   i, e   pp. 286/3/2-321/2/3

Tosca and Cavaradossi (see excerpt 1 for vocal descriptions) are in this scene.

Mario Cavaradossi is brought out from his cell to the terrace of Castel Sant'Angelo. With only one hour left to live, he is permitted to write a last letter to his beloved Tosca, which he does while singing the nostalgic aria "E lucevan le stelle." Tosca arrives unexpectedly, tells her lover about the murder of Scarpia and instructs him in his mock execution and their plans for escape.

LA TRAVIATA

Giuseppe Verdi (1813-1901)

Paris, 1840

EXCERPT 1   B&H   i, e   pp. 16/2/1-47/4/3   9½ min.
                GS/Kal   i, e   pp. 18-46
                Ric   i, e   pp. 27-74/2/2
                Ric   i   pp. 20/1/5-51

This portion of act 1 includes the drinking song "Libiamo ne'-lieti calici" and the duet between Violetta, soprano (C3-Bb4) with

flexibility, and Alfredo, lyric tenor (E2-Bb3). A chorus of party
guests include Flora, mezzo-soprano; Gastone, tenor; the Doctor,
the Baron, the Marquis, basses; Gaston is the only one with solo
lines.

Violetta, entertaining guests in her home, has persuaded Alfredo
Germont, whom she has just met, to sing a drinking song in which
she and the other guests join. When the guests go off to dance in an
adjoining ballroom, Violetta is seized by a sudden faintness. The
concerned Alfredo stays behind; as Violetta revives, he tells her
that he has loved her since he first saw her a year ago. She takes it
all lightly but does give him a camellia which she tells him he may
bring back to her when faded. He is delighted that they will meet
again.

EXCERPT 1a   B&H i, e pp. 36/3/6-44/1/4   4½ min.
                 GS/Kal i, e pp. 36/3/3-42
                 Ric i, e pp. 54/3/5-67/2/4
                 Ric i pp. 39/2/5-47/2/4

The duet between Violetta and Alfredo only.

EXCERPT 2   B&H i, e pp. 76-81; 88-125/2/2;   31 min.
                         129/3/1-129/5/6
                GS/Kal i, e pp. 70-75; 81-115/5/3; 120/3/1-
                         120/5/6
                Ric i, e pp. 113-22; 130-93/3/3; 201/3/1-202
                Ric i pp. 77-83; 90-132/1/4; 137/2/1-137/4/6

This scene features the leading characters of the opera. Violetta
and Alfredo, described in excerpt 1, need solid techniques and dramatic subtlety. Germont, baritone (C2-Gb3), needs maturity and
strength in the upper register for his aria "Di Provenza." Also included are Alfredo's "De' miei bollenti spiriti," and an extended
duet for Violetta and Germont. Supporting roles are Annina, soprano or mezzo-soprano; Giuseppe, tenor; and a Commissioner,
bass.

Violetta and Alfredo have been spending three happy months
together at a country house near Paris. Alfredo learns that Violetta
has sold many of her belongings in order to keep their secluded
home. Alfredo, ashamed, hurries to Paris to obtain funds. While he

is gone, his father arrives, finding Violetta to be much more of a
gracious lady than he had imagined. Nevertheless, he asks her to
give up Alfredo for the sake of his sister's marriage. Upon Alfredo's
return, Violetta utters a tender farewell and leaves a note telling
Alfredo it is good-bye forever. The heartbroken Alfredo is comforted in vain by his father; seeing a party invitation on the desk,
the young man burns with jealousy and rushes off to seek revenge.

EXCERPT 2a   B&H   i, e   pp. 89/2/1-112   15 min.
               GS/Kal i, e   pp. 82/1/3-103
               Ric   i, e   pp. 132/2/1-72
               Ric   i   pp. 91/2/1-117

The duet for Violetta and Germont from excerpt 2.

EXCERPT 3   B&H   i, e   pp. 201-9/2/4; 210/5/4-   22½ min.
                        220/2/8; 221/4/1-28/3/3; 231/1/2-41
              GS/Kal   i, e   pp. 191-99; 201/5/4-11/3/1;
                        213/1/3-19/5/2; 222/2/1-32
              Ric   i, e   pp. 320-33/3/1; 335/4/3-52/3/1;
                        354/3/2-65/4/3; 370/2/1-87
              Ric   i   pp. 207-15/4/2; 217/4/4-27/4/1;
                        229/2/3-36/3/1; 239-49

Again the leading characters are Violetta, Alfredo, and briefly,
Germont, all described in excerpts 1 and 2. Important supporting
roles are Annina, soprano or mezzo-soprano, and the Doctor, bass.
The offstage chorus can be cut if necessary.
   Violetta is in her bedroom, forsaken and deathly ill, attended
only by her maid, Annina. Her doctor reassures Violetta but in an
aside to Annina he confides that her mistress has very little time
to live. Violetta rereads a letter of reconciliation from Alfredo's
father, promising Alfredo's return, but she fears she will die before
he comes back. Alfredo does finally arrive and together they sing
of a brighter future in the duet "Parigi, o cara, noi lascieremo."
As she tries to get dressed, she falters; the Doctor and the remorseful Germont enter in time for a few parting words before she expires.

EXCERPT 3a   B&H   i, e   pp. 201-9/2/4;   10 min.
                                210/5/4-210/5/5
                 GS/Kal   i, e   191-99; 201/5/4-201/5/5
                 Ric   i, e   pp. 320-33/3/1; 335/4/3-335/4/4
                 Ric   i   pp. 207-15/4/2; 217/4/4-217/4/5

The opening portion of excerpt 3 with Violetta, Annina, and the Doctor only.

EXCERPT 3b   B&H   i, e   pp. 205-9/2/4; 210/5/4-   12 min.
                                20/2/8; 221/4/1-28/3/3; 231/1/2-/4/4
                 GS/Kal   i, e   pp. 195/2/3-99; 201/5/4-11/3/1;
                                213/1/3-19/5/2; 222/2/1-/4/5
                 Ric   i, e   pp. 326/3/1-33/3/1; 335/4/3-52/3/1;
                                354/3/2-65/4/3; 370/2/1-71
                 Ric   i   pp. 211/3/4-15/4/2; 217/4/4-27/4/1;
                                229/2/3-36/3/1; 239

Annina, Violetta, and Alfredo only; includes Violetta's aria and the duet.

IL TROVATORE

(The Toubadour)

Giuseppe Verdi (1813-1901)

Spain, Mid-Fifteenth Century

EXCERPT 1   B&H   i, e   pp. 22-30/2/5; 33-50/2/1;   15 min.
                                51/1/2-52
                 GS/Kal   i, e   pp. 20-27/2/5; 29/2/3-46/2/4;
                                47/2/1-48
                 Ric   i   pp. 21-29/1/4; 31/2/3-48/2/5;
                                49/1/6-50

The leading characters in this excerpt are Leonora, lyric-spinto soprano (Ab2-Db5) with agility and a trill; Manrico, lyric or dramatic tenor (D2-Bb3); and Count di Luna, baritone (C2-Bb3). Inez, soprano or mezzo-soprano, is a supporting role.

In the gardens of the palace of Aliaferia, Leonora strolls with her companion Inez. Singing the aria "Tacea la notte placida," Leonora confides her interest in an unknown troubadour who has serenaded her. As the ladies enter the palace, the Count di Luna appears just before the troubadour's song is heard offstage. Leonora comes out of the palace and mistakes the Count for the troubadour. After she realizes her mistake, the two rivals for her love draw swords and rush away to fight a duel.

EXCERPT 1a   B&H   i, e   pp. 22-30/2/5; 33-35   7½ min.
               GS/Kal   i, e   pp. 20-27/2/5; 29/2/3-31
               Ric   i   pp. 21-29/1/4; 31/2/3-33

Leonora and Inez only in a portion of excerpt 1.

EXCERPT 1b   B&H   i, e   pp. 36-50/2/1; 51/1/2-52   7 min.
               GS/Kal   i, e   pp. 32-46/2/4; 47/2/1-48
               Ric   i   pp. 34-48/2/5; 49/1/6-50

The trio for Leonora, Manrico, and the Count only.

EXCERPT 2   B&H   i, e   pp. 53-89/4/5; 90/3/6-91   19 min.
               GS/Kal   i, e   pp. 49-86/2/6; 87/1/5-87/4/14
               Ric   i   pp. 51-89; 90/3/5-91

This scene features Azucena, mezzo-soprano (A2-A4 or C5), in her arias "Stride la vampa" and "Condotta ell'era in ceppi." These arias require dramatic power as well as agility. A vocal description of Manrico can be found in excerpt 1. A group of gypsies sings the famous "Anvil Chorus"; two minor roles are old Gypsy, bass, and Messenger, tenor.

Around the gypsy campfire, Azucena, an old gypsy woman, recounts the vision of her mother being burned for witchcraft. After the others have left, she continues her story to Manrico, whom she has brought up as her son. In an attempt to avenge her mother's death, she wanted to throw the infant brother of the Count di Luna into the fire; instead, in her frenzy, she burned her own child and adopted the infant Manrico in his stead. She then asks Manrico why he spared di Luna's life in the duel, and encourages him to kill his enemy.

EXCERPT 2a   B&H   i, e   pp. 66-89/4/5; 90/3/6-91   12 min.
              GS/Kal   i, e   pp. 63-86/2/6; 87/1/5-87/4/14
              Ric   i   pp. 66-89; 90/3/5-91

Azucena, Manrico, and Messenger only.

EXCERPT 3   B&H   i, e   pp. 186-204/2/2;   11½ min.
                   206/4/1-207
             GS/Kal   i, e   pp. 178-93/3/2; 196/4/2-97
             Ric   i   pp. 184-201/1/1; 204/2/1-205

The "Tower Scene" including Leonora's "D'amor sull'ali rosee" and Manrico's "Ah! che la morte ognora," with their duet (both characters described in excerpt 1). The supporting role of Ruiz, tenor, and an offstage men's chorus complete the scene.

Leonora, with the assistance of Ruiz, approaches the dungeon tower where Manrico is imprisoned. As she sings her aria, her thoughts turn toward her beloved. Manrico is heard, his closing words being "Do not forget me! Leonora, farewell!" An impressive ensemble is heard as the chanting priests provide the accompaniment with their "Miserere."

EXCERPT 4   B&H   i, e   pp. 208-22   7½ min.
             GS/Kal   i, e   pp. 198-213
             Ric   i   pp. 206-23

The characters are Leonora and Count di Luna, both described in excerpt 1.

The Count approaches Leonora outside the prison tower. She offers to marry the Count if he will free Manrico. So great is the Count's passion for Leonora that he consents. But Leonora, wishing to be faithful to Manrico unto death, secretly swallows poison from a ring she is wearing. Their duet ends with his anticipation of having Leonora for his own, and her asides that his prize will be a cold and lifeless bride.

EXCERPT 5   B&H   i, e   pp. 223-50   15 min.
             GS/Kal   i, e   pp. 214-39
             Ric   i   pp. 224-52

The characters are Azucena, Manrico, Leonora, and Count di Luna, described in excerpt 1 and 2.

Inside the dungeon, Manrico and Azucena await their execution, Azucena thinking with horror of the flames leaping around her. Manrico calms her and urges her to rest as they join in a nostalgic duet, "Ai nostri monti." Leonora rushes in with the news of Manrico's freedom. As the Count enters to claim his bride, Leonora perishes from the poison she has taken. Realizing that Leonora has cheated him, the Count orders Manrico to an immediate execution and drags Azucena to the window to witness the death of her son. She then tells the Count that Manrico was actually his brother, and rejoices that her mother's death has finally been avenged.

EXCERPT 5a   B&H   i, e   pp. 223-31   7 min.
               GS/Kal   i, e   pp. 214-22
               Ric   i   pp. 224-33

The duet between Azucena and Manrico only.

VANESSA

Samuel Barber (1910-)

Vanessa's Castle in a Northern County, About 1905

EXCERPT 1   GS (revised)   e, g   pp. 10/1/2-51   21½ min.

The opening scene features Vanessa, a lyric-spinto soprano with some florid singing and many sustained passages (Bb2-B4). She is a beautiful baroness about forty years old. Erika, her niece, about twenty, is a lyric mezzo-soprano (Db3-A4) whose singing lies in a high tessitura. Anatol, a man in his early twenties, is a tenor with dramatic and sustained singing from D2 to Bb3. The Old Baroness does not sing in this scene.

Vanessa watches a snowstorm raging outside, while her niece Erika reads aloud. A few minutes after Vanessa's mother, the old Baroness, who has refused to speak to her daughter for years, goes to bed, the sound of a sleigh is heard. Vanessa asks Erika to leave and to let her meet the man alone. Keeping her back to the door, Vanessa addresses the man in the doorway as Anatol and tells him

that she has waited twenty years, always knowing he would come.
Now, unless he loves her, he must leave. The man says that he believes he loves her. Vanessa whirls around to see this is not the man
she had expected and she cries to Erika for help. Erika assists her
aunt from the room and returns to find that the young man's
name is Anatol and he is the son of Vanessa's former lover who is
now dead. He pleads to stay because of the storm and Erika consents. Seated at the supper table prepared for his father, he opens
a bottle of wine and asks Erika's name.

EXCERPT 1a   GS (revised)   e, g   pp. 37/4/2-51   6 min.

This is the portion of excerpt 1 with only Erika and Anatol.

EXCERPT 2   GS (revised)   e, g   pp. 52-127
                            with chorus   25½ min.
                            without chorus   24½ min.

Added to the characters described in excerpt 1 are the Doctor, a
bass-baritone who needs warmth and expression (C2-Eb3). The
Baroness (mezzo-soprano) sings a little in this scene (A2-F4) and
the Minister appears in a mute role. The SATB chorus sings offstage at the end of the excerpt.

It is a bright Sunday morning a month later. Erika tells the Baroness that the night Anatol came, she stayed all night with him in
his room and that he has offered marriage. She might like to marry
him but by now Vanessa loves him quite blindly. Vanessa and Anatol return from ice skating and are shortly visited by the Doctor
who reminisces about old garden parties and dances.

The Baroness insists that Erika must speak to Anatol about marriage. She does, and at first Anatol hesitates saying he can't really
offer eternal love but they might have a good time traveling around
Europe together. As the others leave for church, Erika remains behind and when she hears the first hymn being sung she cries out
that she will not marry Anatol but will let Vanessa have him, "she
who for so little had to wait so long."

EXCERPT 3   GS (revised)   e, g   pp. 150-62/1/4   5½ min.

A scene for Vanessa and Anatol (see vocal descriptions in excerpt 1).

It is New Year's Eve and the Doctor is scheduled to announce the engagement of Vanessa and Anatol at a party. Vanessa is upset because Erika and the Baroness have not come downstairs. Anatol comforts her with assurances about Erika and with light words of love.

EXCERPT 4   GS (revised) e, g   pp. 187-219   18 min.

Vanessa, Erika, Baroness, Anatol, Doctor (see vocal descriptions in previous excerpts), and servants (mute) are included in this scene.

Erika has run out into the night in her party dress muttering, "His child—must not be born!" Now it is dawn and the Baroness, Doctor, and Vanessa are awaiting the searching party led by Anatol. Soon they return bearing the unconscious Erika, saying she was found in a small ravine, her dress damp with blood. When the others have left the room, Erika calls to the Baroness and tells her the child will not be born, whereupon the Baroness leaves the room never to speak to Erika again.

EXCERPT 4a   GS (revised) e, g   pp. 187-98   7 min.

A portion of excerpt 4 with only Vanessa, Doctor, and Baroness (mute).

EXCERPT 5   GS (revised) e, g   pp. 224-63   19 min.

This uses the principal characters as described in earlier excerpts.

Vanessa and Anatol have been married and are preparing to leave. Vanessa asks to have the last word with her niece, and again she questions Erika about her relationship with Anatol. Erika refuses to tell who the man was for whom she almost took her life. As the married couple is ready to depart, the five principal characters stand in their places and in effect step out of the drama to sing a quintet commenting philosophically on what has happened.

WERTHER

Jules Massenet (1842-1912)

Wetzlar, Germany, 1772

EXCERPT 1   Int/Kal   f, e   pp. 52/2/1-60/3/1   6 min.

A scene for Sophie, light lyric soprano, and Albert, lyric baritone with some sustained high passages.

In the garden, Sophie greets the unexpected arrival of Albert,
fiancé of her older sister Charlotte. As she bids him goodnight, he
sings of his love for Charlotte in the aria "Quelle prière."

EXCERPT 2   Int/Kal   f, e   pp. 62/2/1-77   12 min.

The characters are Charlotte, mezzo-soprano, and Werther, tenor
with a few sustained high notes. Le Bailli, Charlotte's father,
speaks from offstage in this scene.

Werther, a visitor in the home earlier that day, accompanies
Charlotte home from a ball. They have fallen completely in love
but Charlotte's previous promise to marry Albert leaves Werther
brokenhearted.

(Excerpts 1 and 2 may be performed together, with the inter-
mezzo between.)

EXCERPT 3   Int/Kal   f, e   pp. 89/4/1-100/3/3;   27½ min.
                                102/4/1-37

The major portion of act 2, involving the four main characters;
Werther, Charlotte, Sophie, and Albert, all described in excerpts 1
and 2. The tenor role of Werther requires a strong B3 for his monologue prayer "Oui! ce qu'elle m'ordonne."

Three months after their wedding has taken place, Charlotte and
Albert are seen in the village square. Werther, watching, sings of his
desperate love for Charlotte in the aria "Un autre est son époux!"
Albert tries to comfort Werther; a few minutes later Charlotte sug-
gests that Werther might try falling in love with her sister Sophie.
Sophie arrives and in a sprightly song invites the men to a party;
Werther declines. He confesses to Charlotte that he still loves her

and she insists that he must go away and not come back until Christmas. Werther prays to God for help.

EXCERPT 4   Int/Kal   f, e   pp. 138-98/4/4   34 min.

The four main characters are the same as in the other excerpts with the addition of a silent messenger. This complete third act contains Charlotte's three well-known arias the "Air des Lettres," "Va, laisse couler mes larmes," and "Seigneur Dieu!" as well as the famous aria of Werther, "Pourquoi me réveiller."

It is Christmas Eve. Charlotte is alone in Albert's house, rereading some old letters from Werther. Sophie arrives and, seeing that her sister is disconsolate, attempts to cheer her, insisting that she join the rest of the family for a holiday celebration. After Sophie leaves, Werther appears, keeping his promise to return at Christmas. For a moment Charlotte succumbs to his love, but remembering her marriage vows, she runs away from him into another room, locking the door behind her. Werther leaves the house, swearing that he will die of unrequited love. Albert returns to find his wife troubled. He is handed a note from Werther asking for the loan of his pistols. The weapons are sent off; Charlotte, realizing the possible significance of the request, rushes out hoping to reach Werther before it is too late.

EXCERPT 4a   Int/Kal   f, e   pp. 138-63/4/2   18 min.

The portion of the act with Charlotte and Sophie only, including Charlotte's first two arias.

EXCERPT 4b   Int/Kal   f, e   pp. 163/4/3-92/3/2   13 min.

A scene for Charlotte and Werther only, from "Seigneur Dieu!" through "Pourquoi me réveiller" and the duet.   •

EXCERPT 5   Int/Kal   f, e   pp. 205/4/2-29   13 min.

The final scene between Charlotte and Werther, both described in excerpt 2. The voice of Sophie, lyric soprano, and an ensemble of children which could be taken by three-part women's voices, are heard offstage.

Charlotte arrives at Werther's study too late; Werther has already shot himself with a pistol borrowed from her husband. Before he dies, Werther hears Charlotte confess that she has loved him. She throws herself across his body as the sound of Christmas carols is heard in the distance.

EXCERPT 5a   Int/Kal   f, e   pp. 205/4/2-18/1/3   7½ min.

The duet for Charlotte and Werther only.

WUTHERING HEIGHTS

Carlisle Floyd (1924-)

The Moor Country of Northern England, 1835 (Prologue), 1817-1821

EXCERPT 1   B&H   e   pp. 22-50   12 min.

The role of Catherine Earnshaw (Cathy) requires a soprano (D3-C5) who looks seventeen but can sustain lyric and dramatic phrases with ease. Mr. Earnshaw, her aged and sick father, should be sung by a bass (Bb1-F3) capable of sustaining a high tessitura. Hindley Earnshaw, the son, is a rather large man in his mid-twenties. The tessitura of his tenor role (F2-Bb3) also lies high. Others in this scene are Heathcliff, baritone, a rather wild gypsy youth who sings only the duet with Cathy; Nelly, mezzo-soprano, the middle-aged kindly maid; and Joseph, tenor, the old servant.

Hindley in his anger over the fact that Mr. Earnshaw treats the gypsy boy Heathcliff as one of the family, strikes the old man, killing him. After Hindley and the servants have taken the body from the room, Cathy throws herself into Heathcliff's arms and the scene ends with a short duet.

EXCERPT 1a   B&H   e   pp. 45/1/4-50/3/4   3 min.

This short portion of excerpt 1 can begin with Cathy looking in the direction in which Hindley and Joseph have supposedly exited with Mr. Earnshaw's body. Cathy shrieks that Hindley has killed her father and he answers from offstage. Then Cathy and Heathcliff cling to each other as they sing the duet.

EXCERPT 2   B&H   e   pp. 61/3/3-79/3/4   8 min.

A scene primarily for Cathy (E3-B4) and Heathcliff (B1-Ab3),
with very short segments for Isabella, soprano, and Edgar, tenor—
the beautiful young daughter and the young son of the wealthy
Linton family. Mute servants may be included.

Cathy and Heathcliff have stolen away from the Earnshaw resi-
dence and are enjoying a beautiful evening of freedom on the
moor. As they near the Linton estate, Cathy sprains her ankle, and
Isabella and Edgar Linton offer to let her stay with them until it is
healed. Heathcliff watches her go into their house and softly calls
her name as the scene ends.

EXCERPT 2a   B&H   e   pp. 61/3/3-75/2/4   6 min.

Only the portion of excerpt 2 involving Cathy and Heathcliff in
their carefree romp on the moor.

EXCERPT 3   B&H   e   pp. 120/3/2-58/1/3   20 min.

Cathy, soprano (C3-Bb4), and Edgar Linton, tenor (E1-B3), are
supported in this dramatic scene by Nelly, the maid, mezzo-
soprano. Cathy must be able to display a variety of emotions in
both her acting and her singing.

Edgar Linton has come to call on Cathy who, after an outburst
of temper aimed at Nelly, calms herself, listens to Edgar's proposal,
and agrees to marry him. When he leaves she apologizes to Nelly
and explains her feelings. When Nelly tells Cathy that Heathcliff
has left Wuthering Heights, Cathy runs out into the night, calling
his name.

EXCERPT 3a   B&H   e   pp. 120/3/2-36/1/5   8 min.

This is the opening of excerpt 3 through Edgar's proposal,
Cathy's acceptance, and his exit.

EXCERPT 3b   B&H   e   pp. 130/2/1-36/1/5   3 min.

After a four-measure introduction, the scene begins with Edgar's
proposal, "Marry me, Cathy," and concludes as she accepts and
Edgar leaves.

EXCERPT 3c   B&H   e   pp. 136/4/3-58/1/3   12 min.

The conclusion of excerpt 3, sung by Cathy and supported by Nelly, may be done as a single scene or could be combined with 3b.

EXCERPT 4   B&H   e   pp. 218/1/1-64/3/5   21 min.
                        with cut 246/2/3-50/3/4   19 min.

This dramatic scene of confrontation requires Cathy (Cb3-B4), now married to Edgar Linton (E3-Bb4); Isabella Linton (Eb3-A#4), who is in love with Heathcliff (Bb1-G3); and Nelly, the maid, whose lines are generally low with occasional high passages (G#2-F#4).

As Isabella is questioning Nelly about Heathcliff's continued attraction to Cathy (Mrs. Edgar Linton), Cathy enters and overhears the conversation. She calls both Heathcliff and Edgar into the room, hoping to learn truths. After Edgar's words have forced the distraught Isabella to leave, Heathcliff once more asks Cathy to go with him. When she refuses the idea, Heathcliff stands immobile and the scene ends with a quartet for Nelly, Cathy, Heathcliff, and Edgar.

DIE ZAUBERFLÖTE

(The Magic Flute)

Wolfgang Amadeus Mozart (1756-1791)

Egypt in the Area of a Temple of Isis and Osiris

EXCERPT 1   B&H   g, e   pp. 8-51   25½ min.
              GS   g, e   pp. 10-46
              Kal   g, e   pp. 10-45/1/6

This scene includes Tamino, lyric tenor with a sustained line (F2-Ab3); Papageno, baritone with facility and a sense of comedy (Bb1-E3); the Queen of the Night, dramatic coloratura soprano with control of the extremely high tessitura (D3-F5); and the

Three Ladies, soprano (D3-A4), soprano or mezzo-soprano (D3-
Ab4), and mezzo-soprano (Ab2-F4), who have exacting ensembles
and coordinated movement.

Prince Tamino, attempting to escape from a huge serpent, falls
unconscious. Three Ladies-in-Waiting of the Queen of the Night
appear, kill the serpent with their spears, and rejoice in an extended trio. When the Ladies have left to tell the Queen about the
Prince they have saved, Tamino recovers consciousness and sees
Papageno, the Queen's birdcatcher, who is singing his song "Der
Vogelfänger bin ich ja." He tells Tamino that this is the realm of
the Queen of the Night and boasts that he, Papageno, has killed
the serpent. The Ladies reappear and place a padlock on Papageno's mouth for telling a lie.

The Ladies show Tamino a miniature of the maiden Pamina and
at once he falls in love with her image and sings "Dies Bildnis ist
bezaubernd schön." The Queen herself appears, tells him about her
lost daughter Pamina and sings the aria "O zittre nicht, mein lieber
Sohn," then disappears. The Ladies remove the padlock from
Papageno's mouth and give him the magic bells and Tamino the
magic flute that will help the two escape the perils which might
befall them in their search for Pamina.

EXCERPT 1a   B&H   g, e   pp. 8-30   14½ min.
               GS   g, e   pp. 10-27
               Kal   g, e   pp. 10-27/3/6

The portion of excerpt 1 with Tamino, Papageno, and the Three
Ladies before the Queen's entrance.

EXCERPT 1b   B&H   g, e   pp. 32-45/1/6   6 min.
               GS   g, e   pp. 33-46
               Kal   g, e   pp. 32-45/1/6

The quintet from excerpt 1 with Tamino, Papageno, and the
Three Ladies after the Queen's exit.
(Excerpts 1a and 1b can be combined into one scene.)

EXCERPT 2   B&H   g, e   pp. 52-59   7 min.
               GS   g, e   pp. 47-53/2/5
               Kal   g, e   pp. 45/2/1-51/2/5

Papageno (see excerpt 1); Pamina, a lyric soprano who has expressive, sustained singing (C3-Bb4); and Monostatos, a lesser role for tenor (D2-G3).

In an apartment in Sarastro's palace, a brutal Moor, Monostatos, is pursuing Pamina with unwelcome attentions. The appearance of Papageno puts him to flight. Papageno recognizes Pamino and assures her that she will soon be rescued by someone who has fallen in love with her—the sort of thing that never seems to happen to him, he laments. Pamina consoles him in an exquisitely simple tune, "Bei Männern, welche Liebe fühlen."

EXCERPT 2a   B&H   g, e   pp. 48-51/2/5   5 min.
              GS   g, e   pp. 50-53/2/5
              Kal   g, e   pp. 48-51/2/5

This is the duet from excerpt 2 for Papageno and Pamina.

EXCERPT 3   B&H   g, e   pp. 60-74/4/3   22½ min.
              GS   g, e   pp. 53/3/1-65
              Kal   g, e   pp. 51/3/1-63

In addition to Tamino, lyric tenor, this scene uses the Three Spirits, (soprano, mezzo-soprano, alto) with exacting ensembles and sustained singing; a priest called the Speaker, bass or baritone; a TTBB offstage chorus; and persons dressed as animals (nonsinging). If only piano is used for accompaniment, it is desirable to add a flute for this scene.

Three Spirits lead Tamino to a grove where there are the entrances to three temples and leave him with the advice to be silent, patient and persevering. He is refused admittance at the first two temple doors. From the third, the Speaker emerges and informs him that Sarastro is not the tyrant the Queen has said, rather a man of wisdom and noble character. As Tamino ponders these things, a hidden chorus encourages him with answers. Tamino plays his magic flute and sings while wild animals come from their lairs and lie at his feet.

EXCERPT 4   B&H   g, e   pp. 95-112   12 min.
              GS   g, e   pp. 82-96
              Kal   g, e   pp. 80-94

In addition to Papageno, Tamino, and the Three Ladies (see excerpt 1 for vocal descriptions), Sarastro appears in this scene with his priests (a minimum of four to sing the TTBB chorus in a workshop presentation). Sarastro has a bass aria requiring an extremely low, sustained sound; and two other priests, tenor and baritone, sing a short duet.

In the Temple of Wisdom, the priests of Isis have assembled to consider whether Tamino is ready to be initiated into the final mysteries. Sarastro prays to Isis and Osiris that strength may be granted to the aspirants of wisdom. As Papageno and Tamino enter, two priests warn them to keep their vow of silence. Left alone Papageno and Tamino are confronted by the Three Ladies who try to persuade them to abandon their quest. Tamino and, more reluctantly, Papageno maintain silence. The priests congratulate them on having passed their first test.

EXCERPT 4a   B&H   g, e   pp. 98-112   6 min.
               GS   g, e   pp. 85-96
               Kal   g, e   pp. 83-94

This scene begins after the exit of Sarastro; it includes Papageno, Tamino, the Two Priests, and the Three Ladies.

EXCERPT 4b   B&H   g, e   pp. 98; 101-12   3 min.
               GS   g, e   pp. 85; 87-96
               Kal   g, e   pp. 83; 85-94

This is the same as excerpt 4a without the Two Priests.

EXCERPT 5   B&H   g, e   pp. 113-23   9½ min.
               GS   g, e   pp. 97-105
               Kal   g, e   pp. 95-103

A scene for Monostatos, Queen of the Night, and Sarastro, each of whom has an aria (see excerpts 1 and 2 for vocal descriptions). Pamina has no singing but only speaking lines in this excerpt.

Pamina is lying asleep and Monastatos, the Moor, steals toward her and indulges in a dance and aria around her. He tries to steal a kiss but a cry stops him; it is the Queen of the Night. She gives her daughter a dagger with the command that she kill Sarastro. In "Der hölle Rache kocht in meinem Herzen" all her fury is vented

in fiery coloratura. Monastatos returns and threatens to reveal the
plot, demanding Pamina's love as price for his silence. Sarastro enters and when Pamina pleads for her mother, Sarastro sings "In
diesen heil'gen Hallen kennt man die Rache nicht."

EXCERPT 6   B&H   g, e   pp. 125-29   6 min.
                     GS   g, e   pp. 106-10
                     Kal   g, e   pp. 104-8

Papageno and Tamino do not sing but are present in this scene
with the Three Spirits and Pamina (see vocal descriptions in excerpt 3).

Papageno and Tamino, still undergoing the test of silence, are
greeted by the Three Spirits who bring them food, drink, the flute,
and magic bells. When Pamina enters, unaware of their vow of
silence, she is overjoyed to find Tamino but when he will not talk
to her she sings the poignant aria "Ach, ich fühl's, es ist verschwun-
den."

EXCERPT 7   B&H   g, e   pp. 130-45   11 min.
                     GS   g, e   pp. 111-23
                     Kal   g, e   pp. 109-21

This excerpt uses Pamina, Papageno, Tamino, Sarastro (see vocal
descriptions in earlier excerpts); the Speaker and an Old Woman
who changes into Papagena have speaking roles. The chorus is TTB.
If piano accompaniment is used, celeste could be added.

The priests bring Tamino in followed by Pamina who is still upset by Tamino's apparent coldness. Sarastro assures them both of
a happy future if they will only be patient. As they depart, Papageno enters and is given a glass of wine. He plays his magic bells
and sings merrily of the tender little wife he would like to have.
Suddenly his wish comes true. An old woman announces herself as
his bride and when Papageno accepts her advances, the old woman
suddenly is transformed into a young beauty. With a cry of "Papagena!" he tries to embrace her but the Speaker intervenes and
takes the young woman away saying that Papageno is not yet
worthy of her.

EXCERPT 7a   B&H   g, e   pp. 132-38   3 min.
                GS   g, e   pp. 112-17
                Kal   g, e   pp. 110-15

This is the portion of excerpt 7 using only Tamino, Pamina, and Sarastro.

EXCERPT 8   B&H   g, e   pp. 146-57/2/5   5½ min.
                GS   g, e   pp. 124-33/2/7
                Kal   g, e   pp. 122-31/2/7

An excerpt using Pamina and the Three Spirits (see vocal descriptions in excerpt 2).

In a garden, Pamina is found delirious with grief. She raises the dagger to kill herself when the Three Spirits stop her, warning her gravely that suicide is punished by the gods. They assure her that Tamino loves her dearly and would be driven insane if he were to hear of this rash act. Pamina rejoices and asks to be led to Tamino.

EXCERPT 9   B&H   g, e   pp. 172-87   7 min.
                GS   g, e   pp. 145-58
                Kal   g, e   pp. 143-56

This scene with Papageno, the Three Spirits, and Papagena (see earlier excerpts for vocal requirements). Needs the celeste even if only piano accompaniment is being used.

Despairing, Papageno resolves to hang himself since he cannot find Papagena. In a suicide attempt he drapes the rope over a tree branch and is interrupted by the Three Spirits who ask him why he doesn't use the magic bells. He jumps at the suggestion and begins his song and dance, wishing for a maiden. The Three Spirits vanish and return with Papagena. The two greet each other ecstatically and chatter about the lovely little Papagenas and Papagenos that will be theirs after they are married.

Selected Bibliography

The authors not only have referred to the original opera libretti for the synopses included in this book but also have found the translations of these libretti and the following books of assistance in the compilation of the plot for each excerpt.

Brockway, Wallace, and Weinstock, Herbert. *The World of Opera.* New York: Pantheon Books, 1962.

Cross, Milton. *The New Milton Cross' Complete Stories of the Great Operas.* Garden City, N.Y.: Doubleday Company, Inc., 1955.

Eaton, Quaintance. *Opera Production.* Minneapolis: University of Minnesota Press, 1961. Reprinted New York: Da Capo Press, 1974.

_____. *Opera Production II.* Minneapolis: University of Minnesota Press, 1974.

Ewen, David. *Encyclopedia of the Opera.* New York: Hill and Wang, Inc., 1955.

Fellner, Rudolph. *Opera Themes and Plots.* New York: Simon and Schuster, 1958.

Grout, Donald Jay. *A Short History of Opera.* New York and London: Columbia University Press, 1966.

Jacobs, Arthur, and Sadie, Stanley. *Opera, A Modern Guide.* New York: Drake Publishers, 1972.

Kobbé, Gustave. *Kobbé's Complete Opera Book.* Edited and revised by the Earl of Harwood. London and New York: Putnam, 1975.

Legerman, David G. *A Treasury of Opera Librettos.* Garden City, N.Y.: Doubleday Company, Inc., 1962.

Morley, Sir Alexander F. *The Harrap Opera Guide.* London: George G. Harrap & Co., Ltd., 1970.

Orrey, Leslie. *The Encyclopedia of Opera.* New York: Charles Scribner's Sons, 1976.

Peltz, Mary Ellis, and Lawrence, Robert. *The Metropolitan Opera Guide.* New York: Random House, Inc., 1942.

Rosenthal, Harold, and Warrack, John. *Concise Oxford Dictionary of Opera.* London: Oxford University Press, 1964.

Schneidereit, Otto. *Operette A-Z.* Berlin: Henschelverlag, 1975.

Schumann, Otto. *Handbuch der Opern.* Wilhelmshaven, Heinrichshofen, 1972.

The Victor Book of the Opera. Revised by Henry W. Simon. New York: Simon and Schuster, 1968.

Index of Operas

Index of Composers

Index of Arias and Ensembles

Index to Editions of Piano-Vocal Scores

The Devil and Daniel Webster: B&H, 1943
Les Dialogues des Carmélites: Ric, 1959
Dido and Aeneas: B&H, 1960; Br, 1952; Kal, #6384; Nov (reprinted by Kal); Ox, 1925
Don Carlos: GS, 1963; Int, 1972; Kal, #6746; Ric, 1970
Don Giovanni: B&H, 1966; GS, 1961; Kal, #6314
Don Pasquale: Kal, 1969; Ric, 1965

L'Elisir d'Amore: GS, 1961; Kal, 1968; Ric, 1975
Die Entführung aus dem Serail: B&H, 1962; Int, 1956; Kal, 1968
Eugene Onegin: GS, 1957; Kal, 1969

Falstaff: GS, 1963; Kal, 1968; Int, 1949; Ric, 1974
La Fanciulla del West: Ric, 1971
Faust: GS, 1966; Kal, #6192
La Favorita: Ric, 1977
Fidelio: B&H, 1948; GS, 1935; Kal, 1969; Pet, 1961
La Fille du Régiment: Int, 1972; Jou, 1916; Kal, #6178; Ric, 1966
Die Fledermaus: B&H, 1951; GS, 1951; Kal, 1968
Der Fliegende Holländer: GS, 1925; Kal, #6514; Pet, #3402
La Forza del Destino: GS, 1968; Int, 1964; Kal, 1968; Ric, 1975
Der Freischütz: GS, 1932; Kal, #6522; Pet, #79

La Gioconda: GS, 1956; Ric, 1975; Int, 1948; Kal, #6360
Giulio Cesare: Int, 1973

Hänsel und Gretel: B&H, 1976; GS, 1969; Kal, #6429; Sch (g), 1923; Sch (e), 1970
Help! Help! The Globolinks!: GS, 1969

L'Incoronazione di Poppea: Fab, 1966; UE, 1960
L'Infedeltà Delusa: UE, 1961
L'Italiana in Algeri: GS, 1966; Ric, 1976

Lakmé: Int, 1973
Lizzie Borden: B&H, 1967
Lohengrin: GS, 1963; Kal, #6499; Pet, #3401
Louise: GS, 1934

The Saint of Bleecker Street: GS (rev. ed.), 1955
Samson et Dalila: GS, 1964; Kal, #6408
The Seagull: Bel, 1975
La Sonnambula: GS, 1929; Kal, #6809
Summer and Smoke: Bel, 1976
Suor Angelica: Ric, 1977
Susannah: B&H, 1967

Il Tabarro: Ric, 1975
The Taming of the Shrew: Ric, 1954
The Tender Land: B&H, 1956
Tosca: GS, 1956; Ric (i), 1974; Kal, #6388; Ric (i, e), 1956
La Traviata: B&H, 1964; GS, 1961; Kal, #6482; Ric (i, e), 1962;
   Ric (i), 1975
Il Trovatore: B&H, 1960; GS, 1926; Kal, #6488; Ric, 1977

Vanessa: GS (rev. ed.), 1964

Werther: Int, 1971; Kal, #6379
Wuthering Heights: B&H, 1961

Die Zauberflöte: B&H, 1944; GS, 1951; Kal, 1967